The Art of
CARDCAPTOR SAKURA

2

staff

SATSUKI IGARASHI

NANASE OHKAWA

MICK NEKOI

MOKONA APAPA

planning and presented by

CLAMP

LOS ANGELES • TOKYO

Translators • Jack Niida and Daisuke Kinouchi

Retouch • Jeremy Canceko

Designer • Anna Kernbaum

Editor • Jake Forbes

Production Manager • Mario M. Rodriguez

Art Director • Matt Alford

VP Production • Ron Klamert

Publisher • Stuart Levy

Email: editor@TOKYOPOP.com
Come visit us online at www.TOKYOPOP.com

A TOKYOPOP® Book

TOKYOPOP® is an imprint of Mixx Entertainment, Inc.
5900 Wilshire Blvd. Ste. 2000, Los Angeles, CA 90036

ISBN: 1-59182-013-8

First TOKYOPOP printing: September 2002

10 9 8 7 6 5 4 3 2 1

Printed in the USA

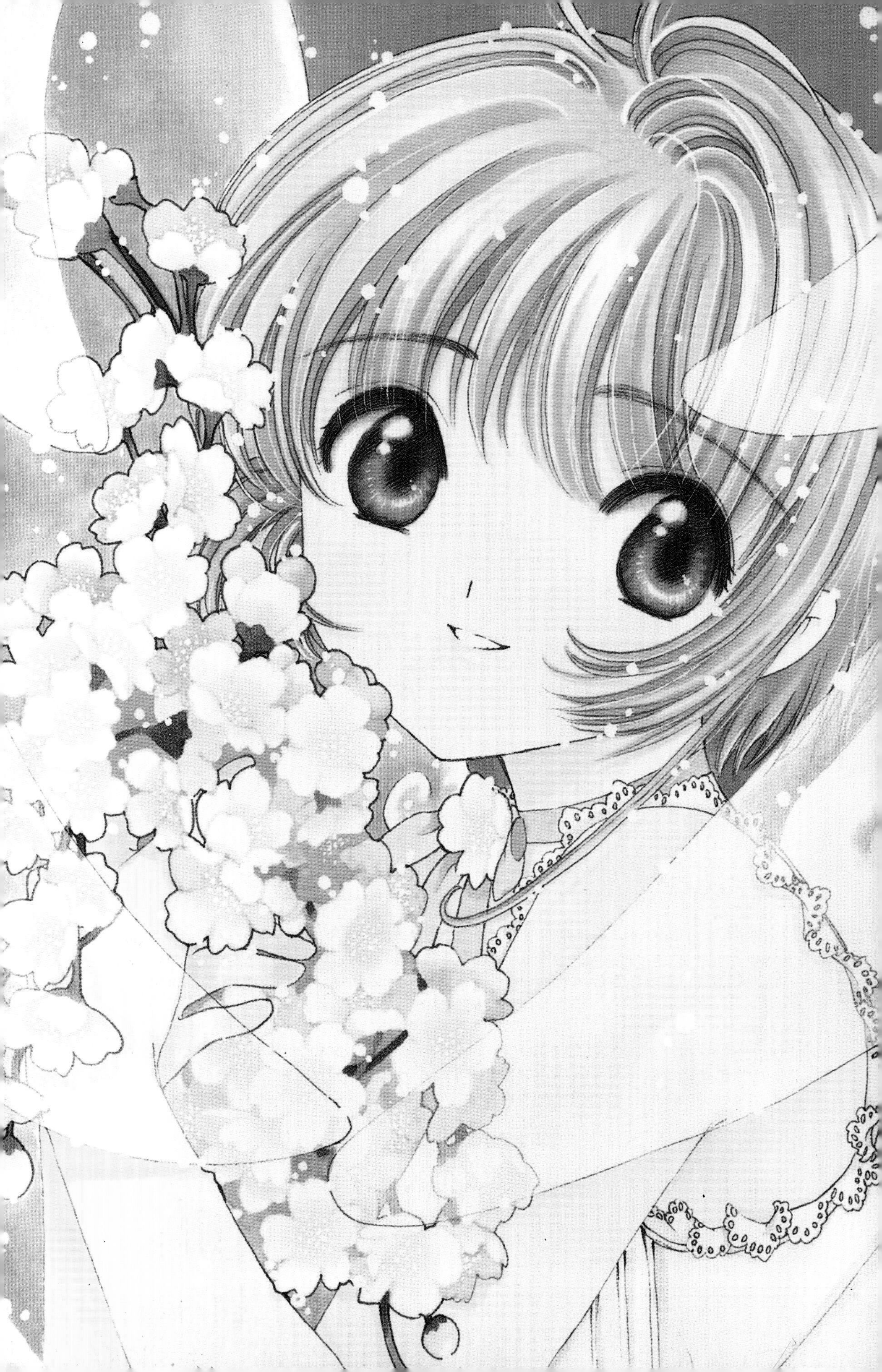

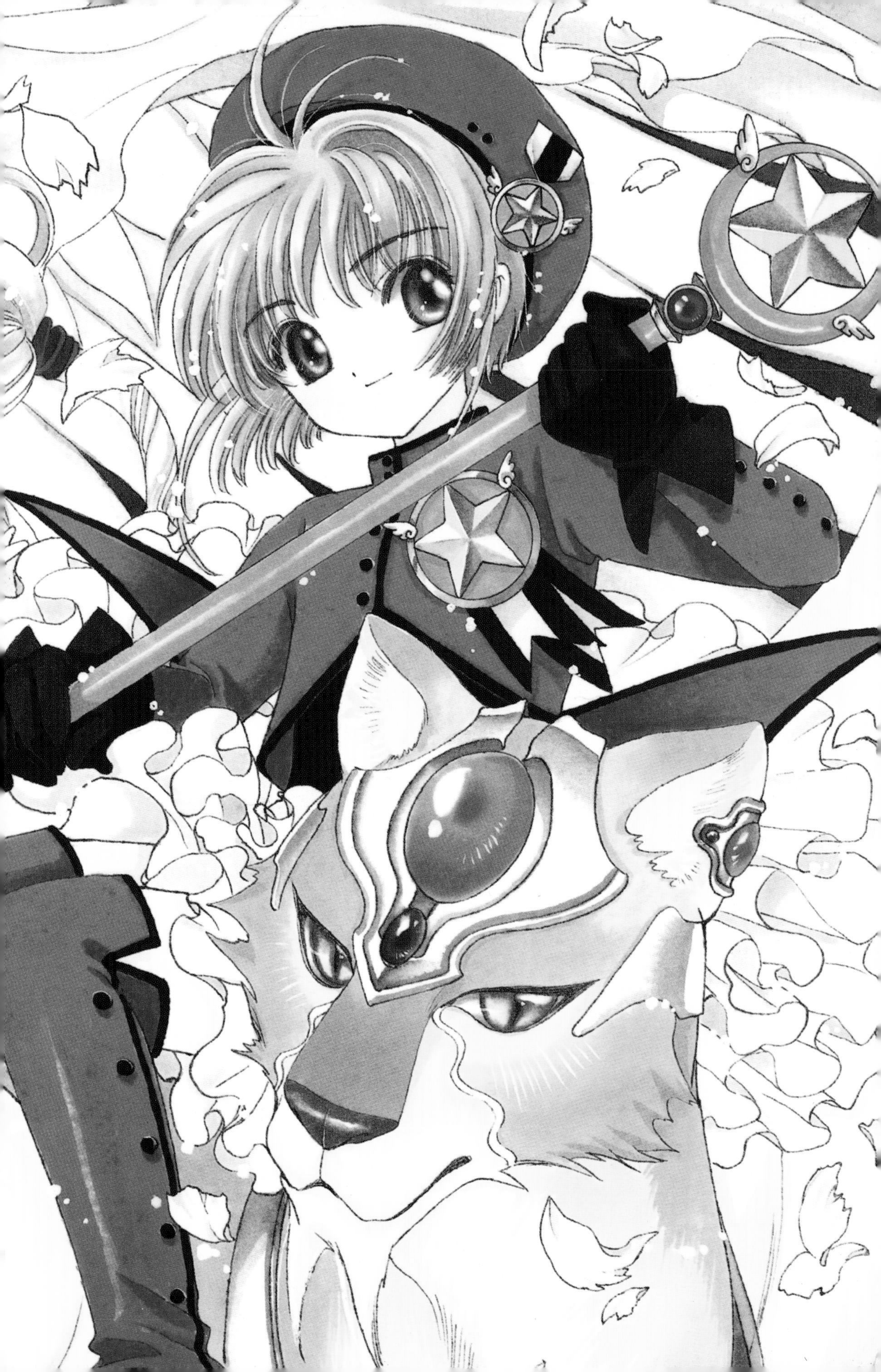

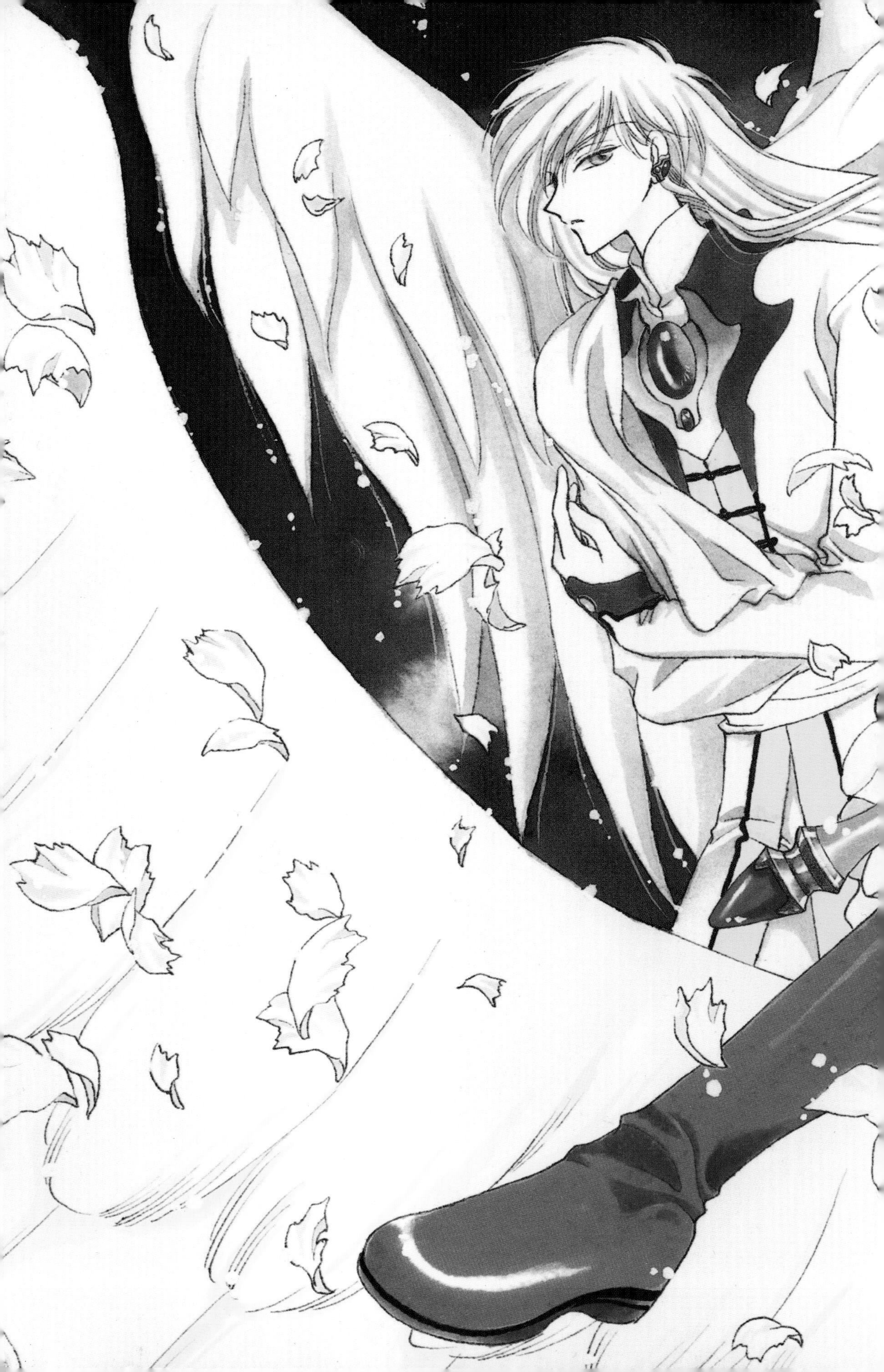

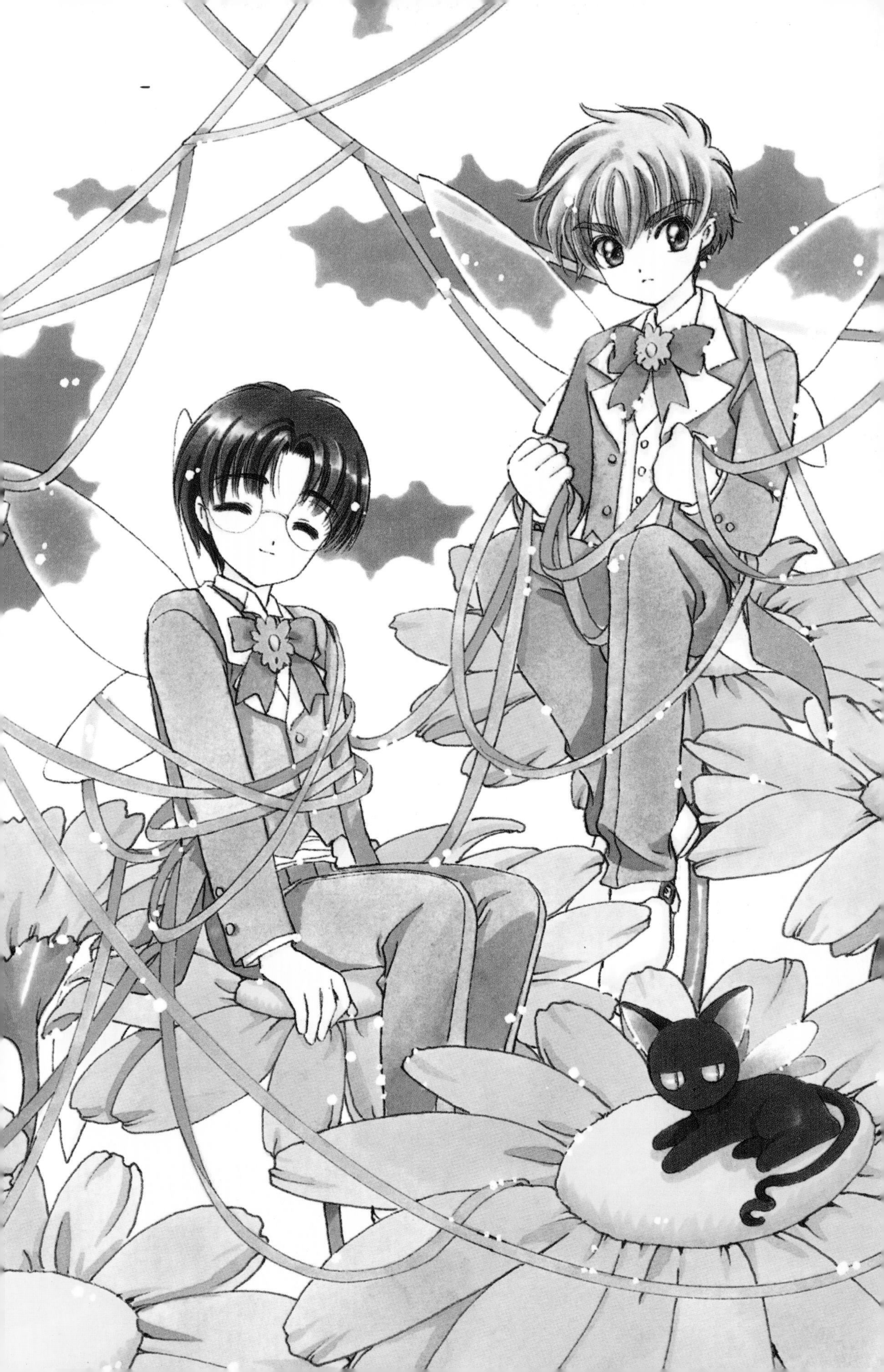

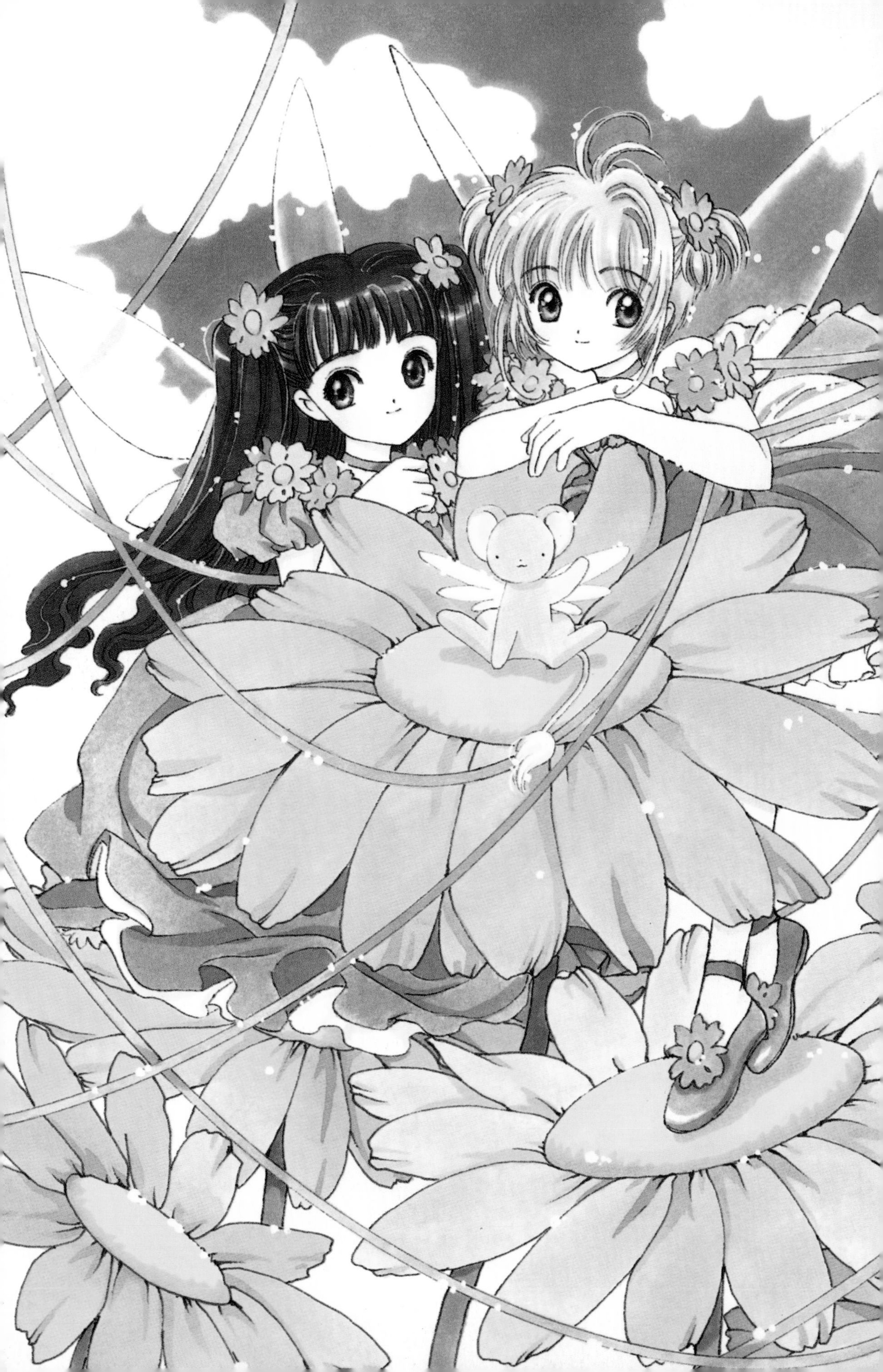

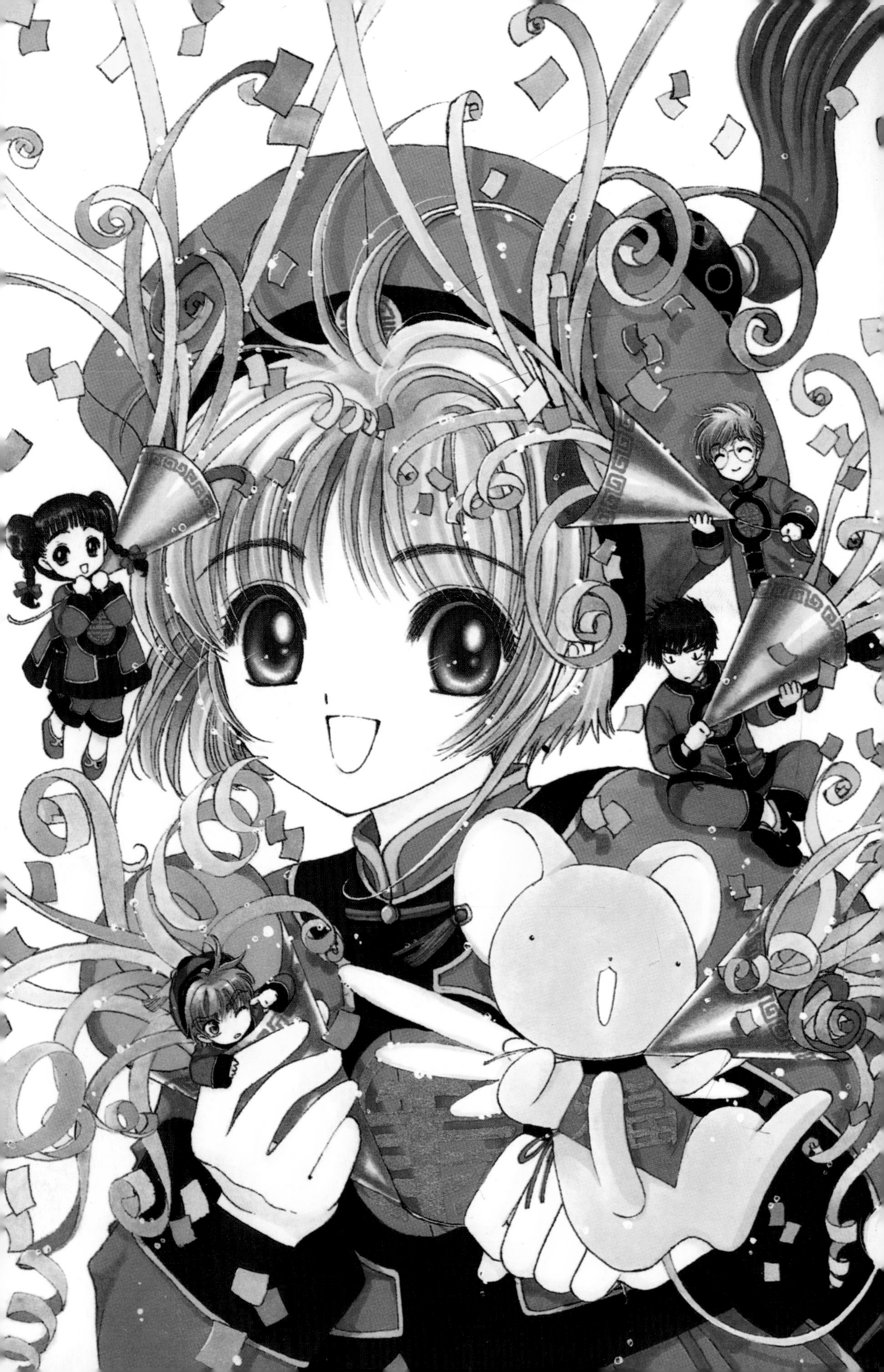

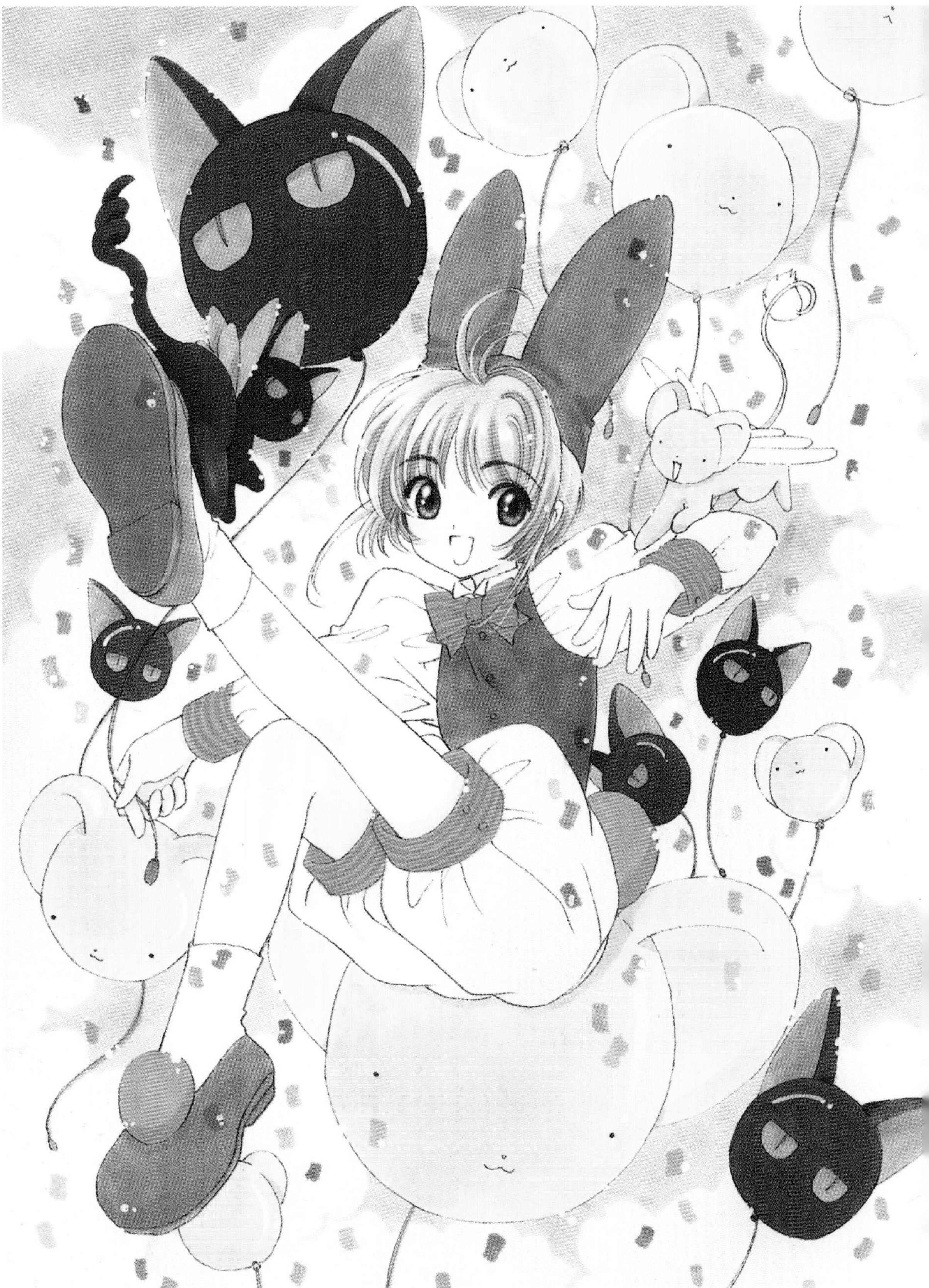

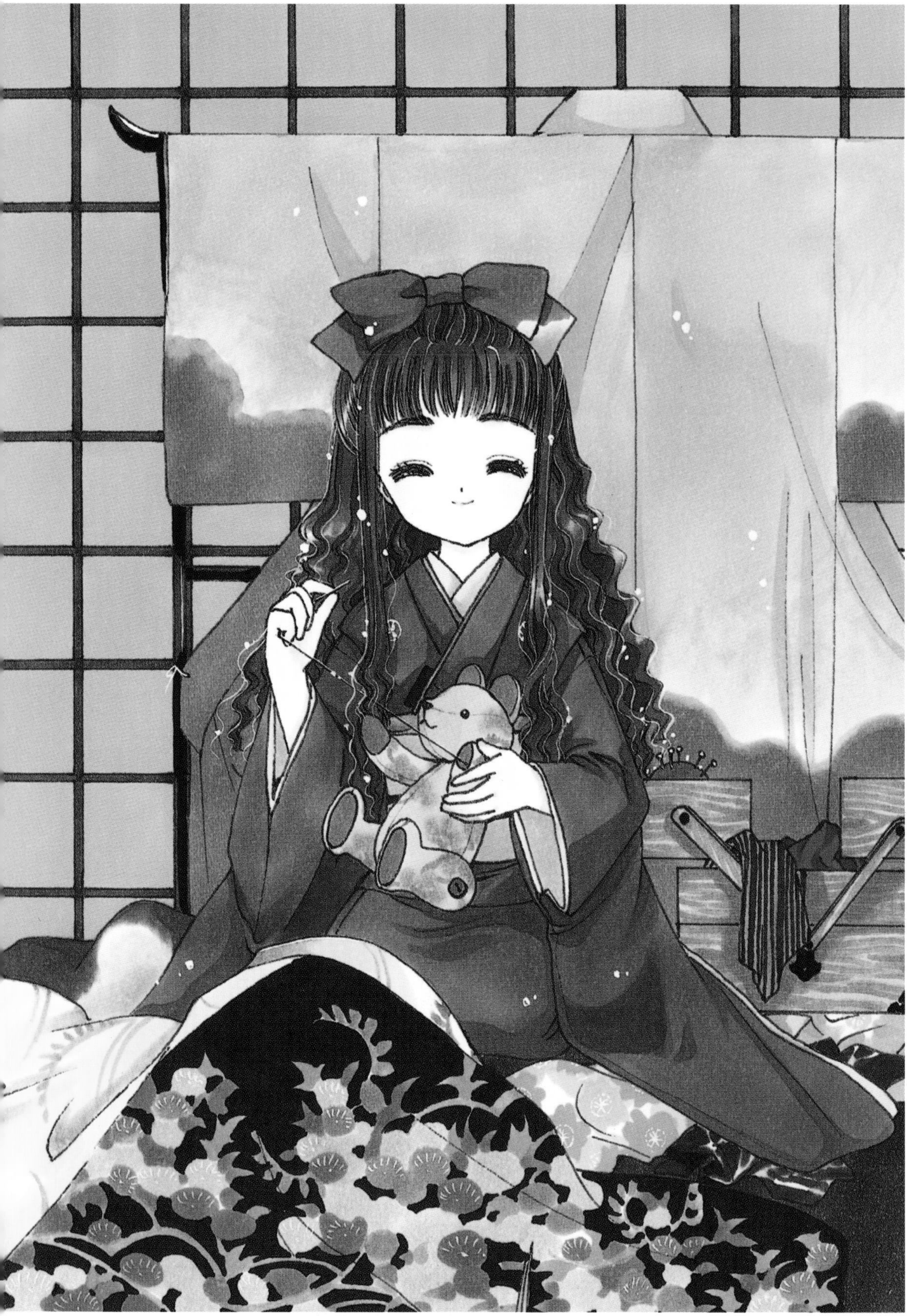

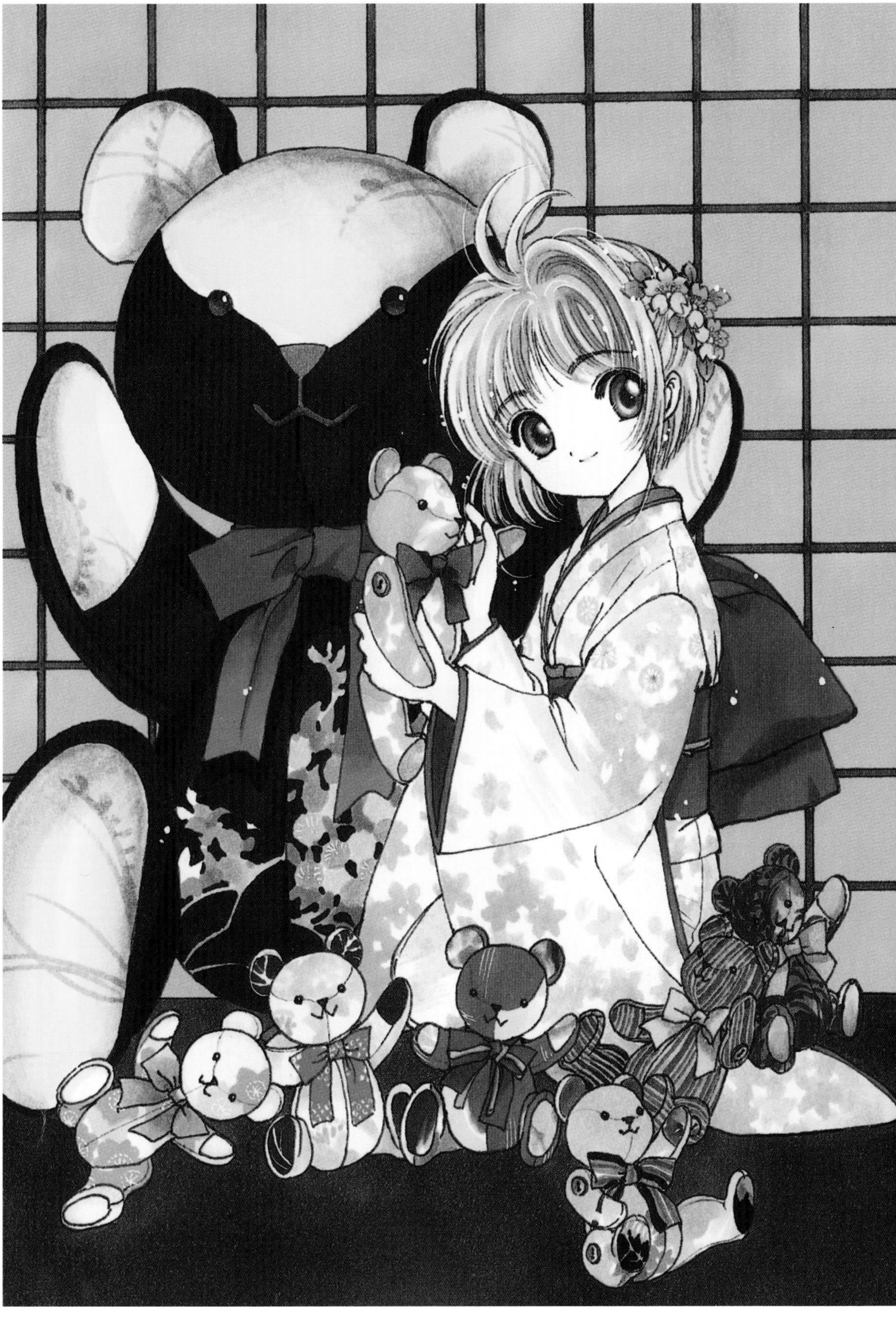

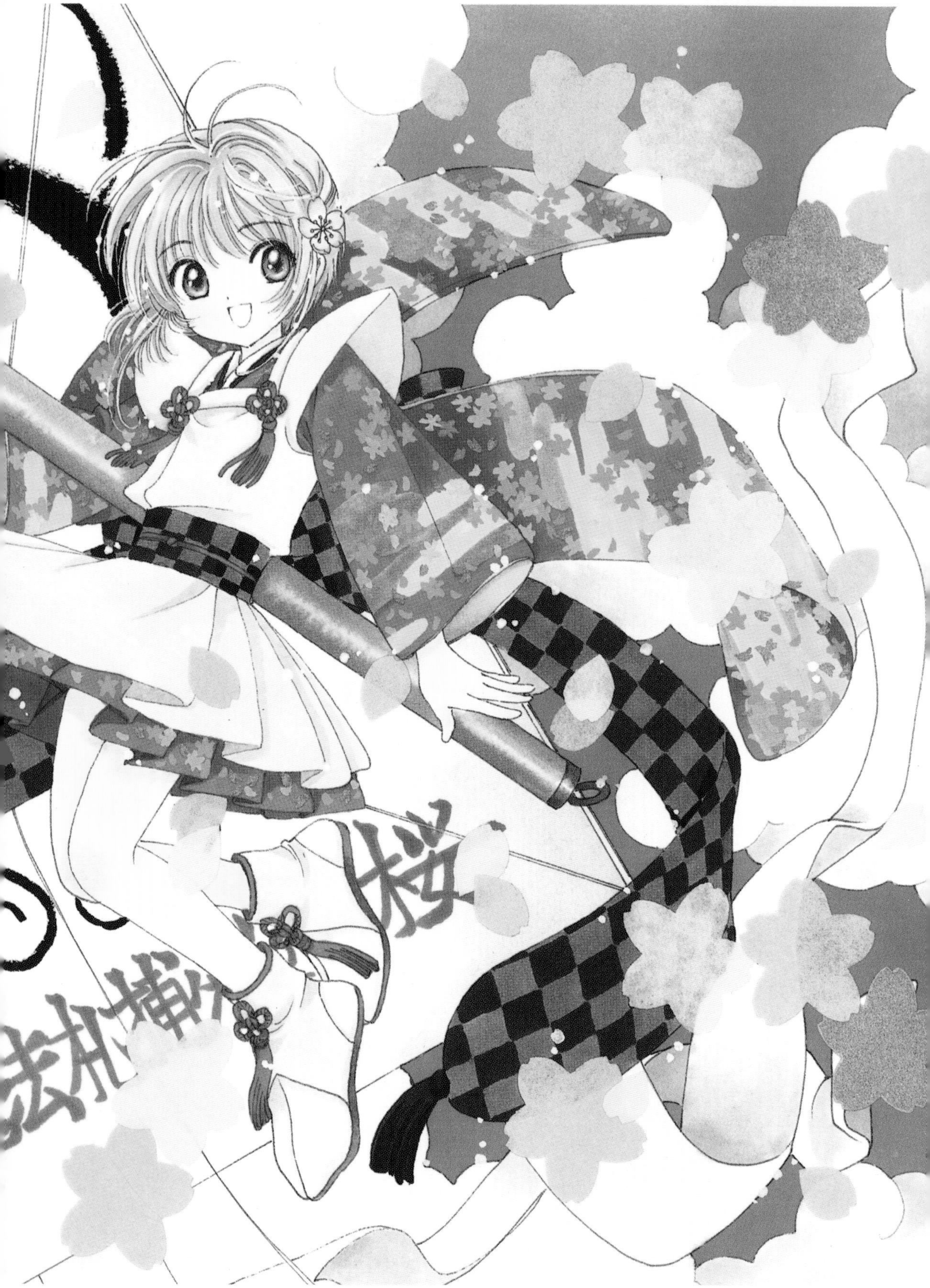
桜

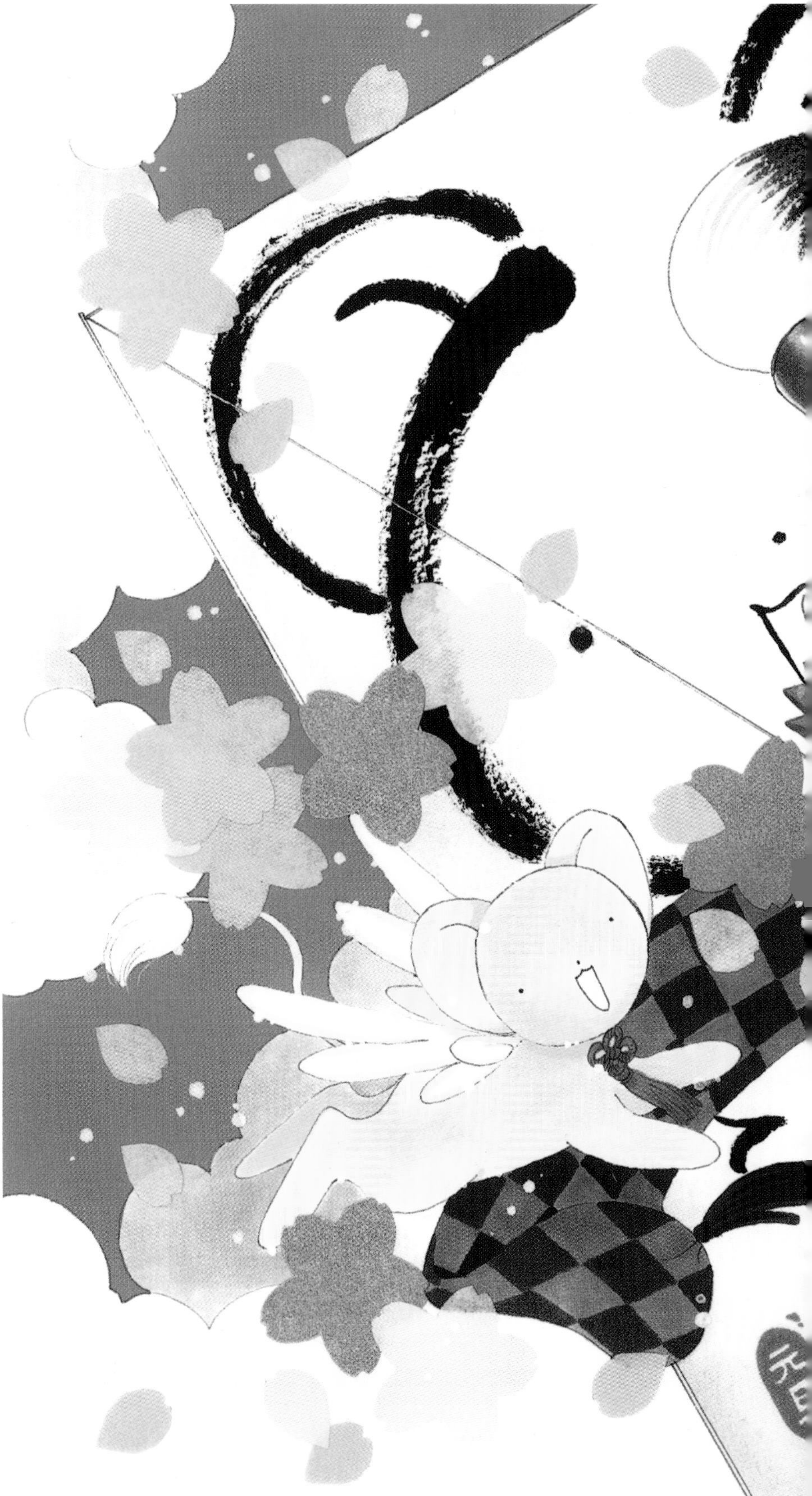

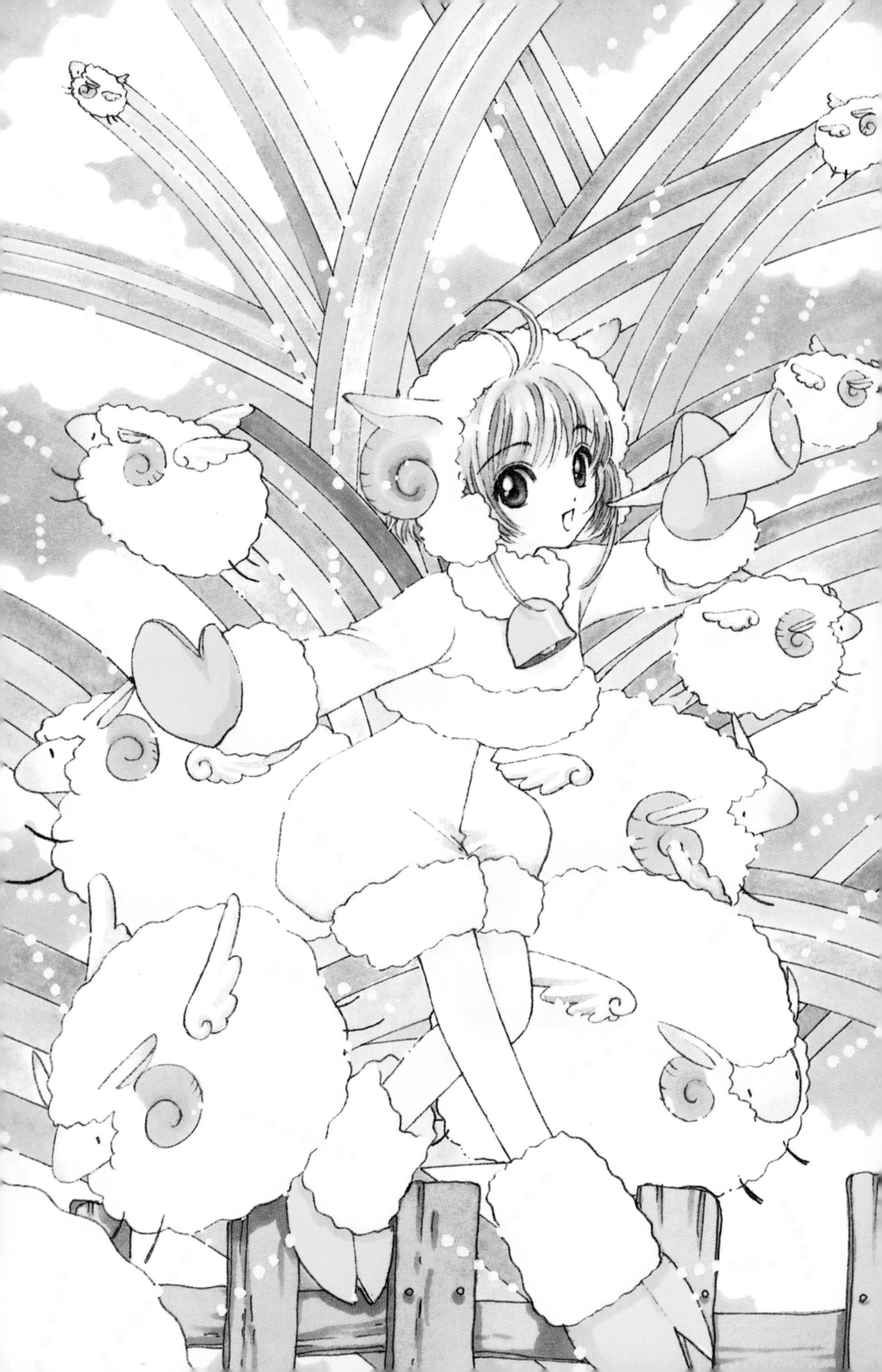

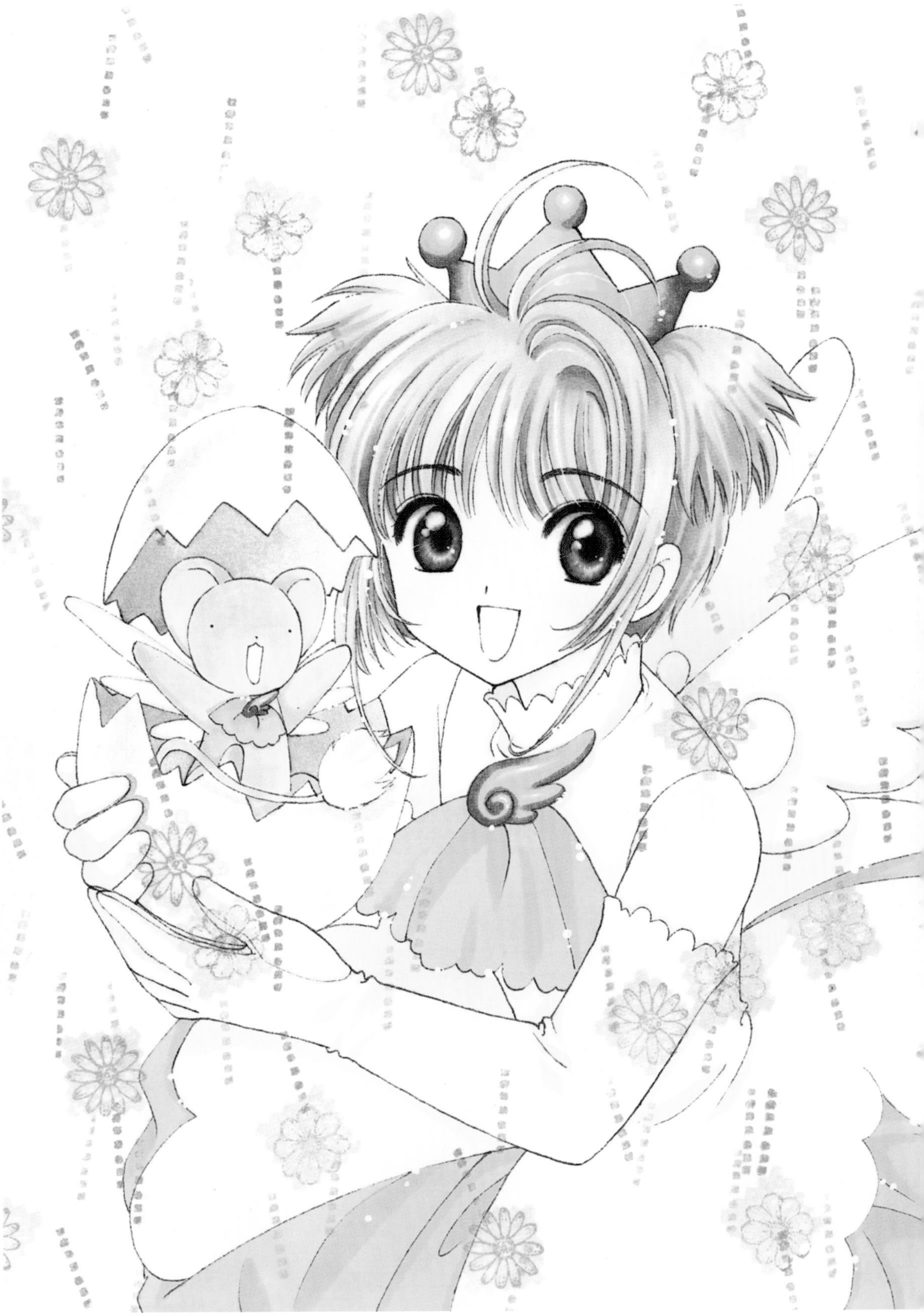

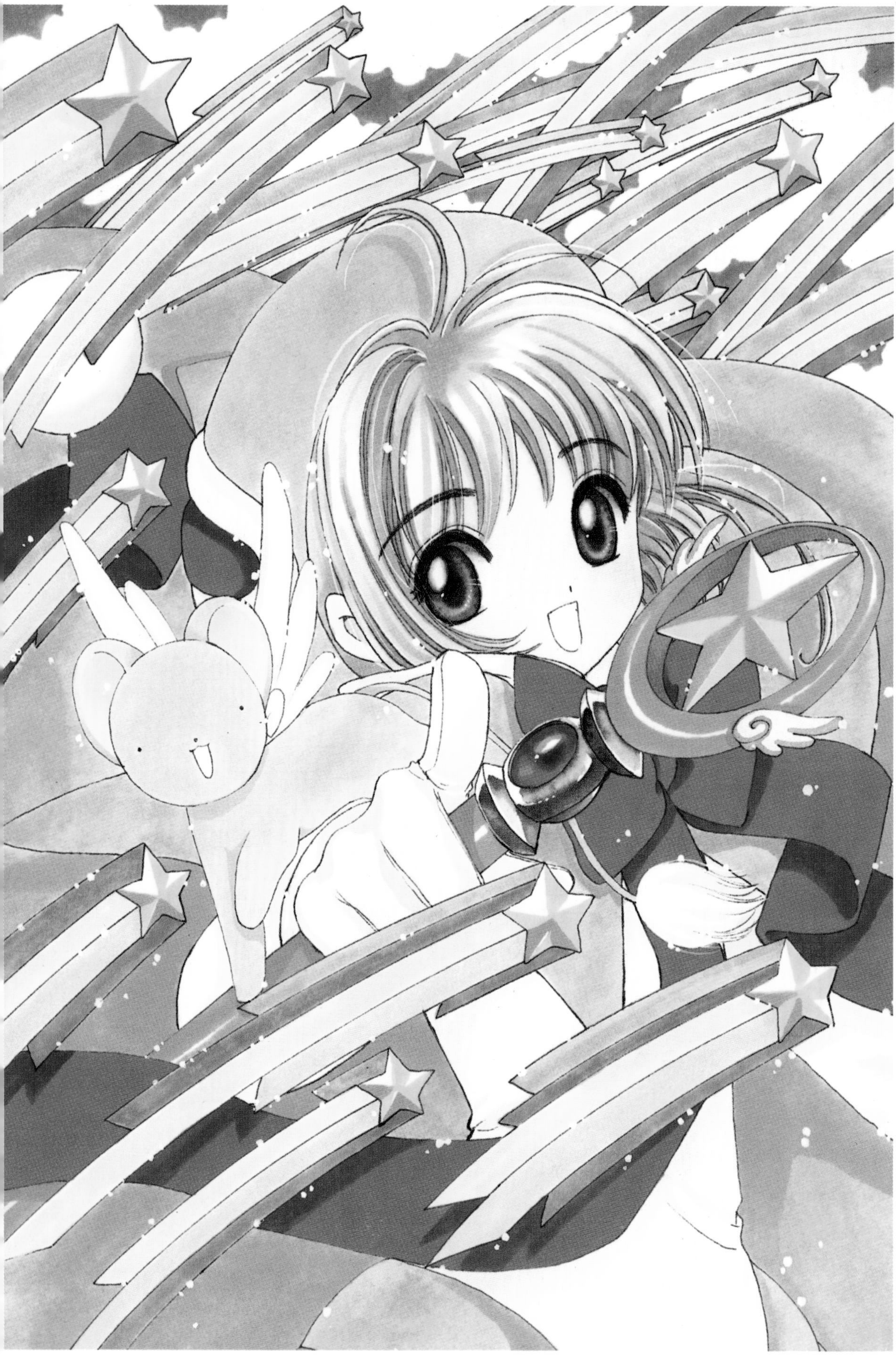

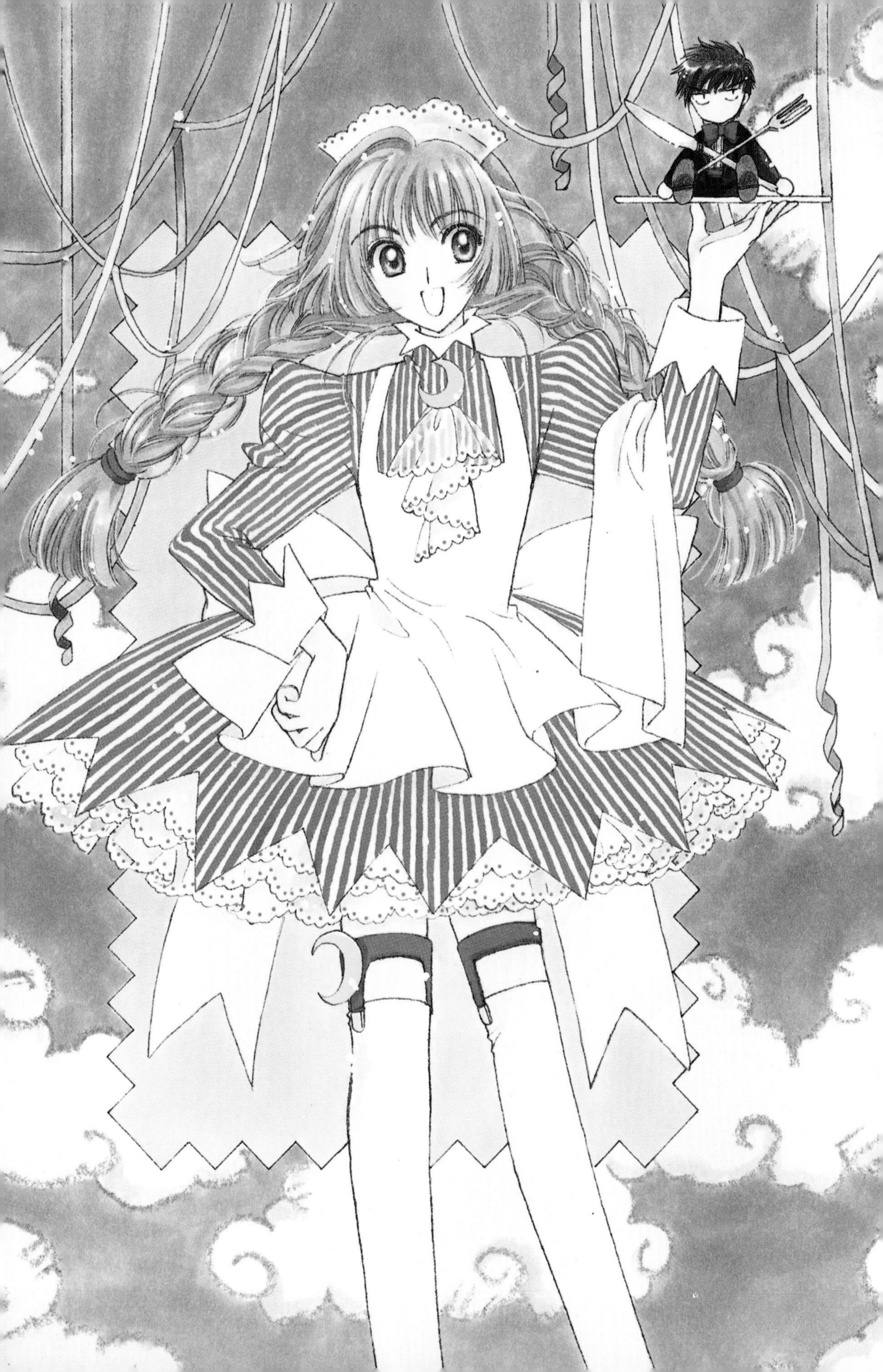

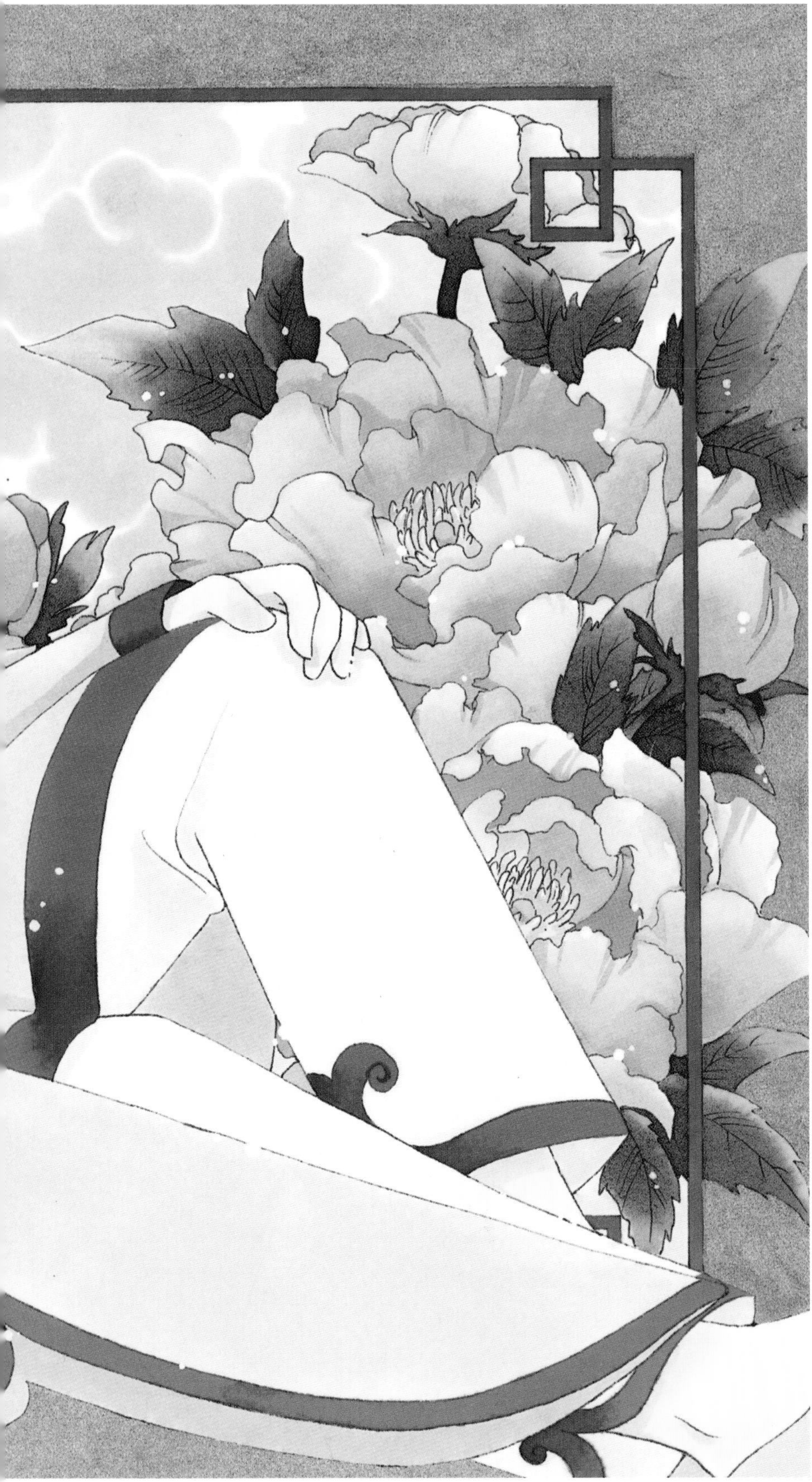

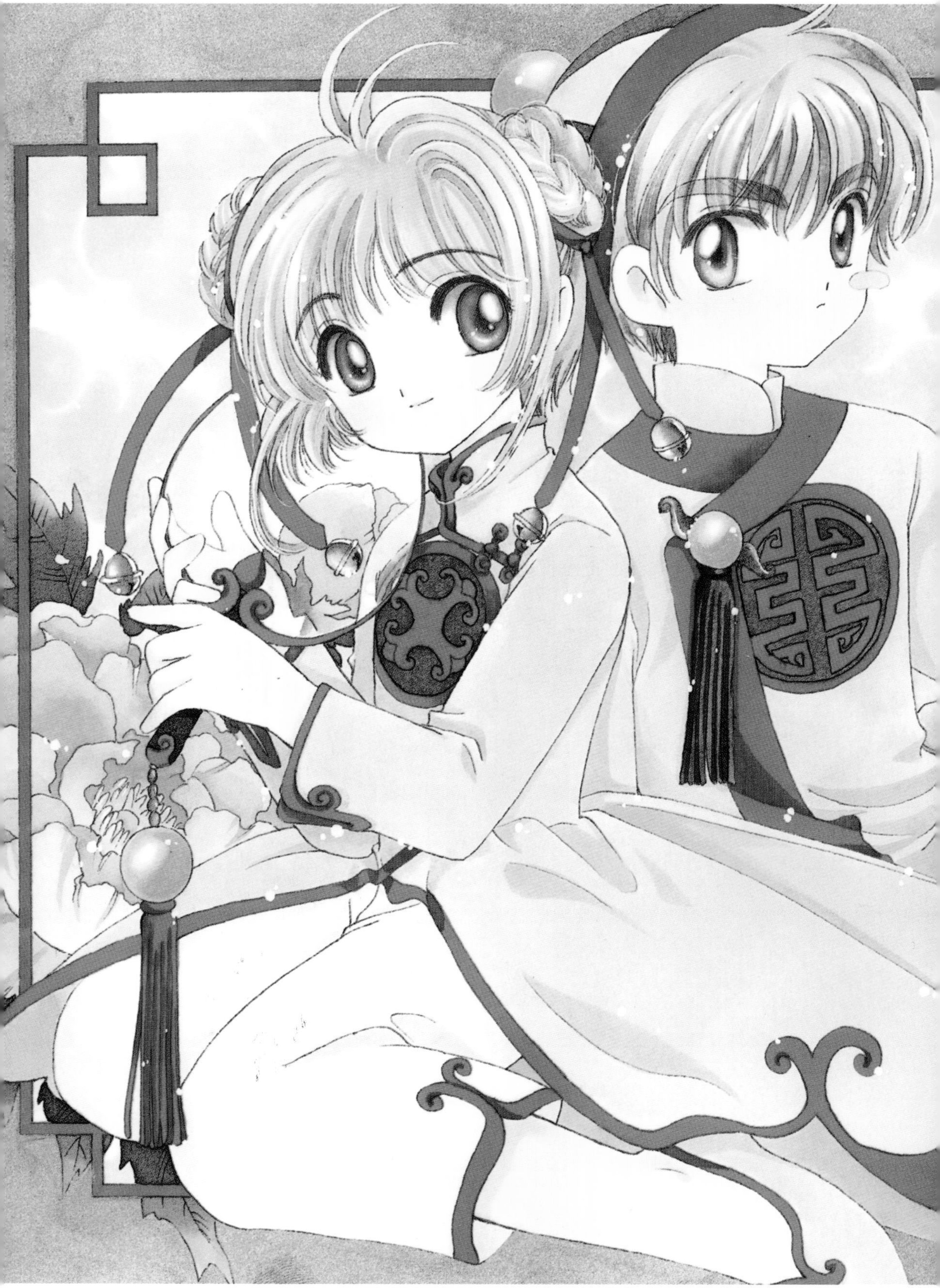

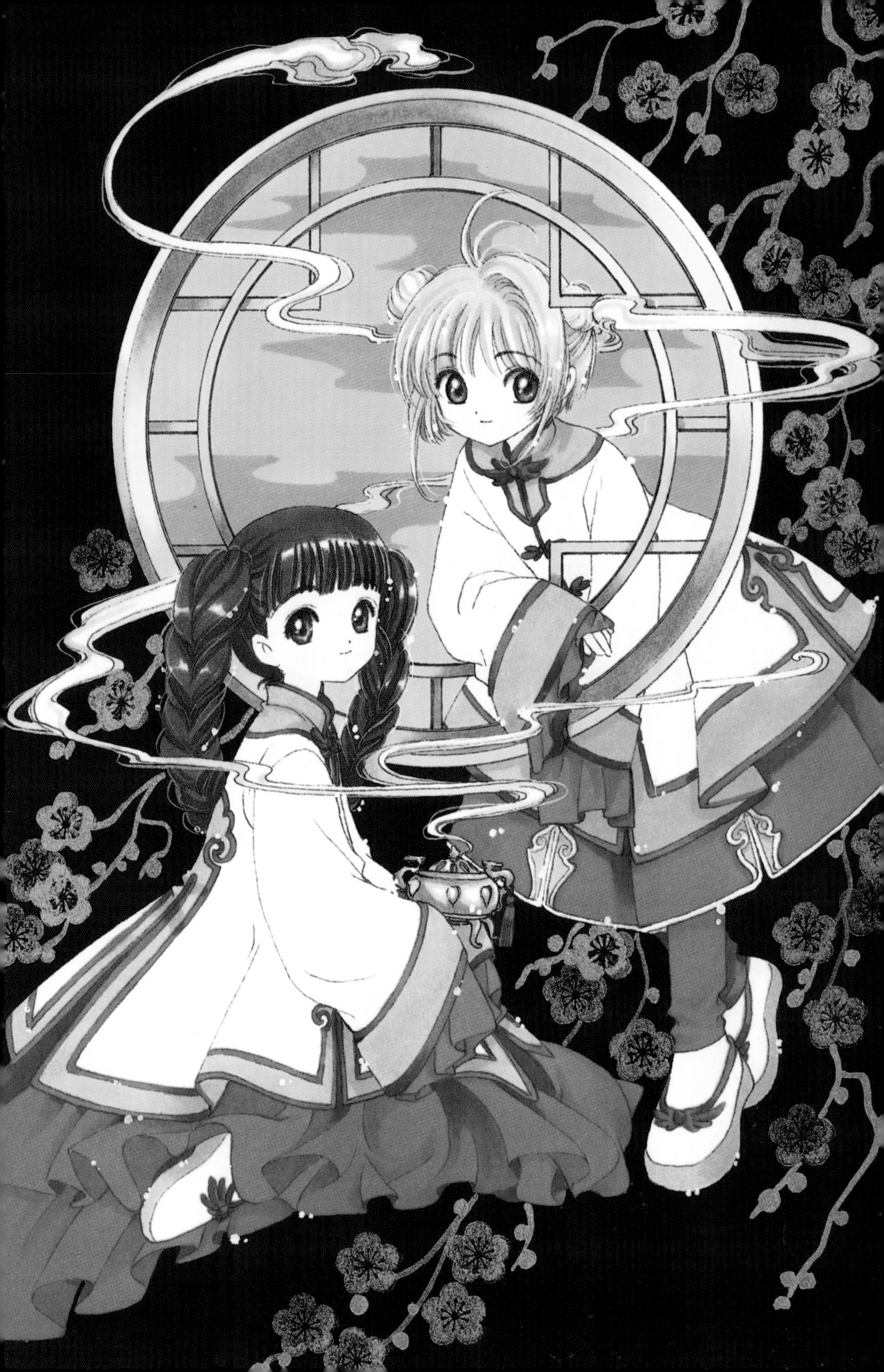

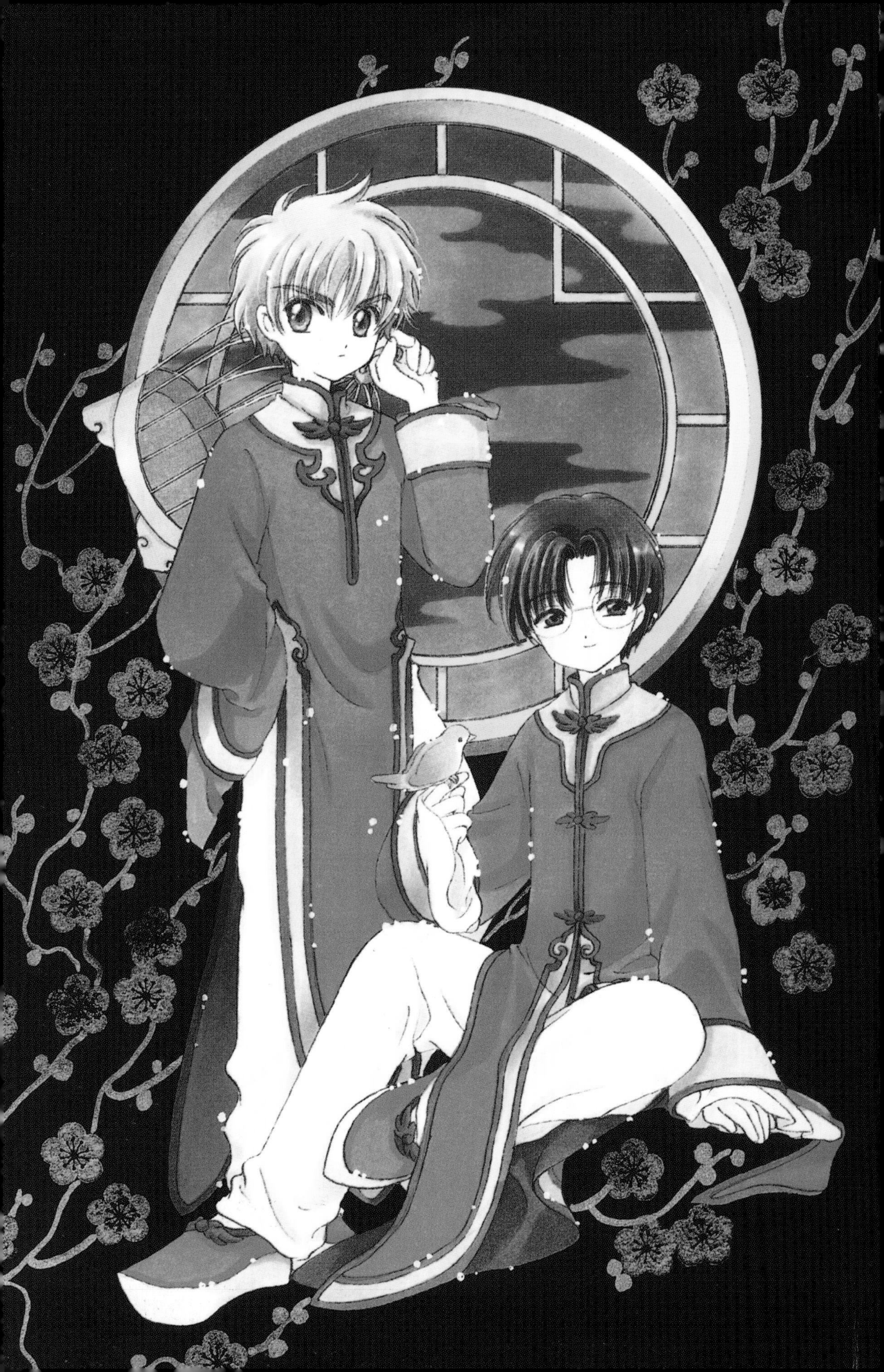

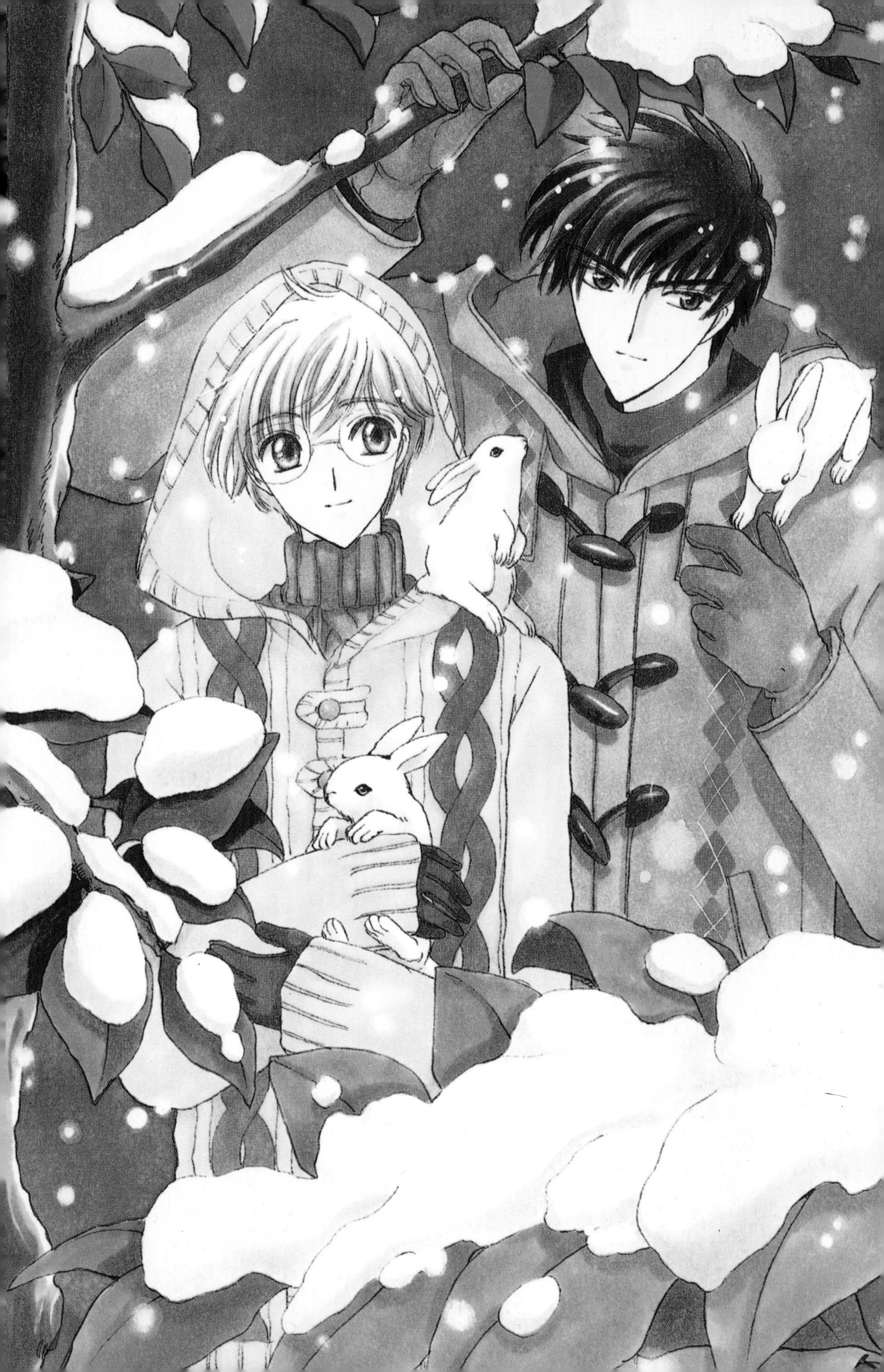

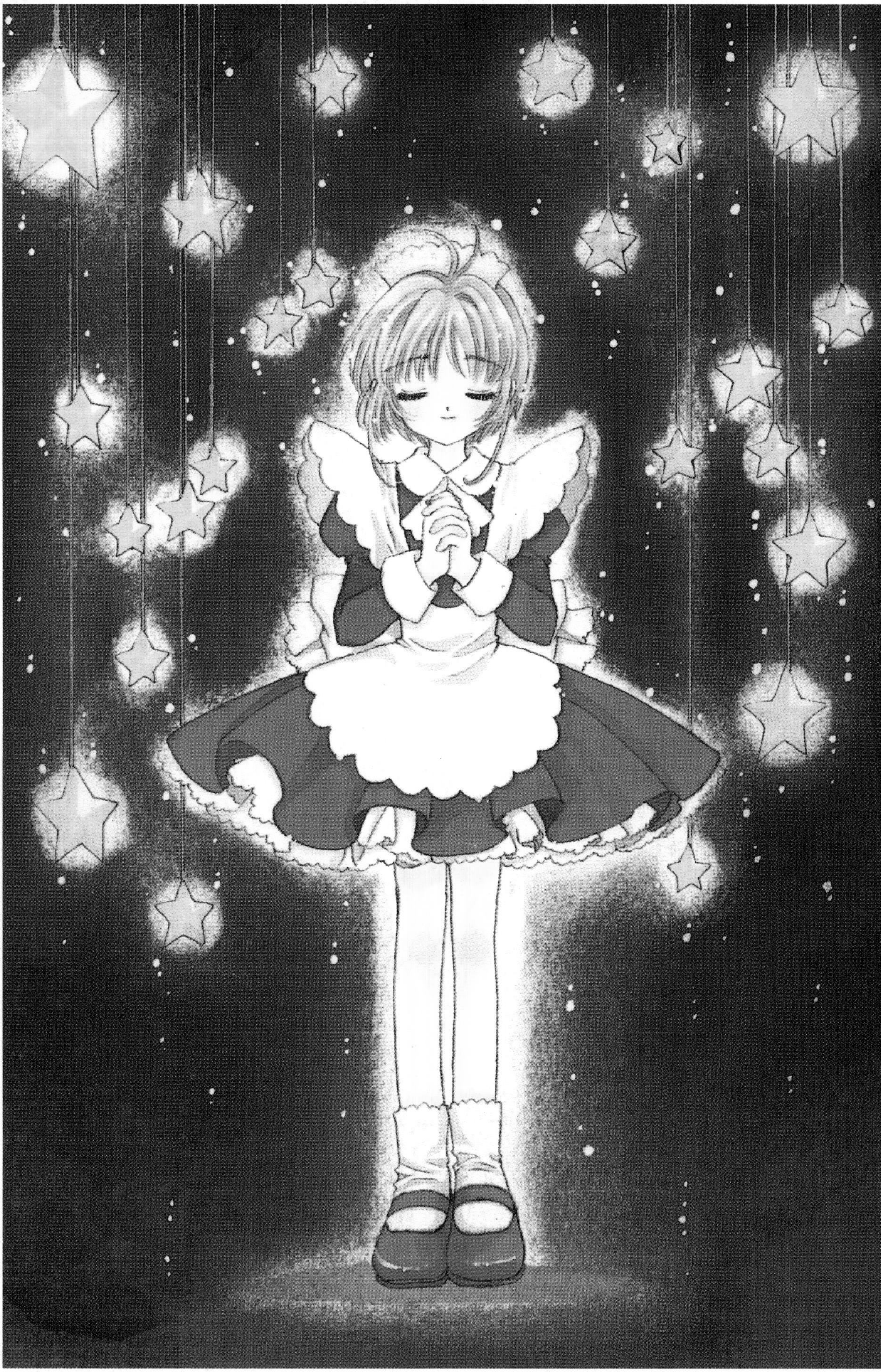

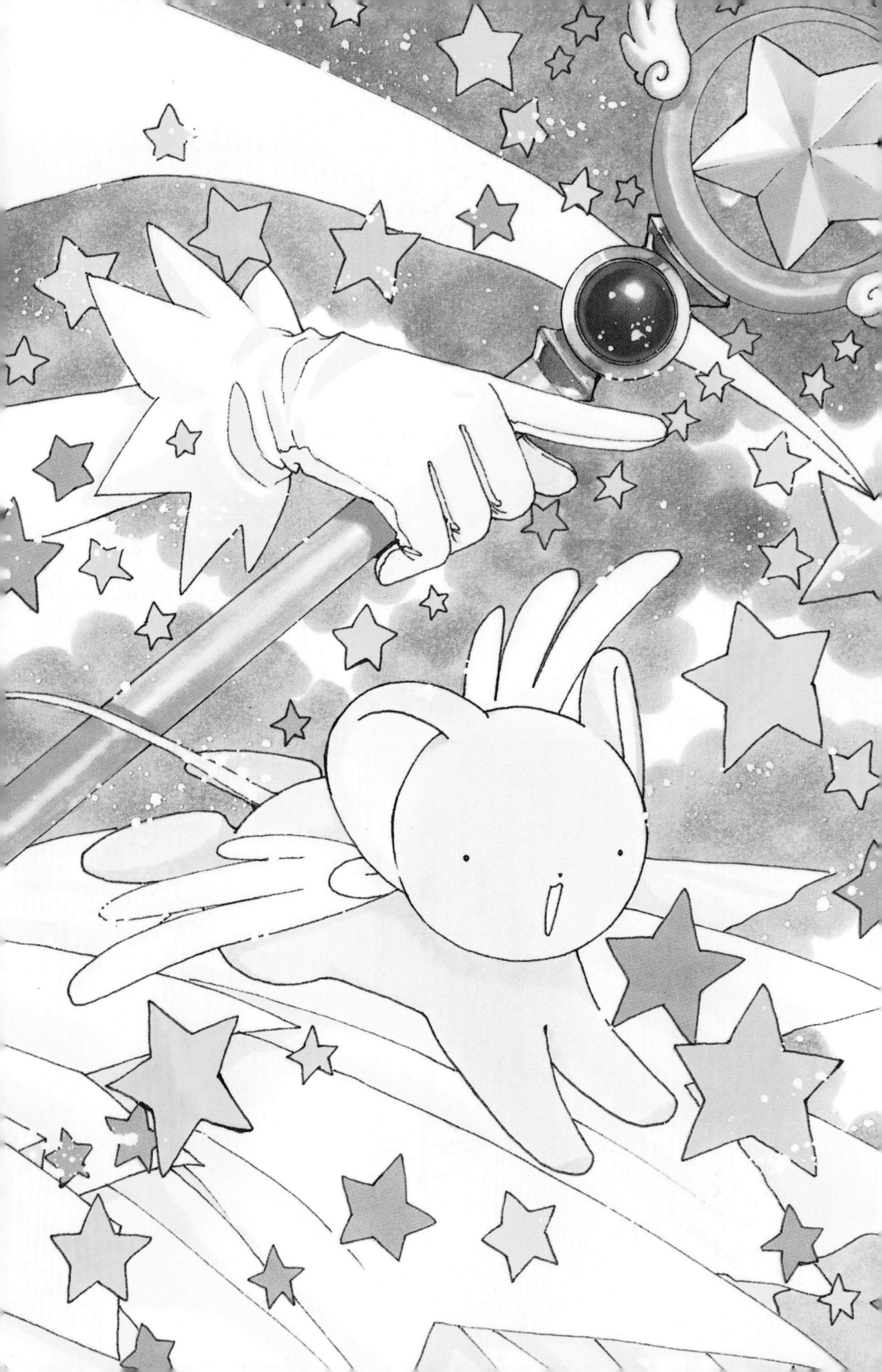

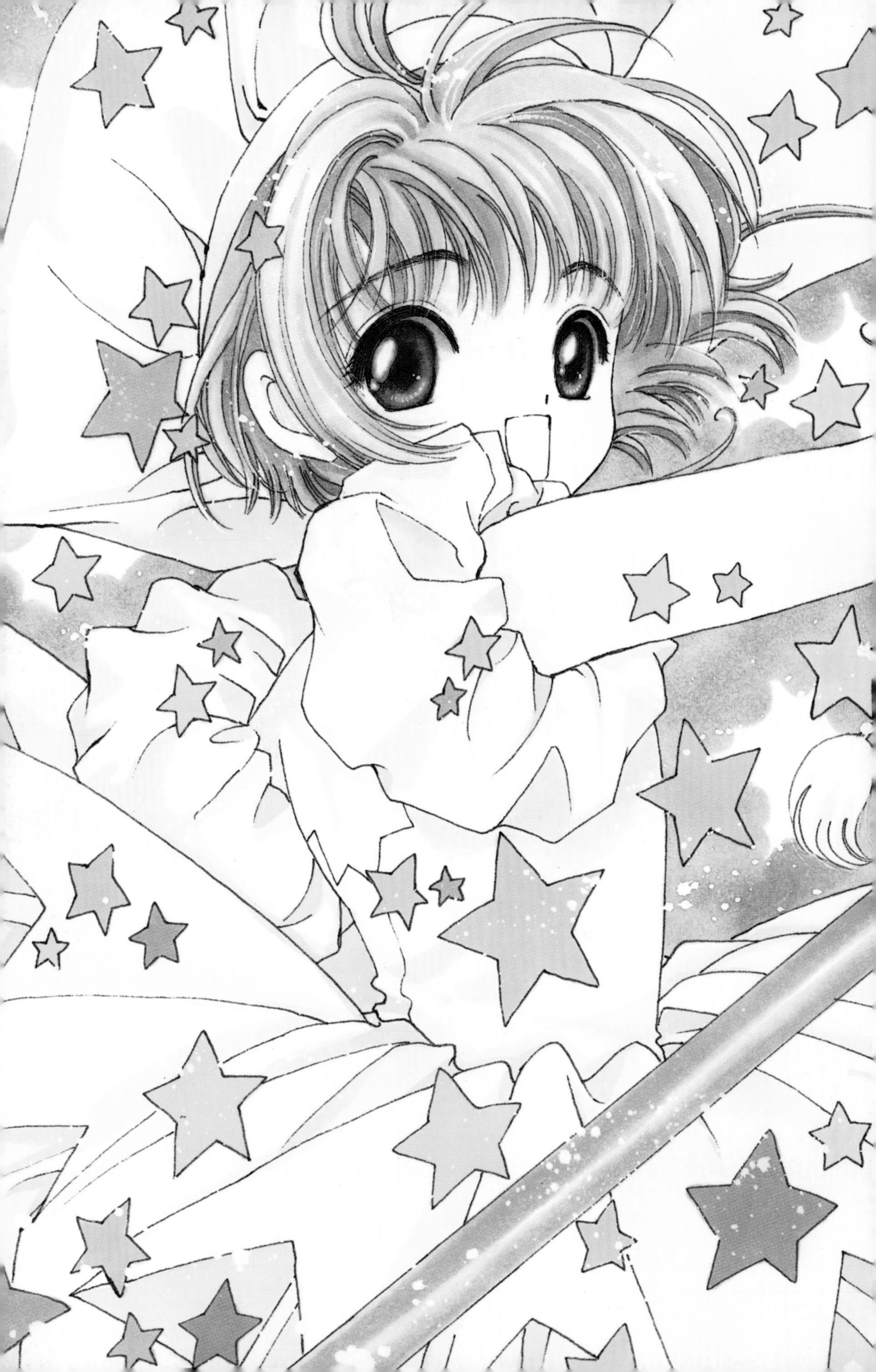

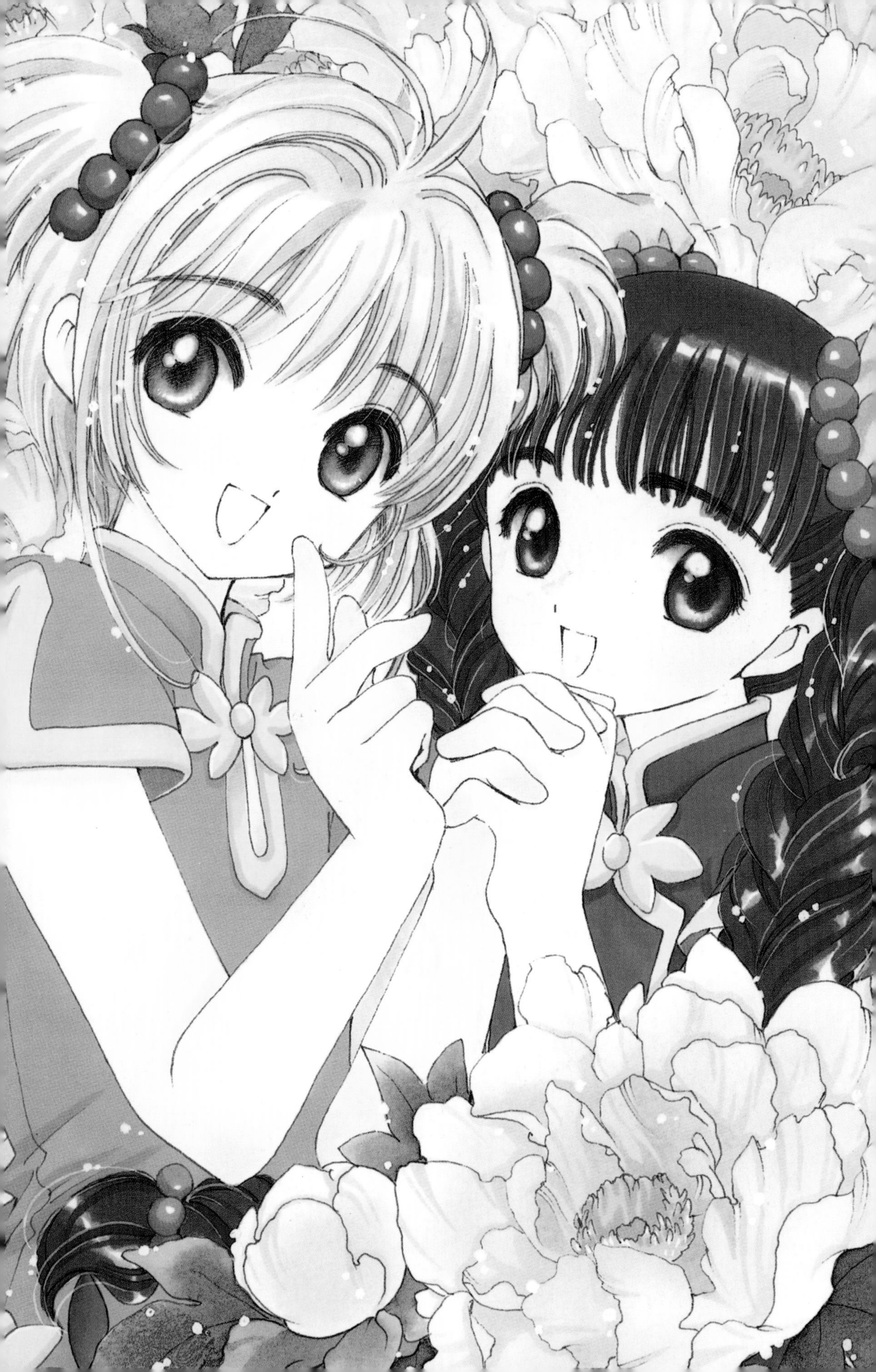

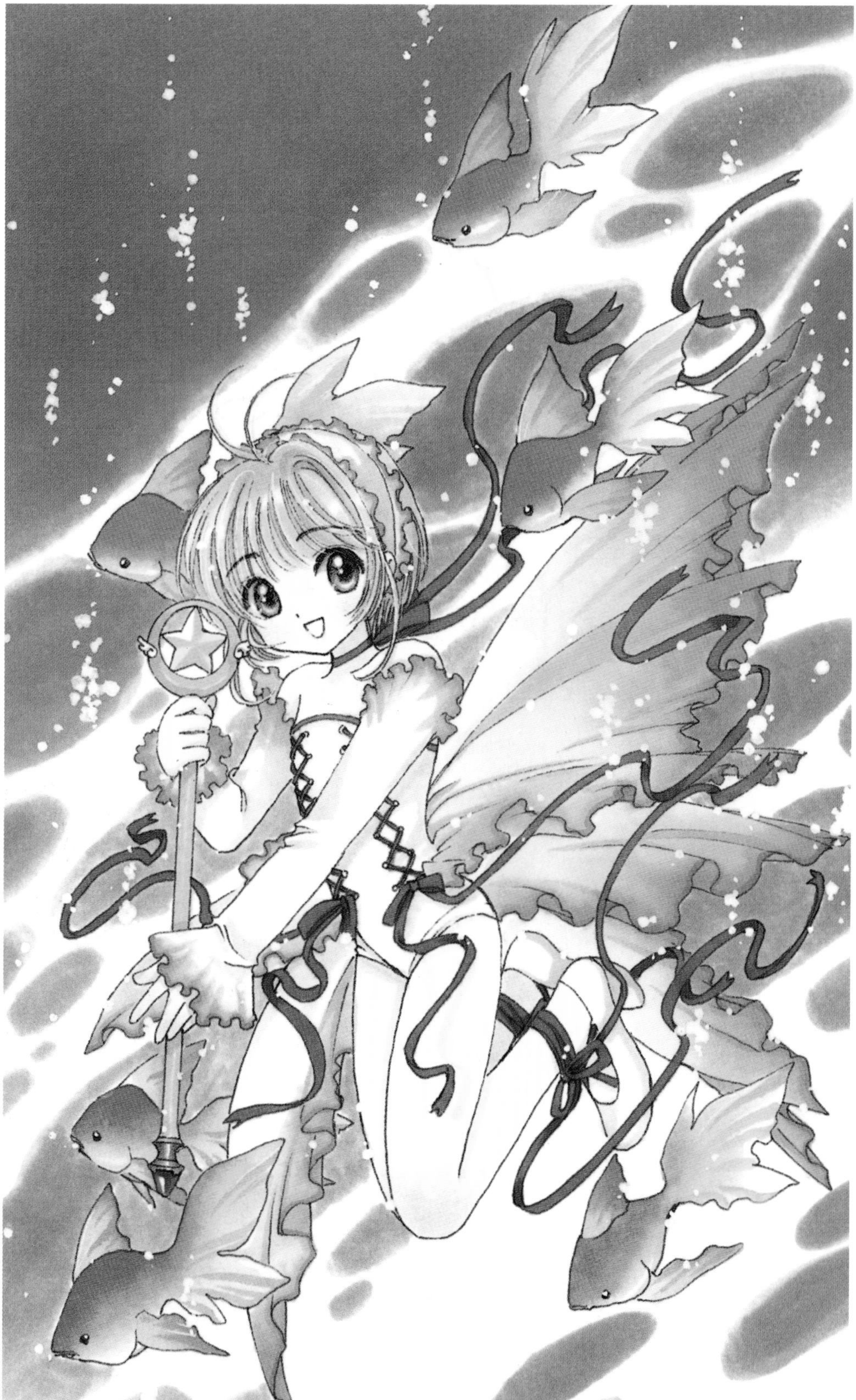

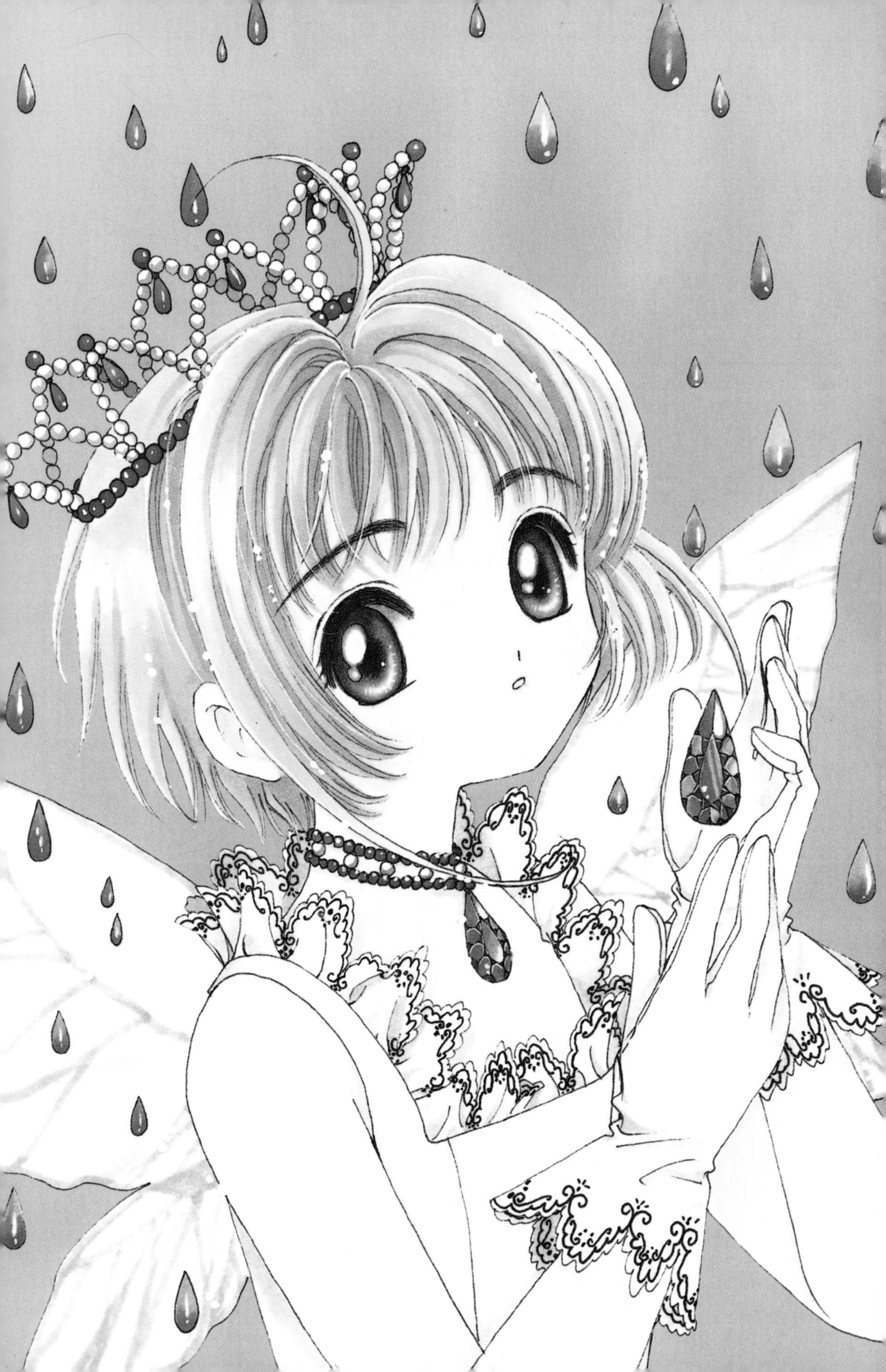

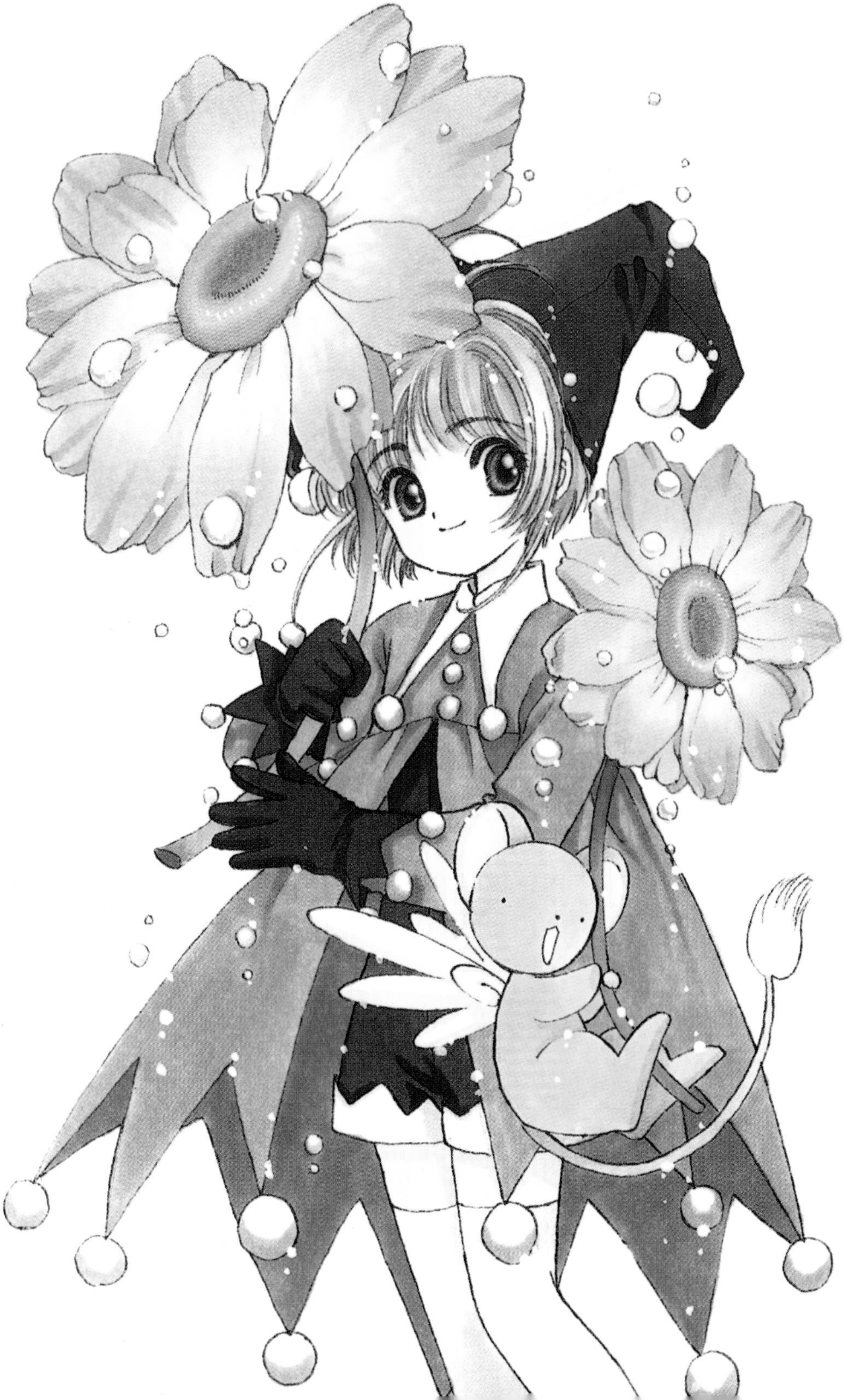

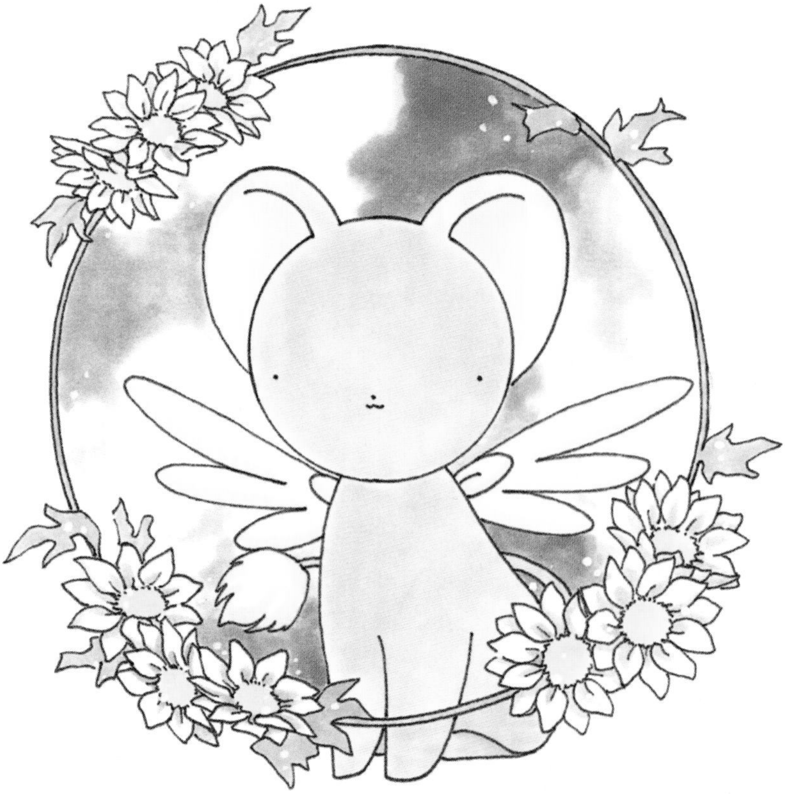

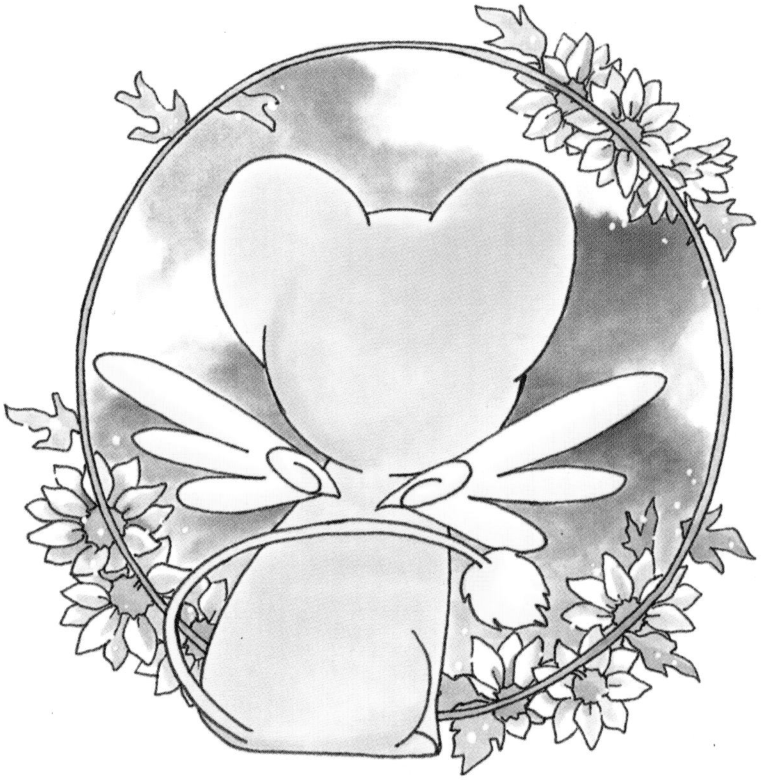

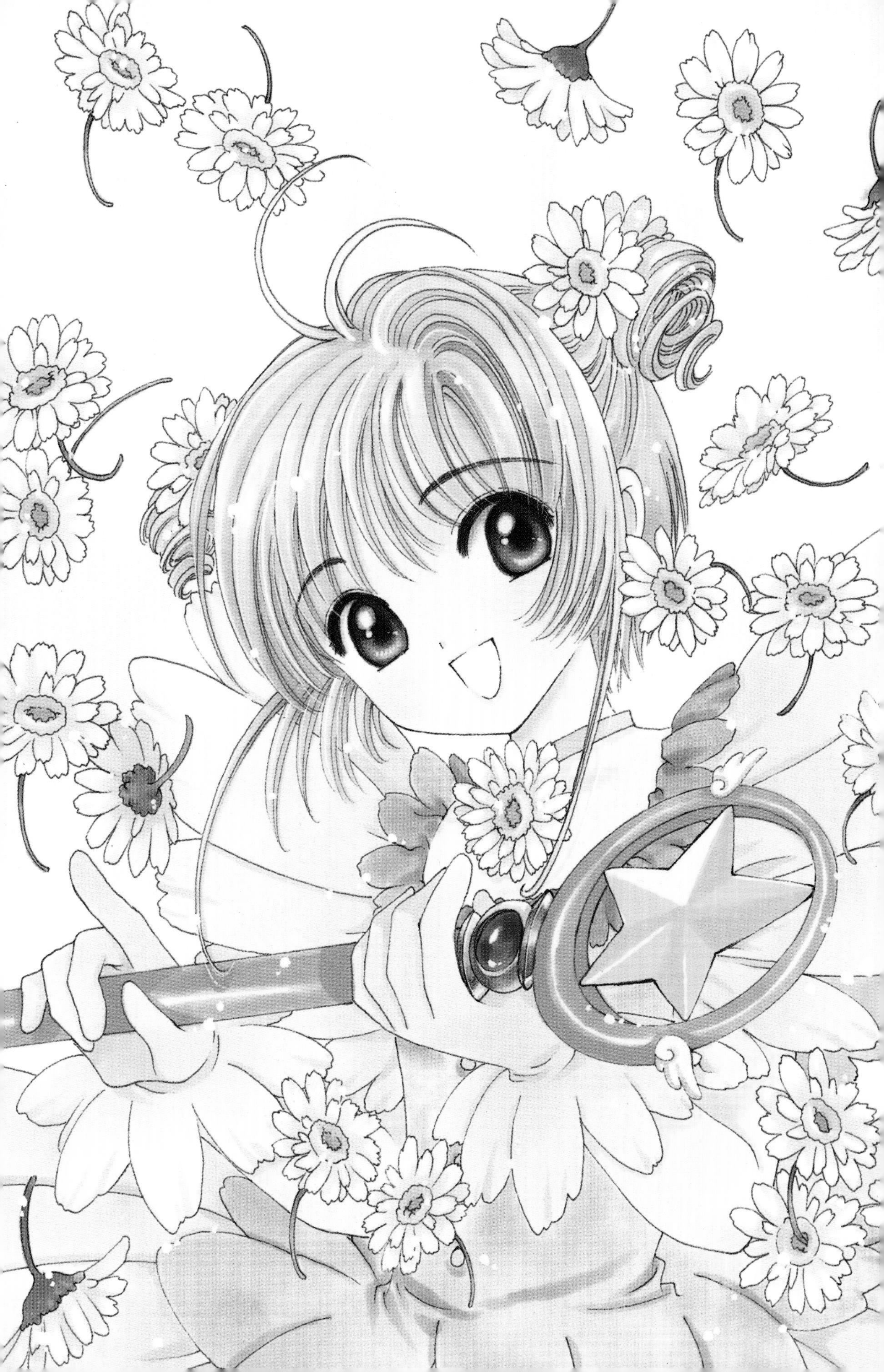

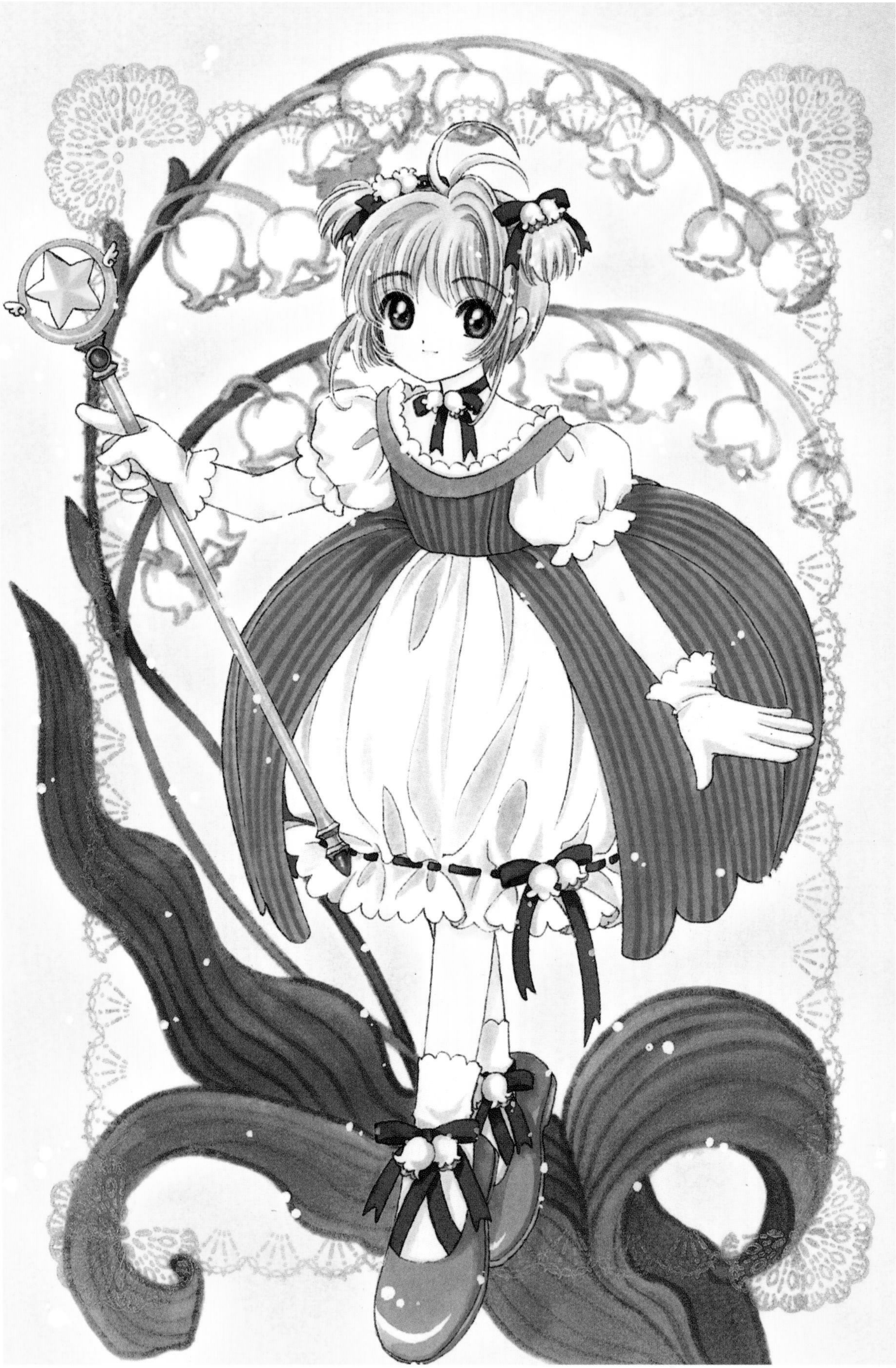

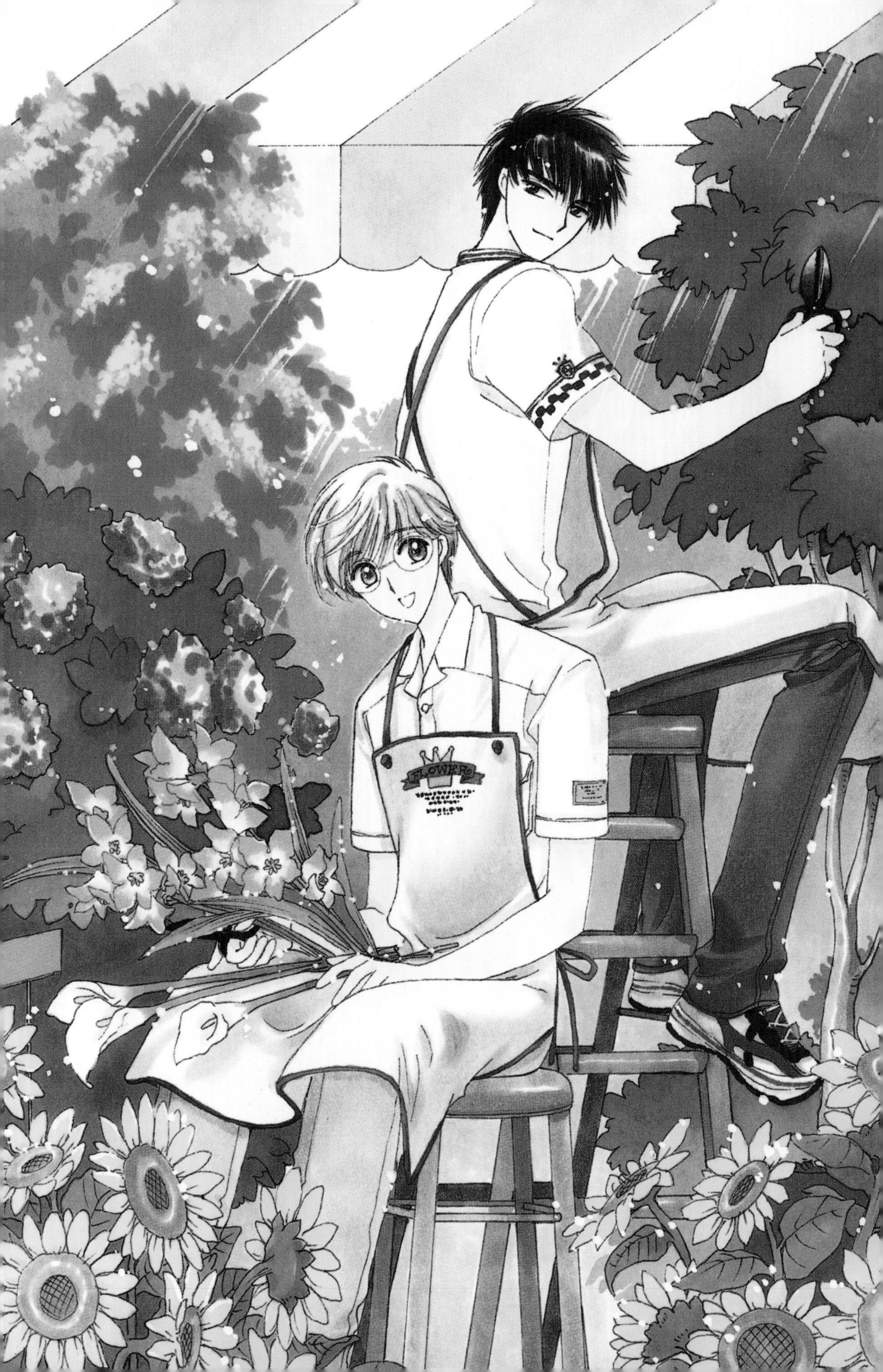

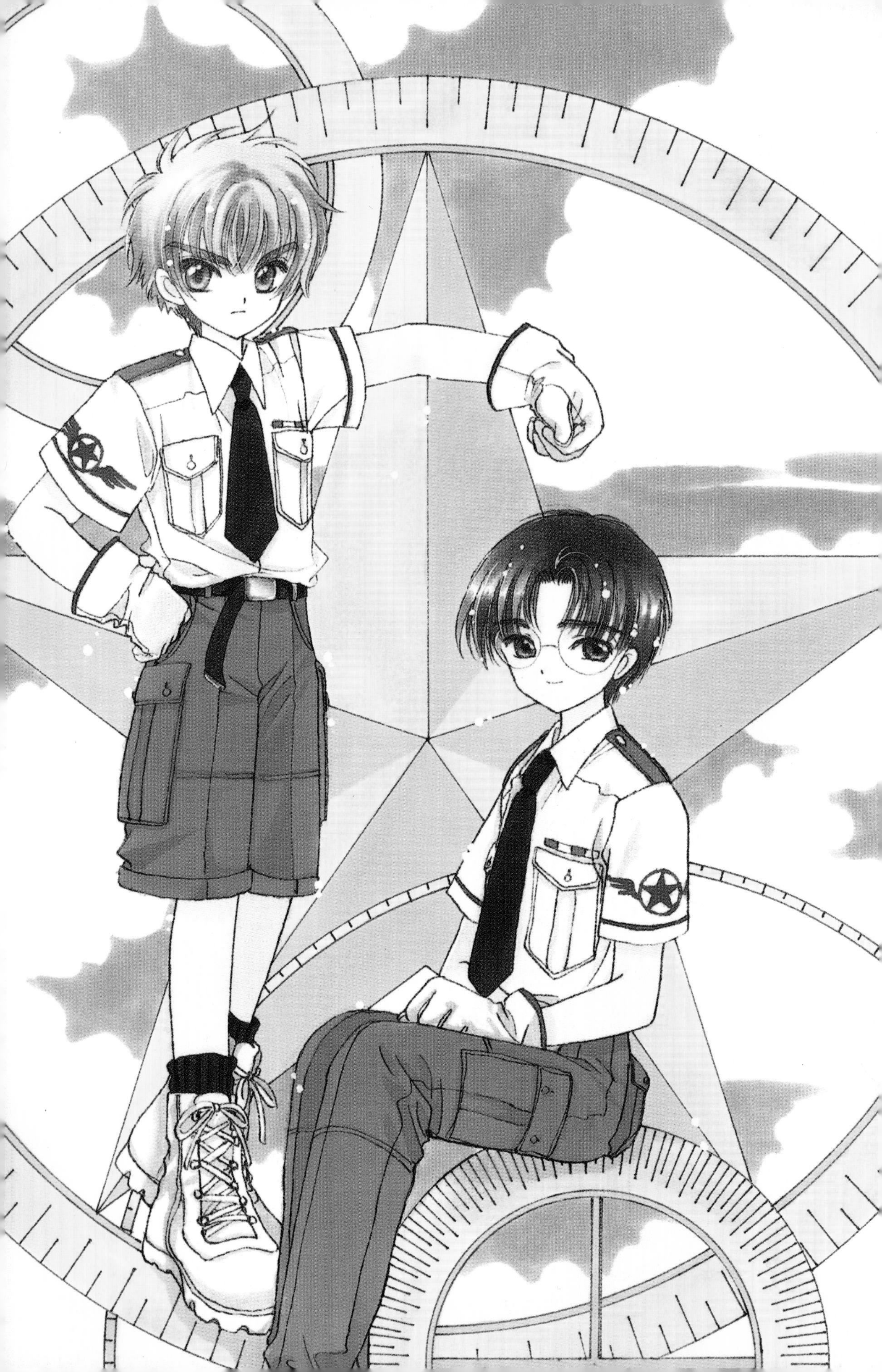

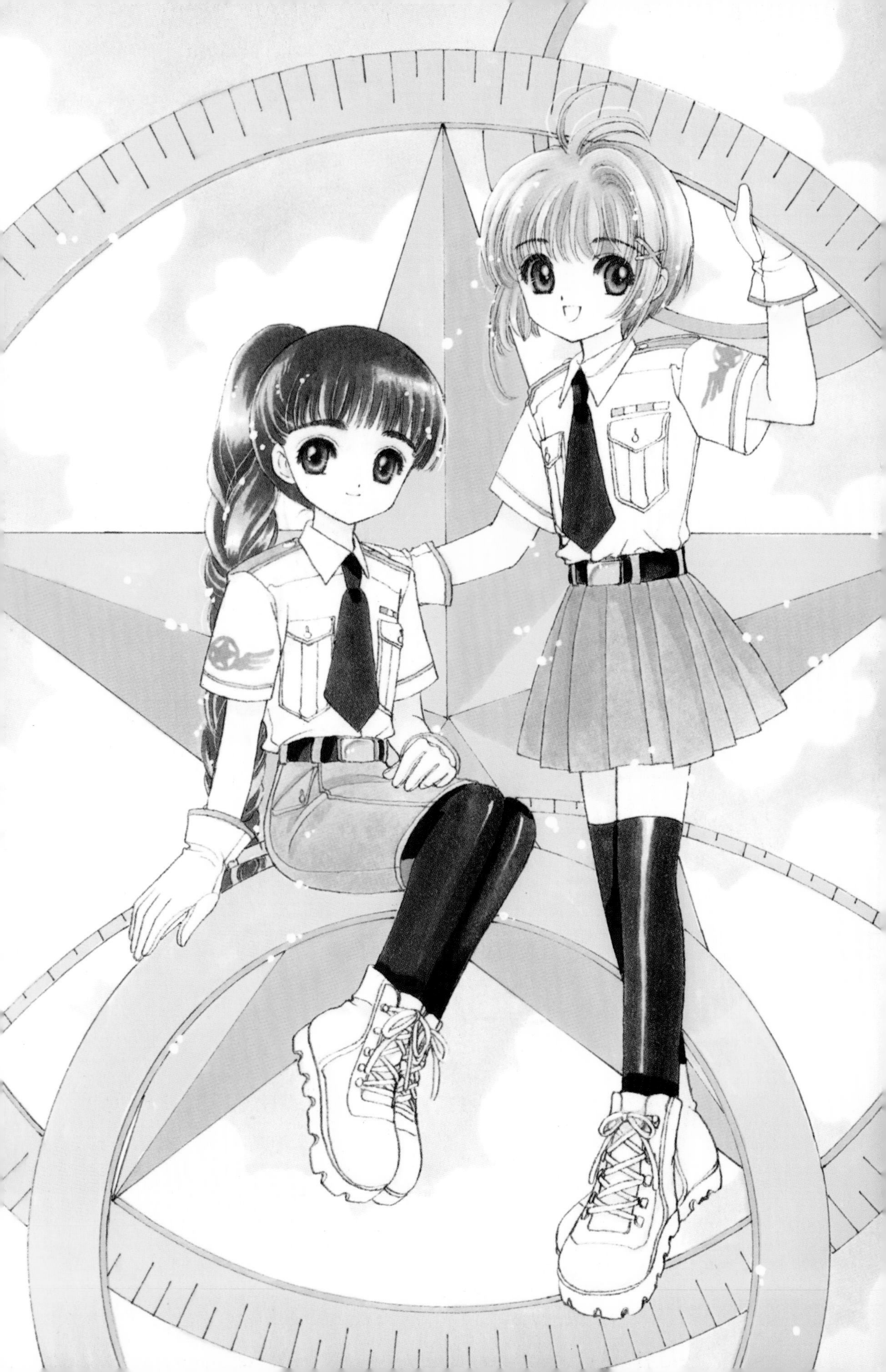

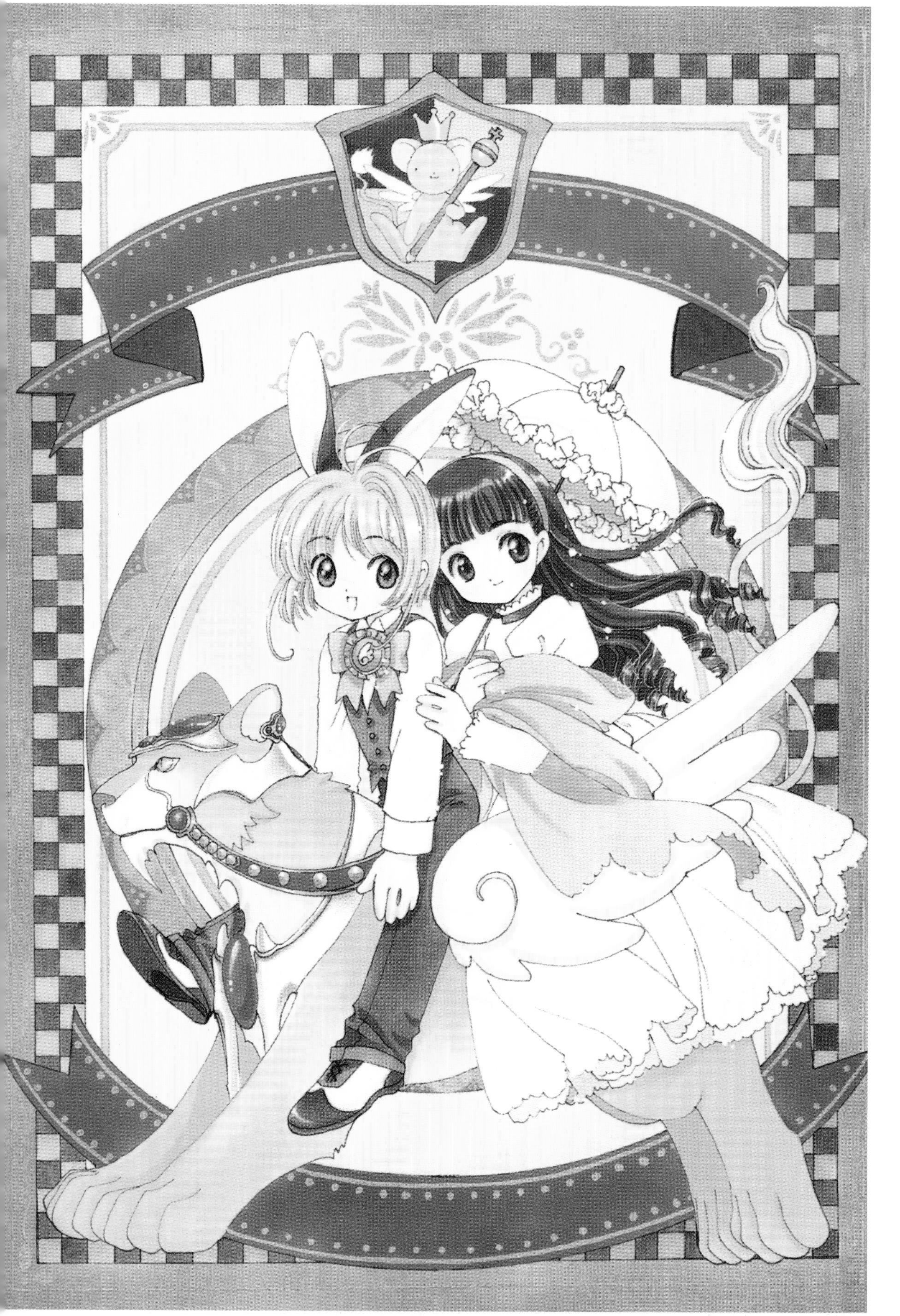

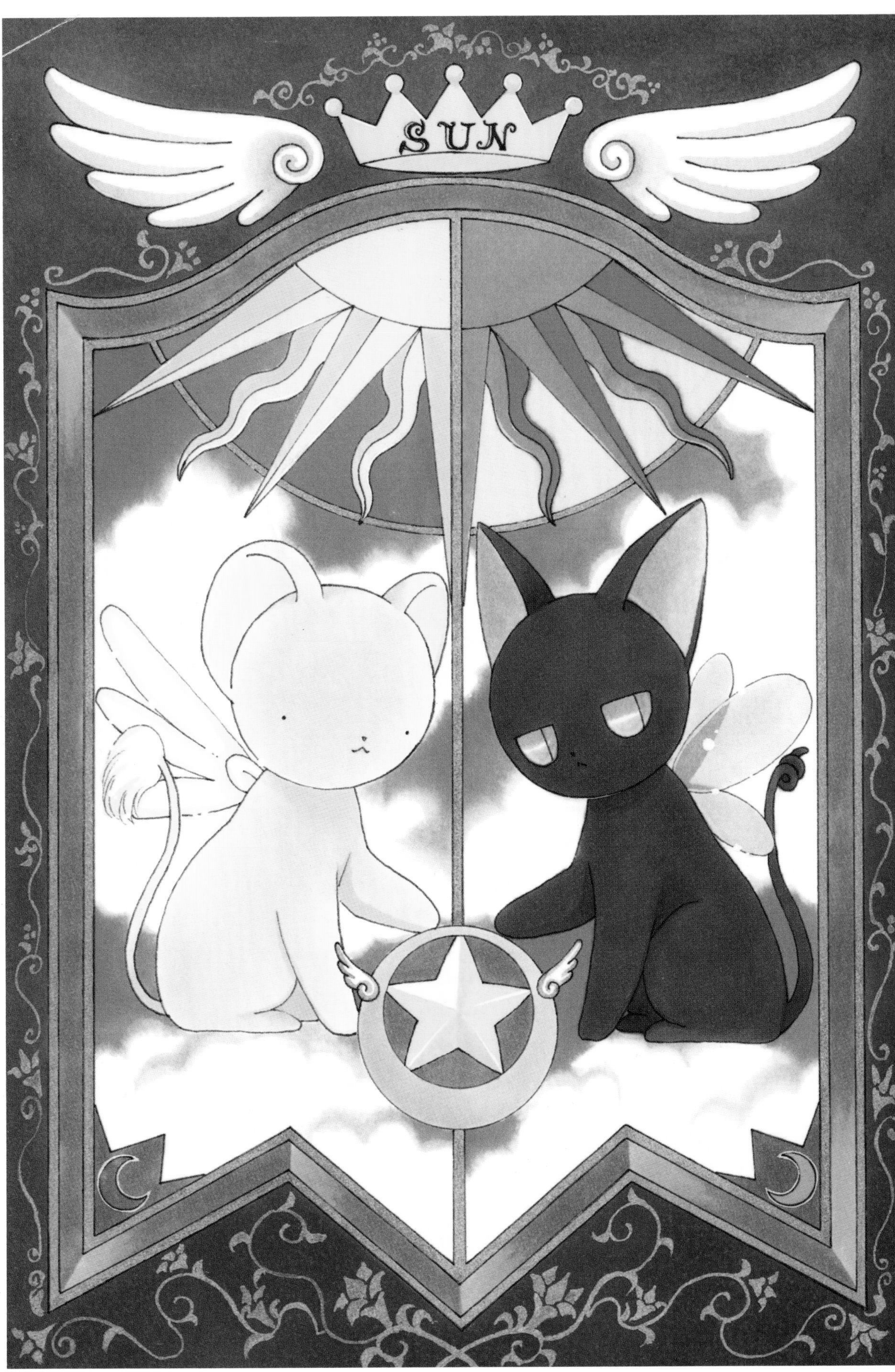
SUN

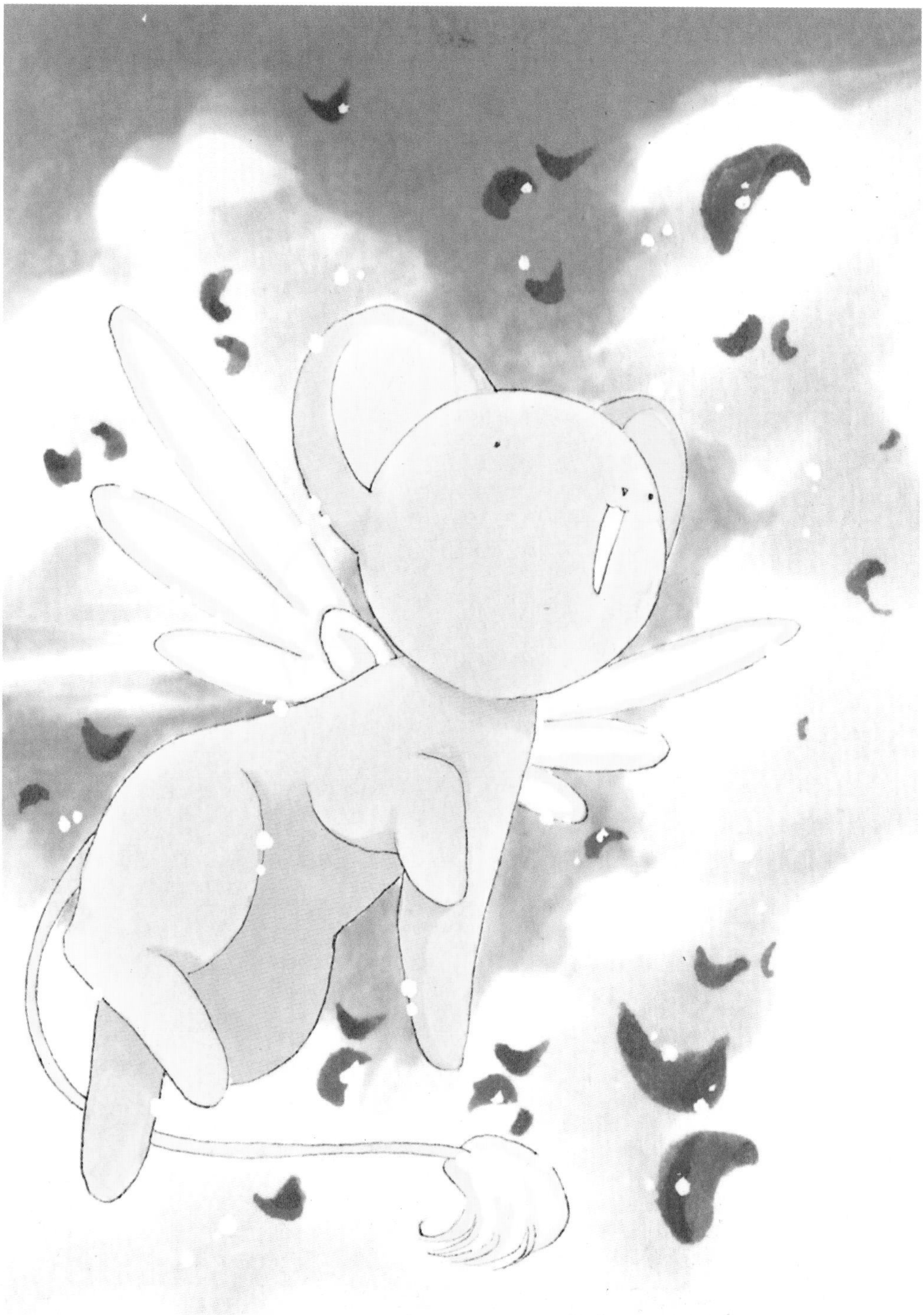

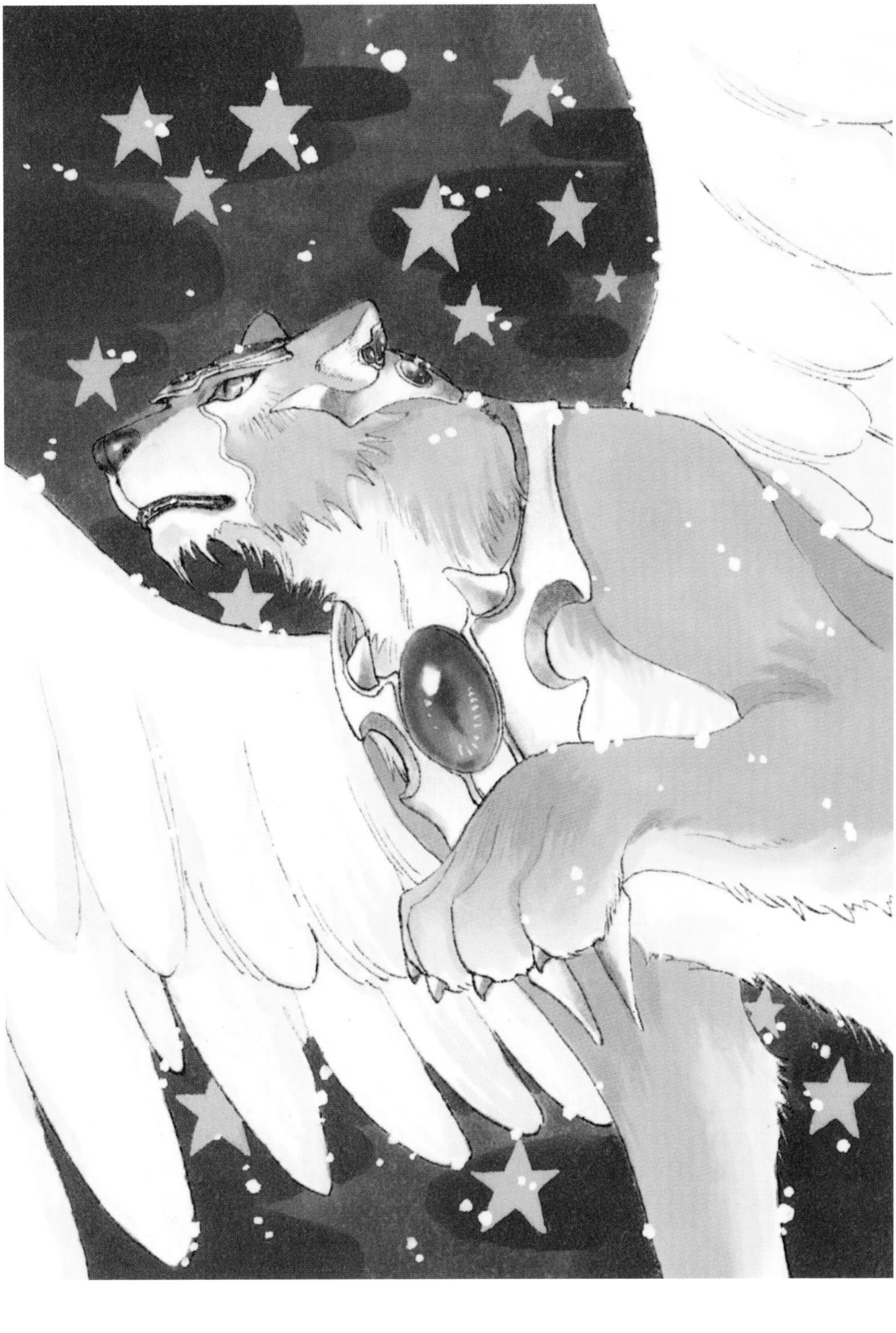

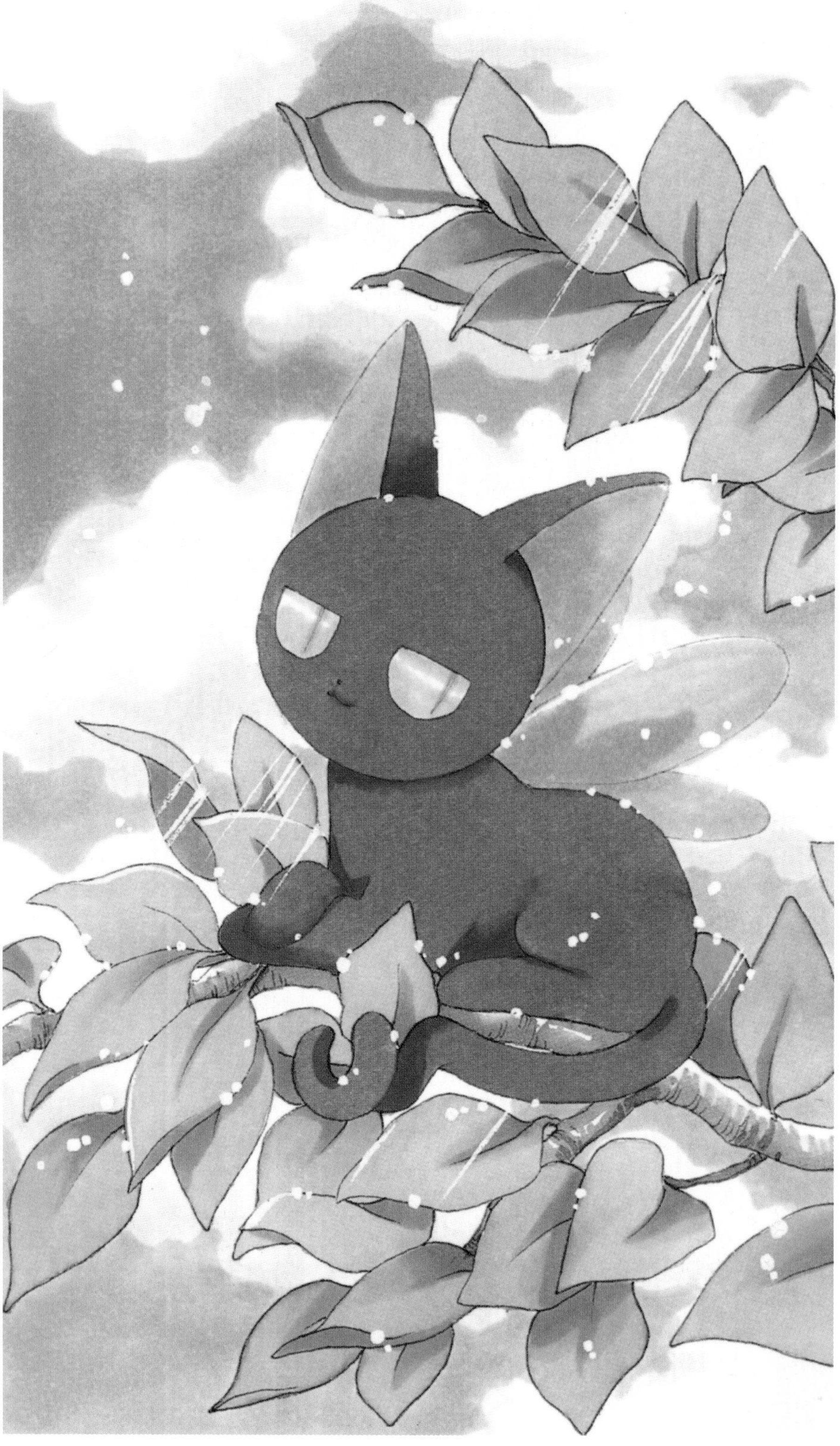

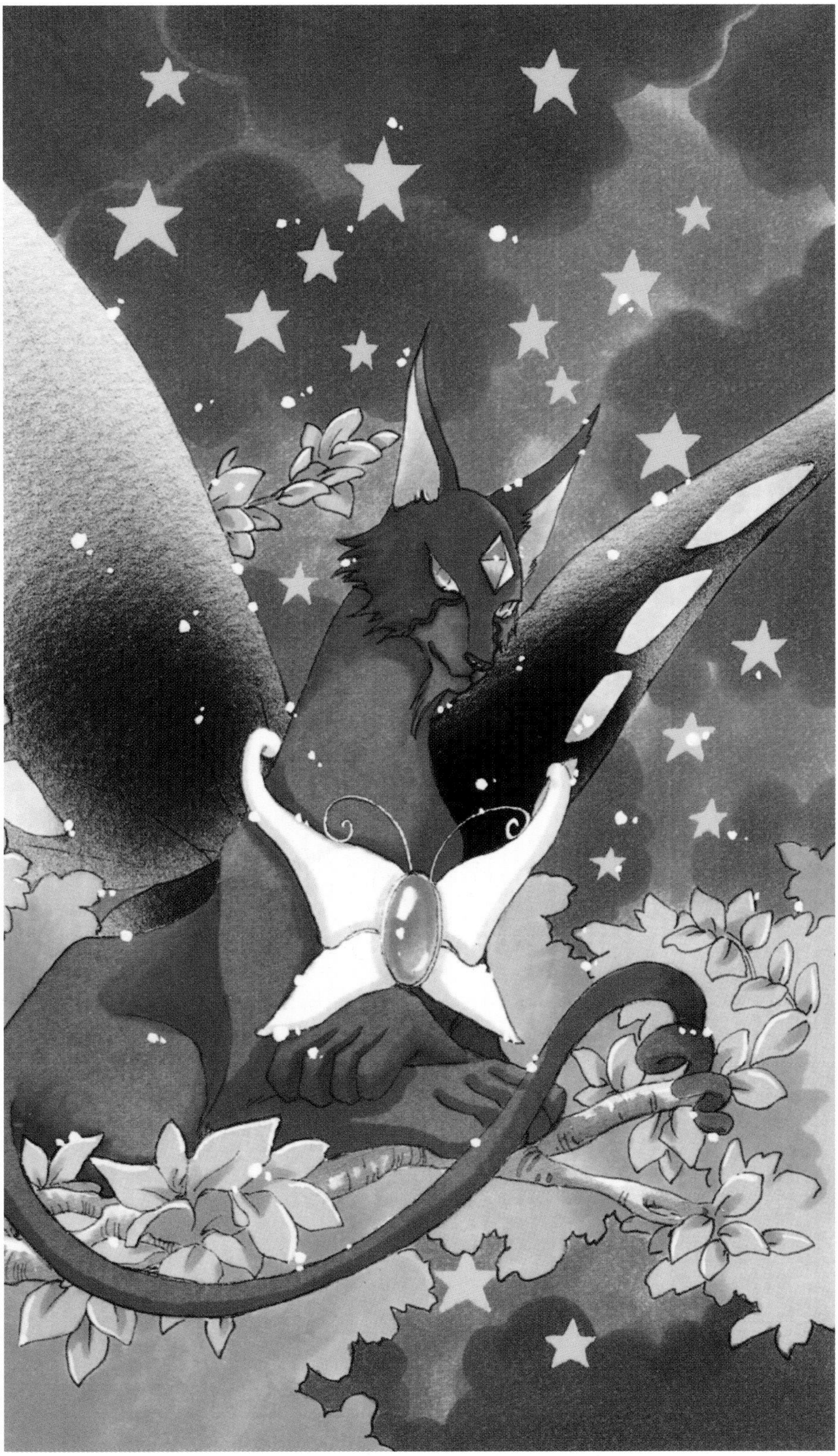

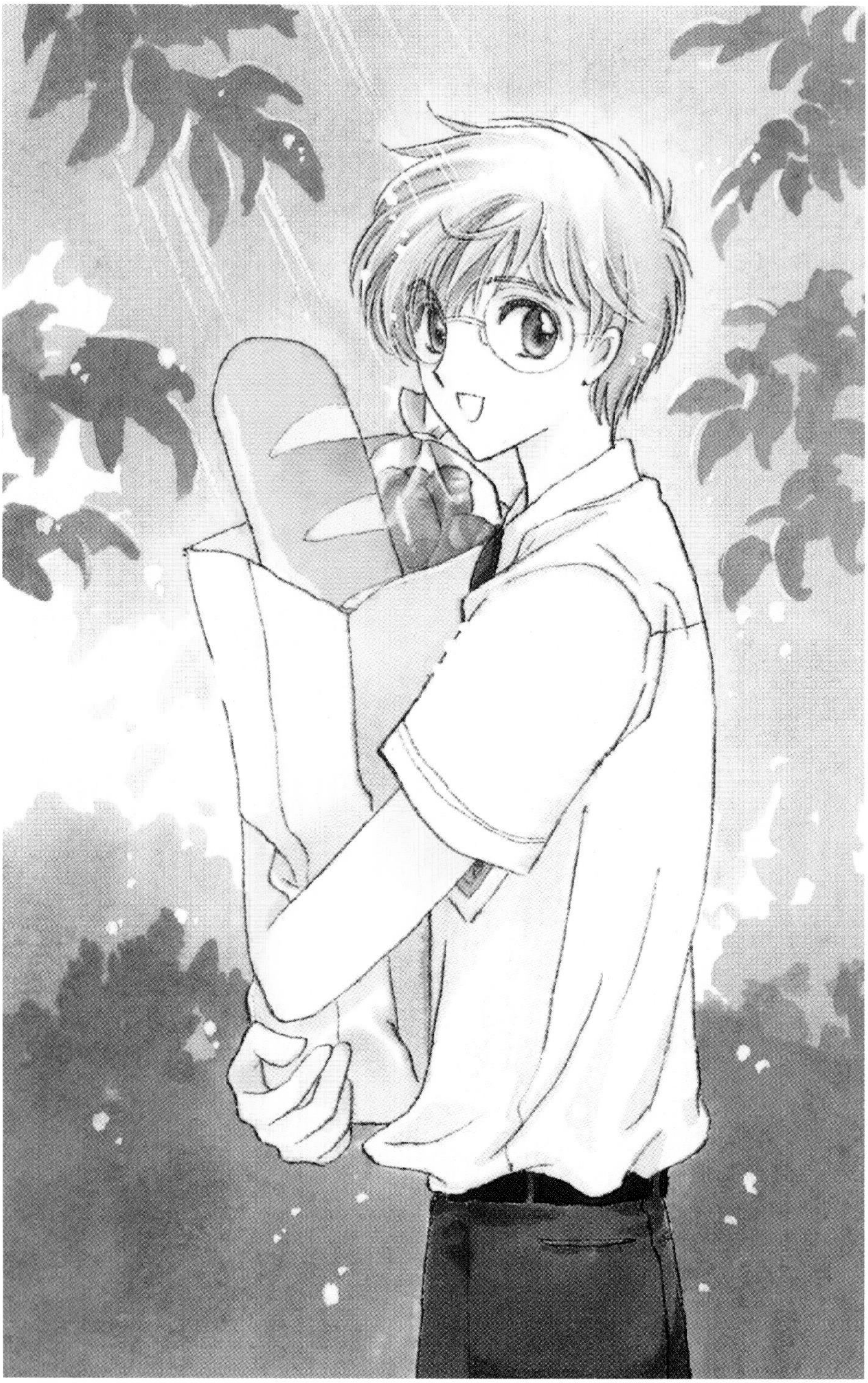

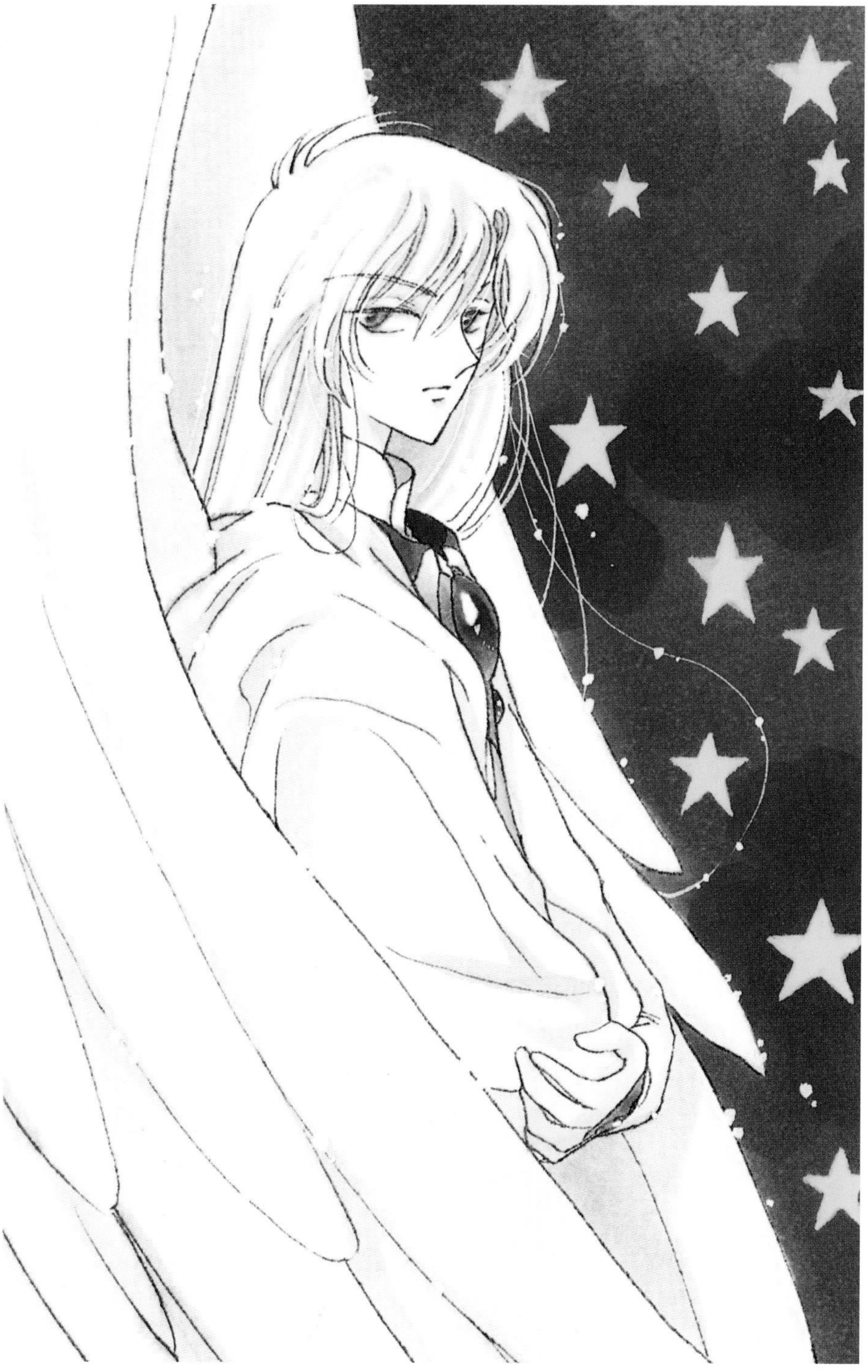

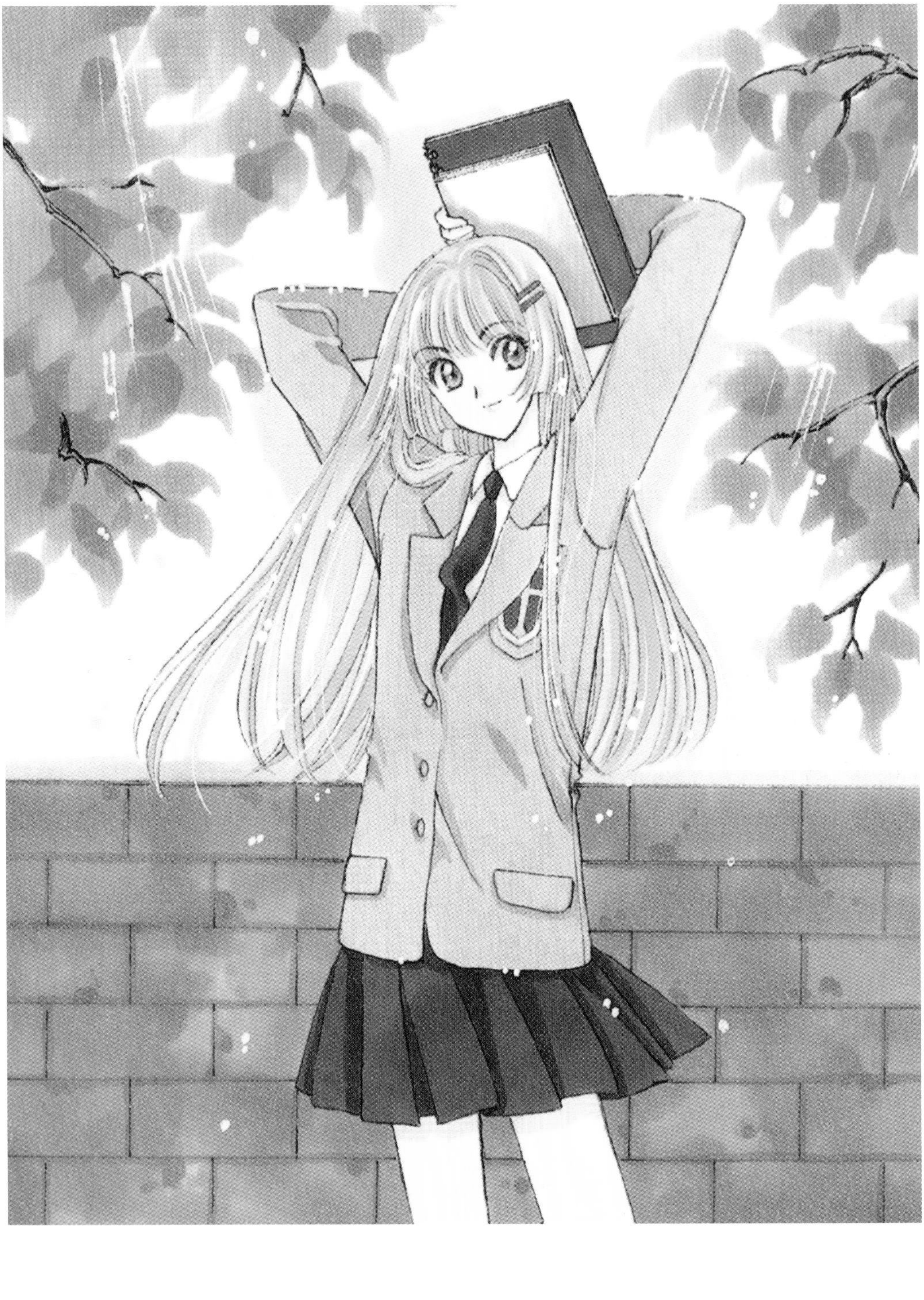

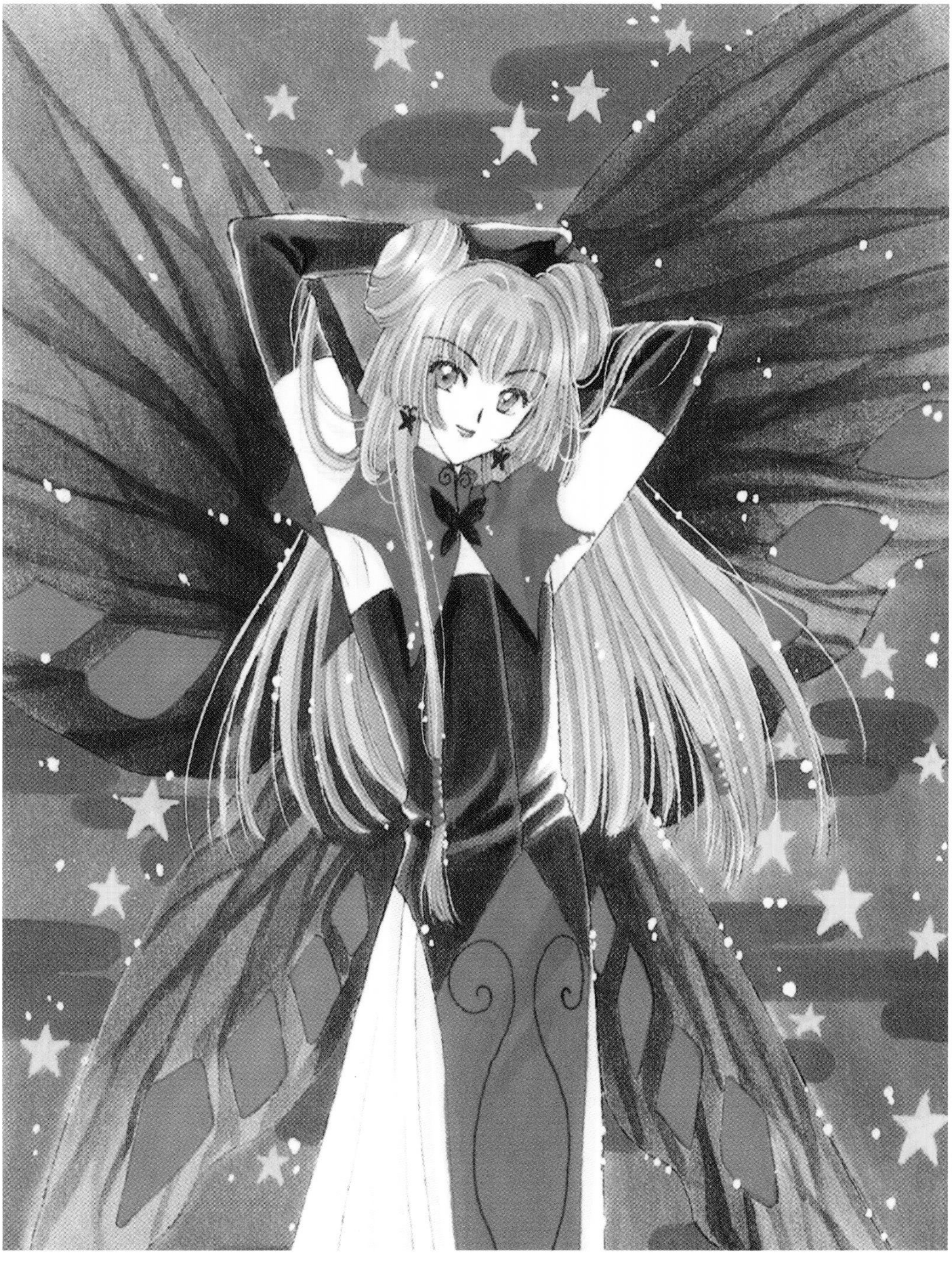

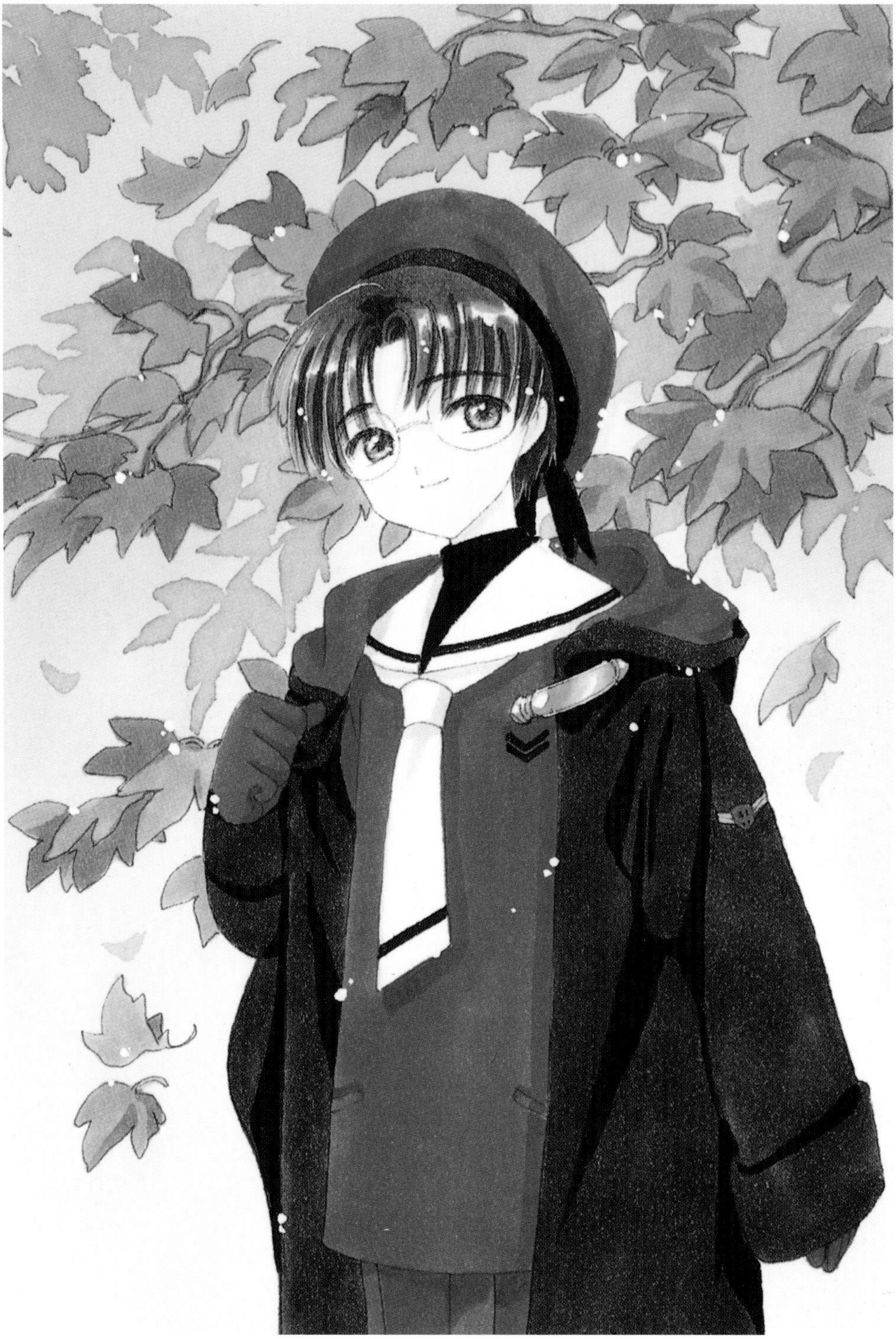

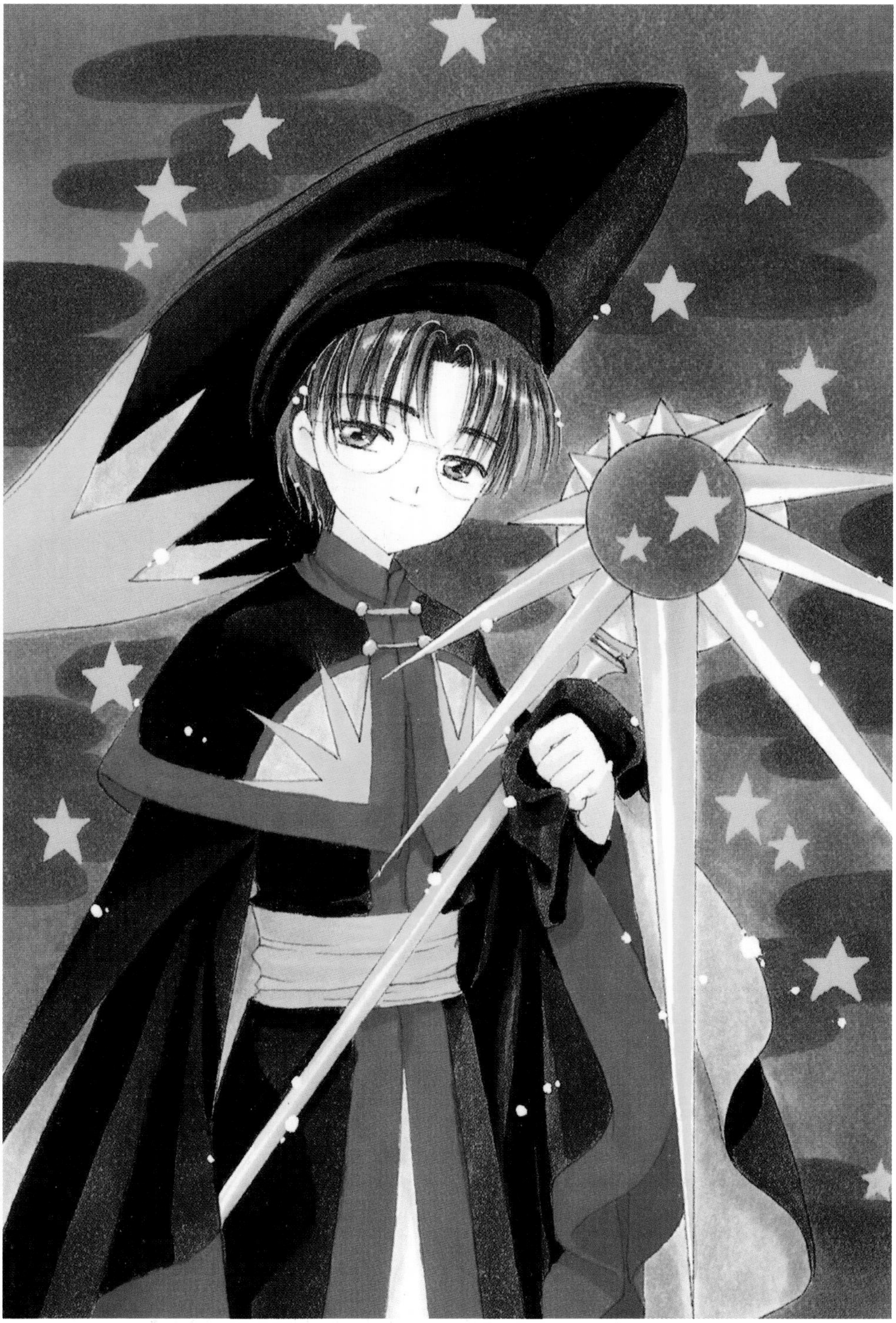

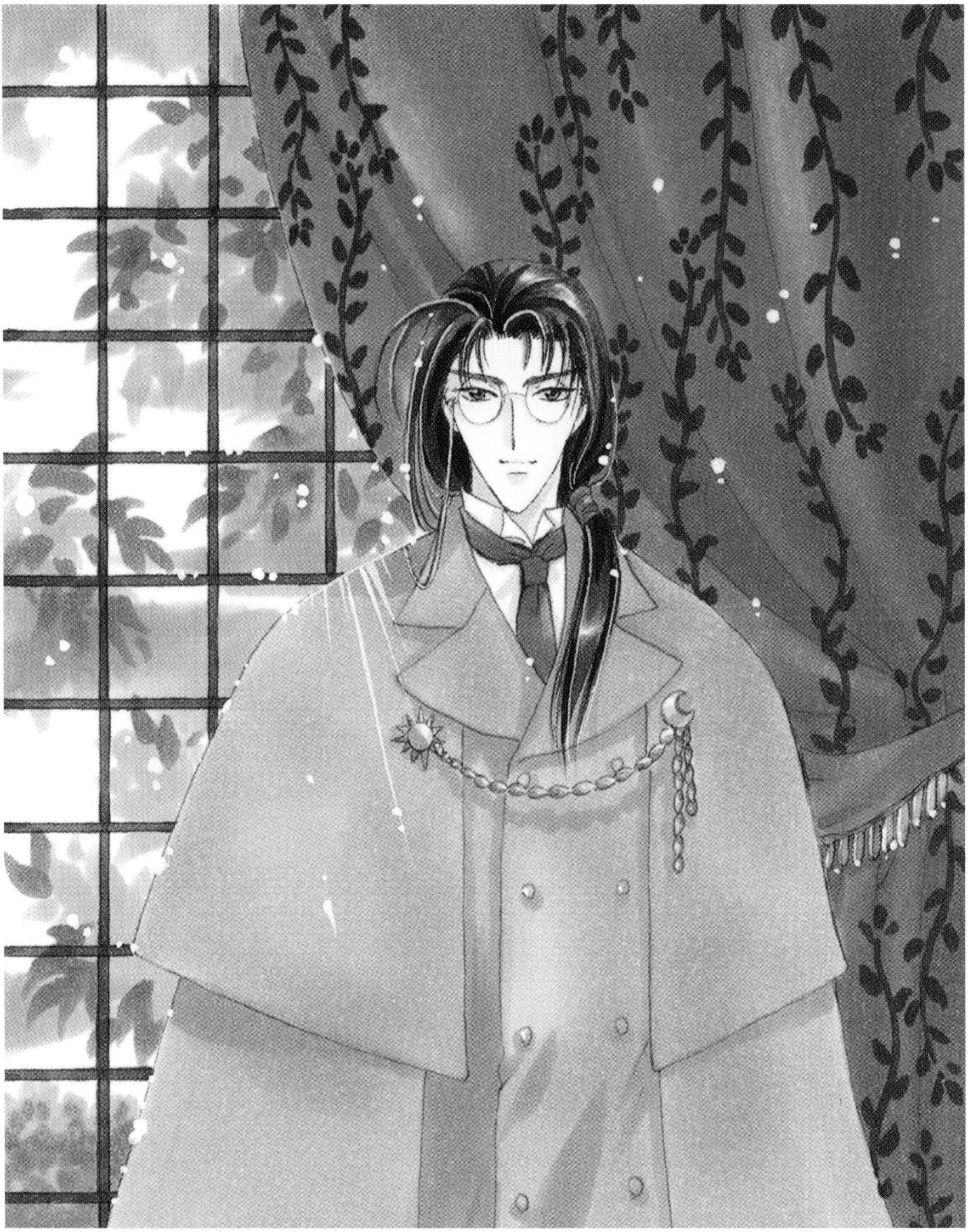

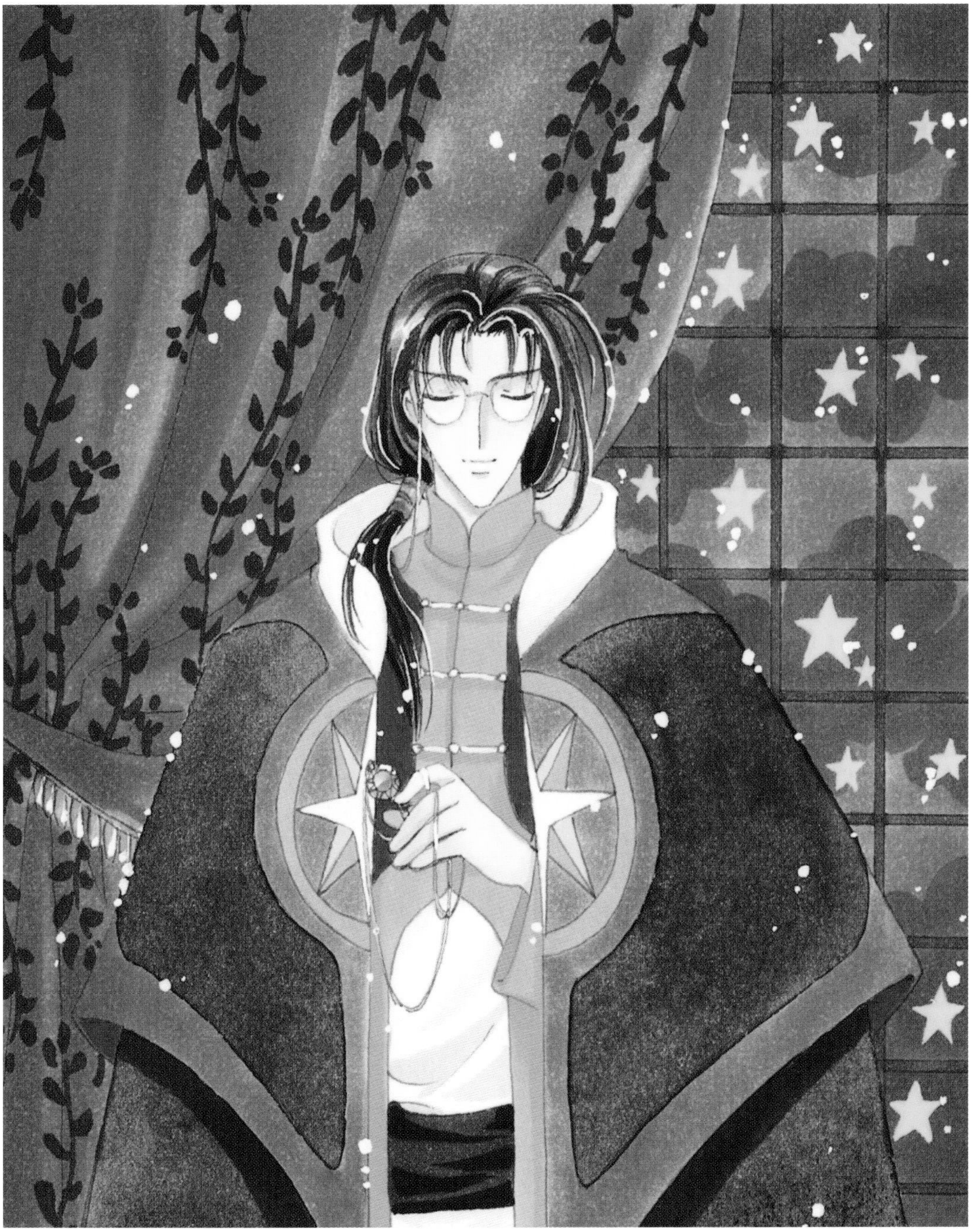

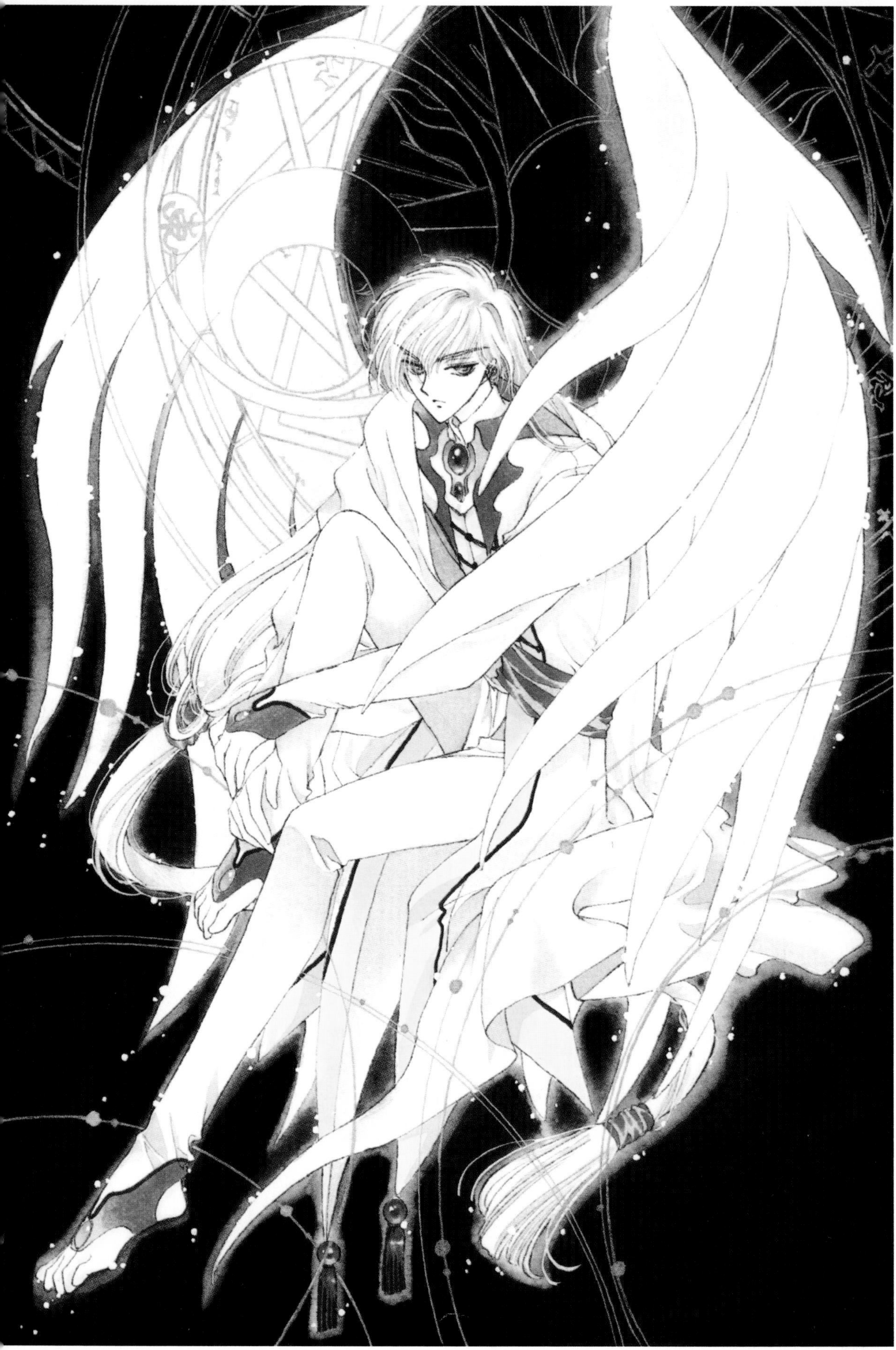

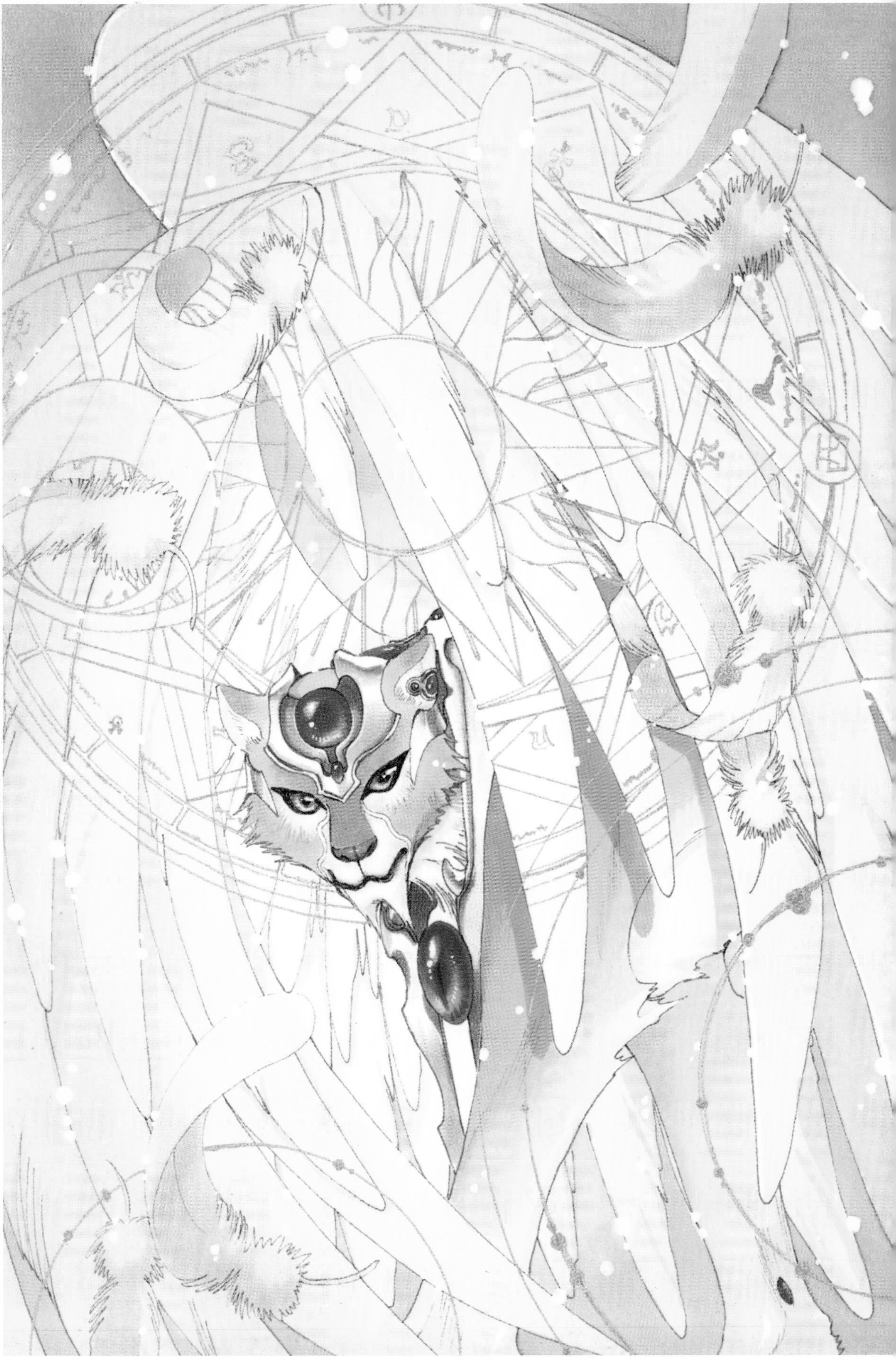

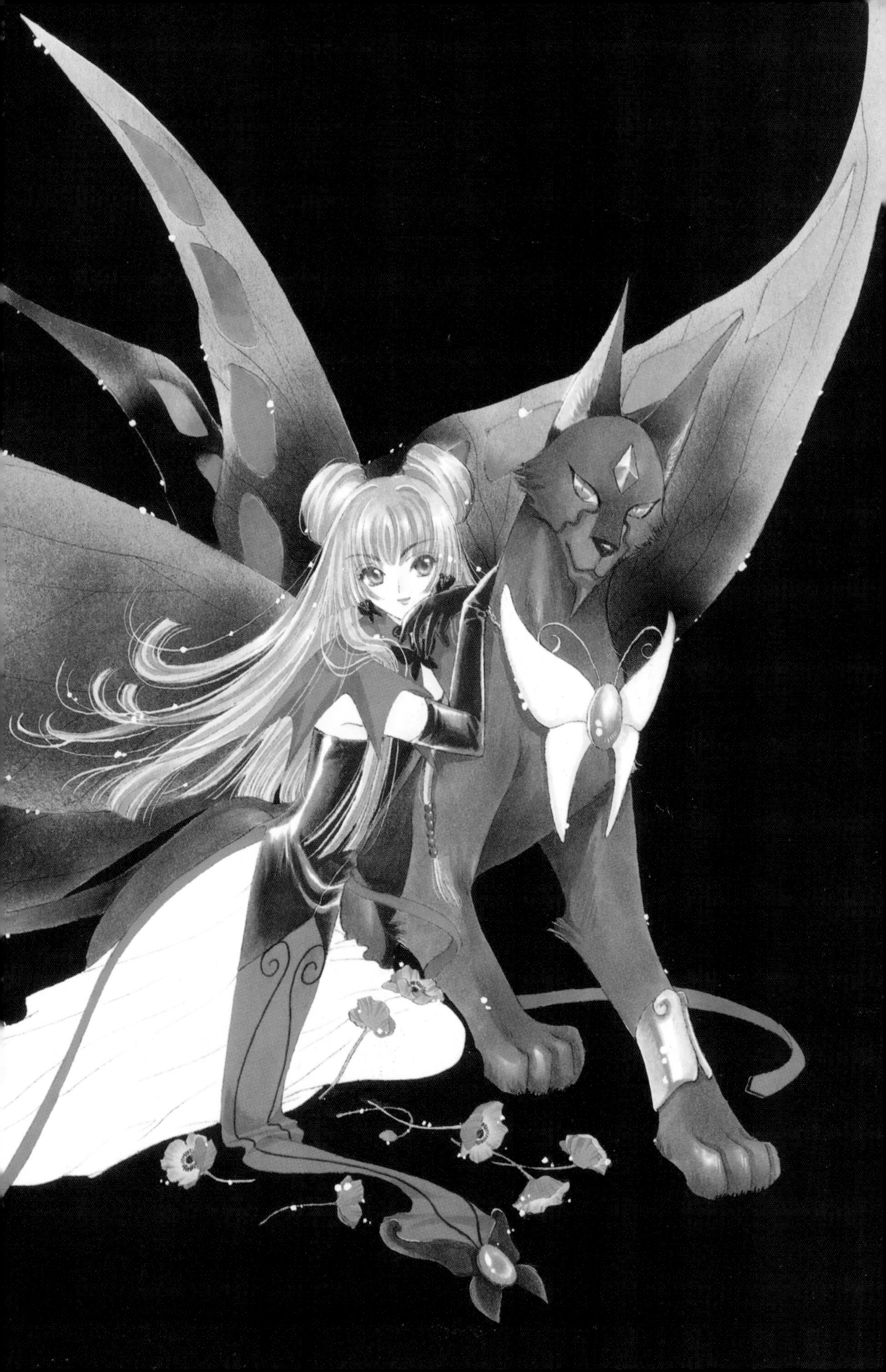

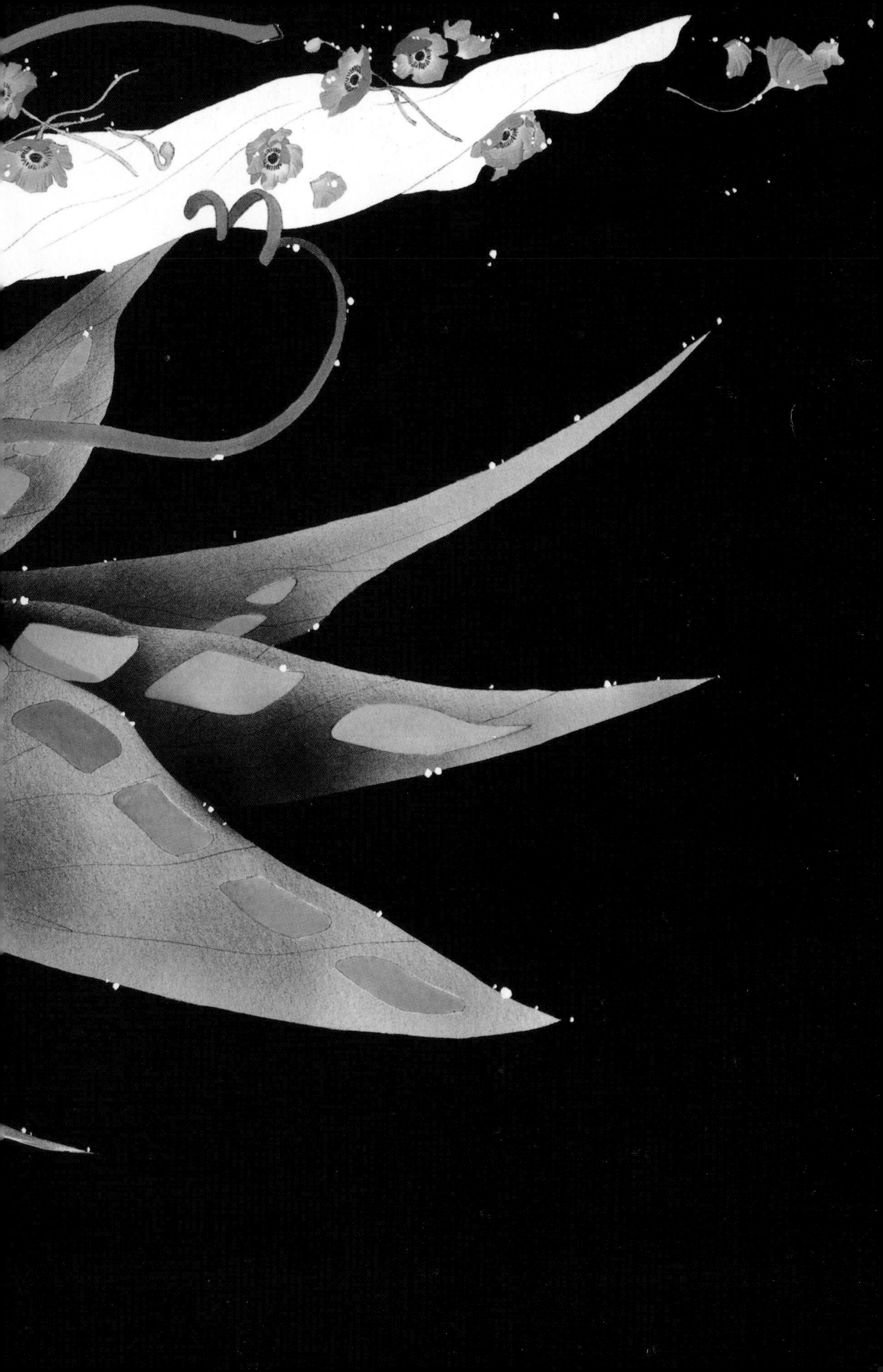

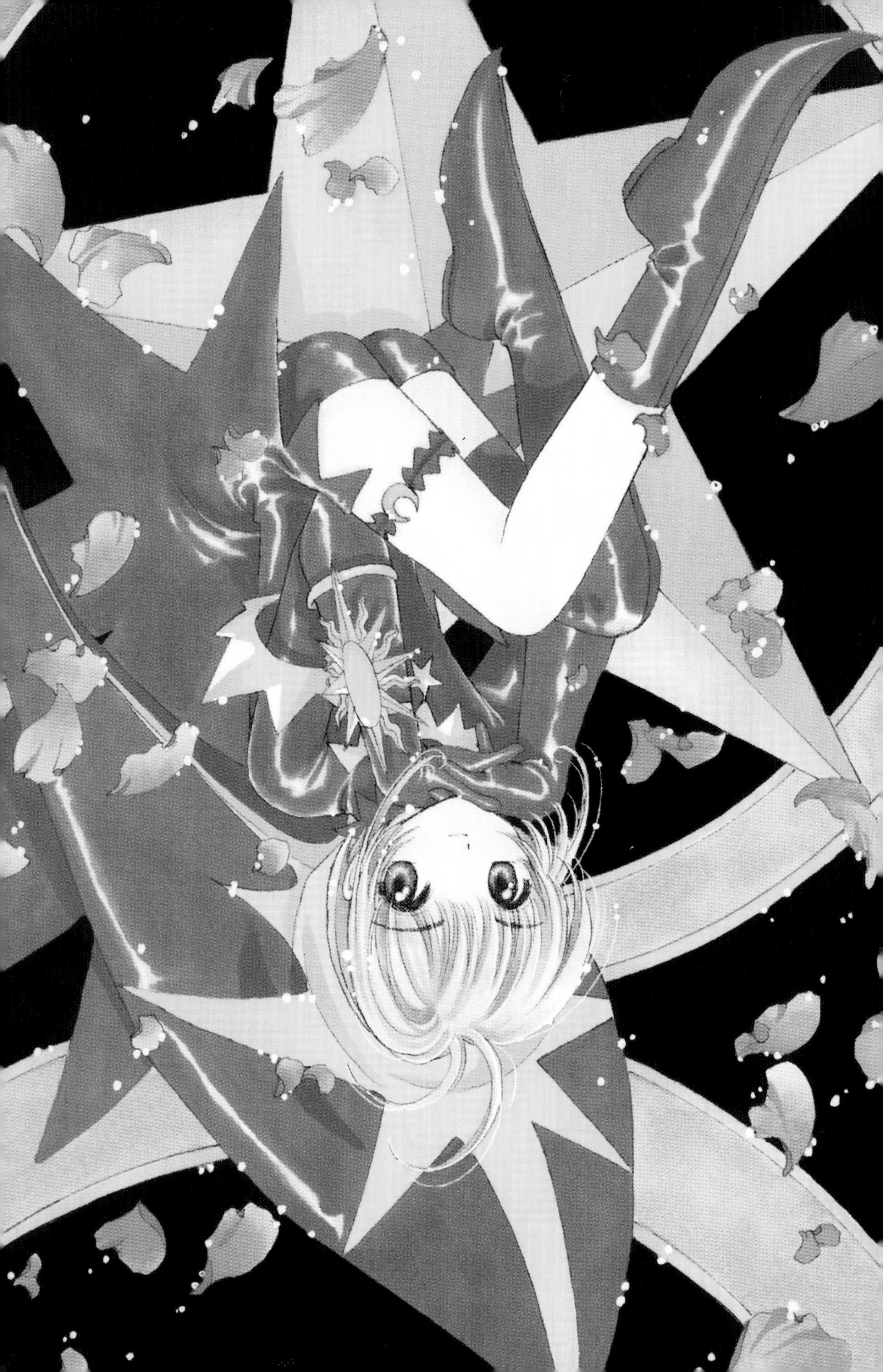

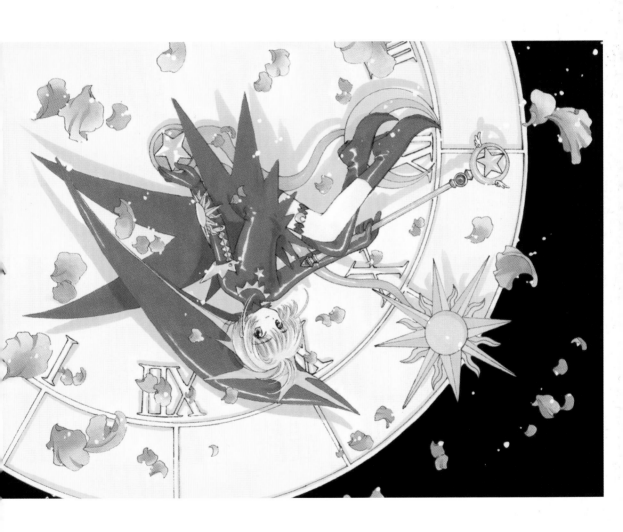

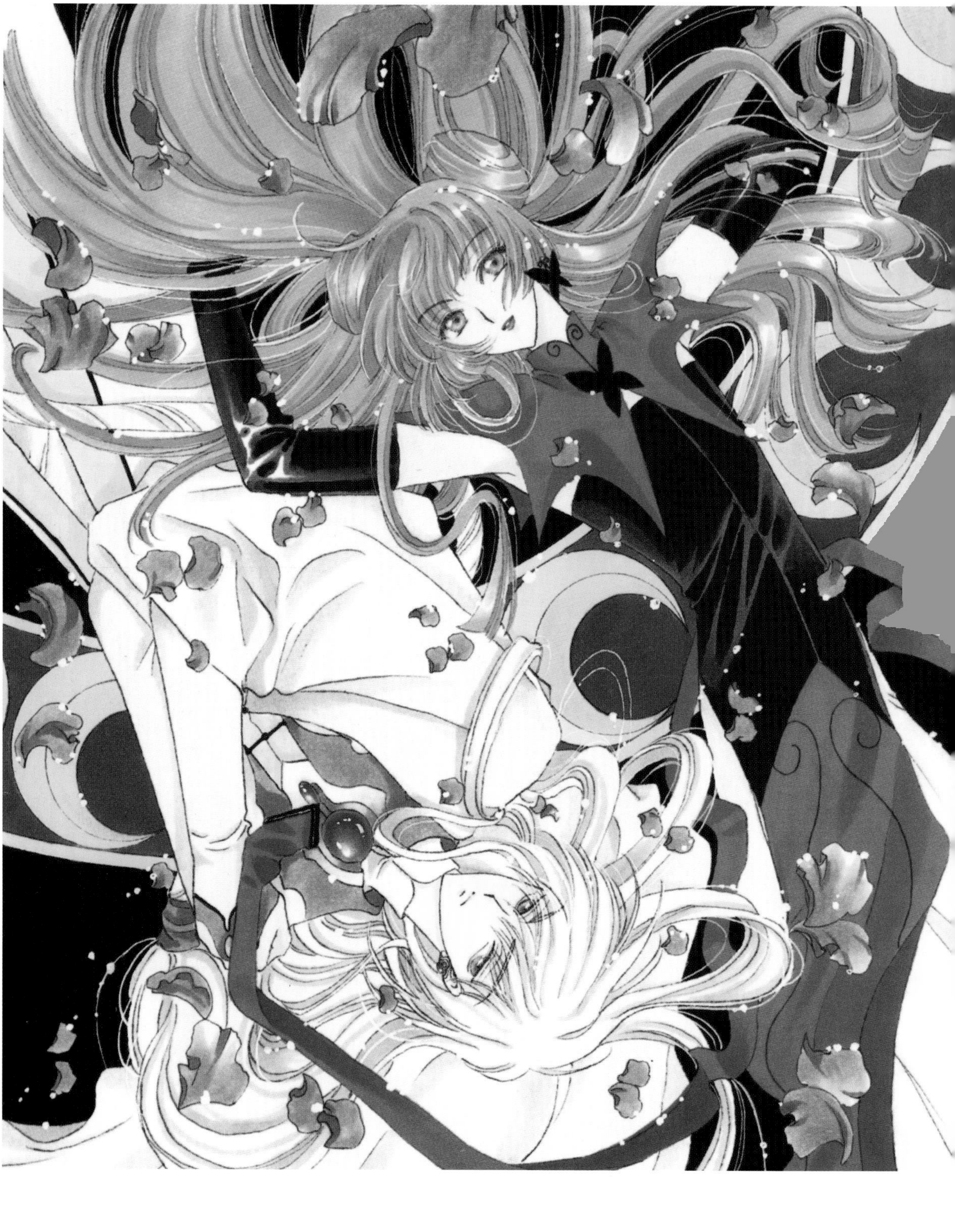

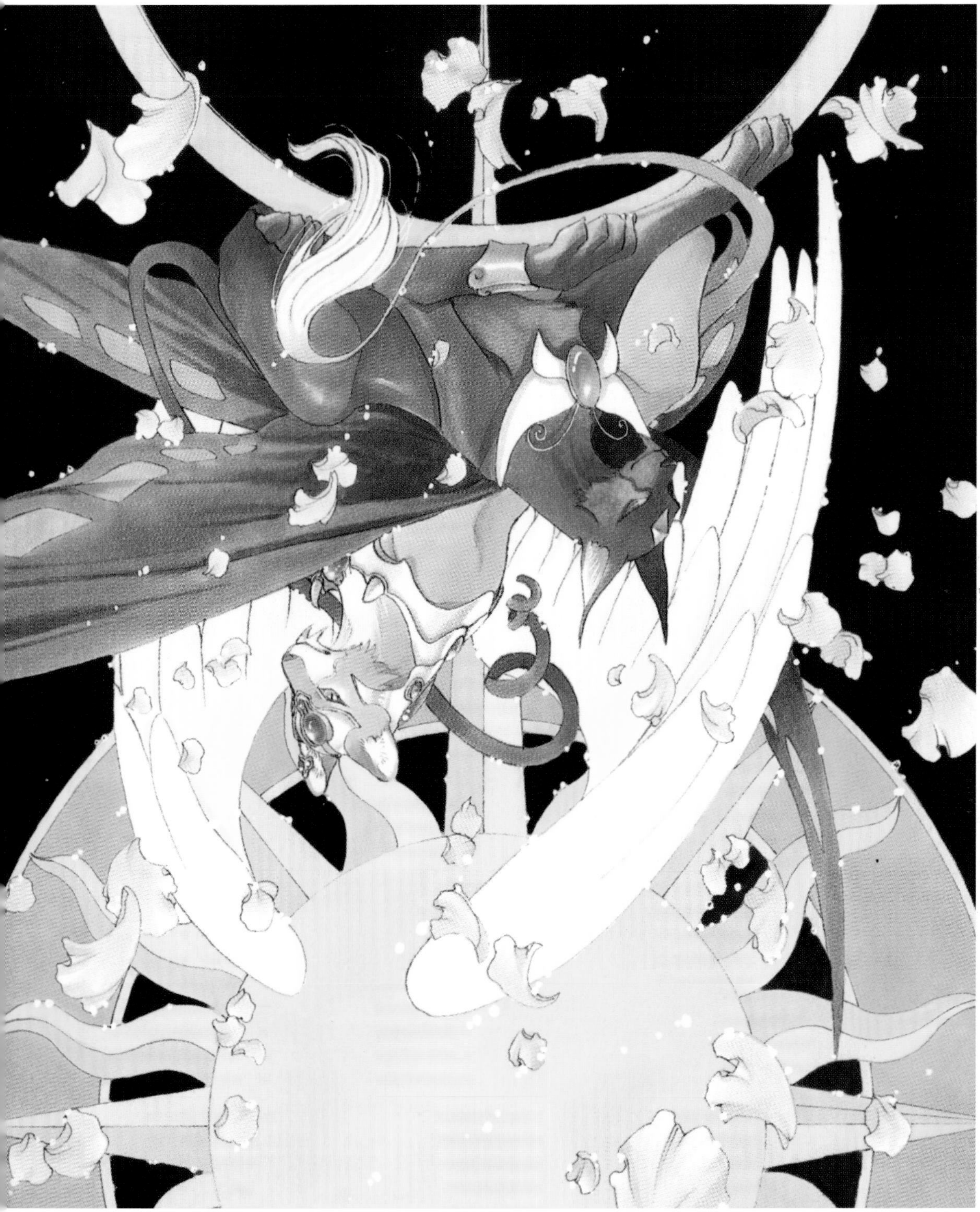

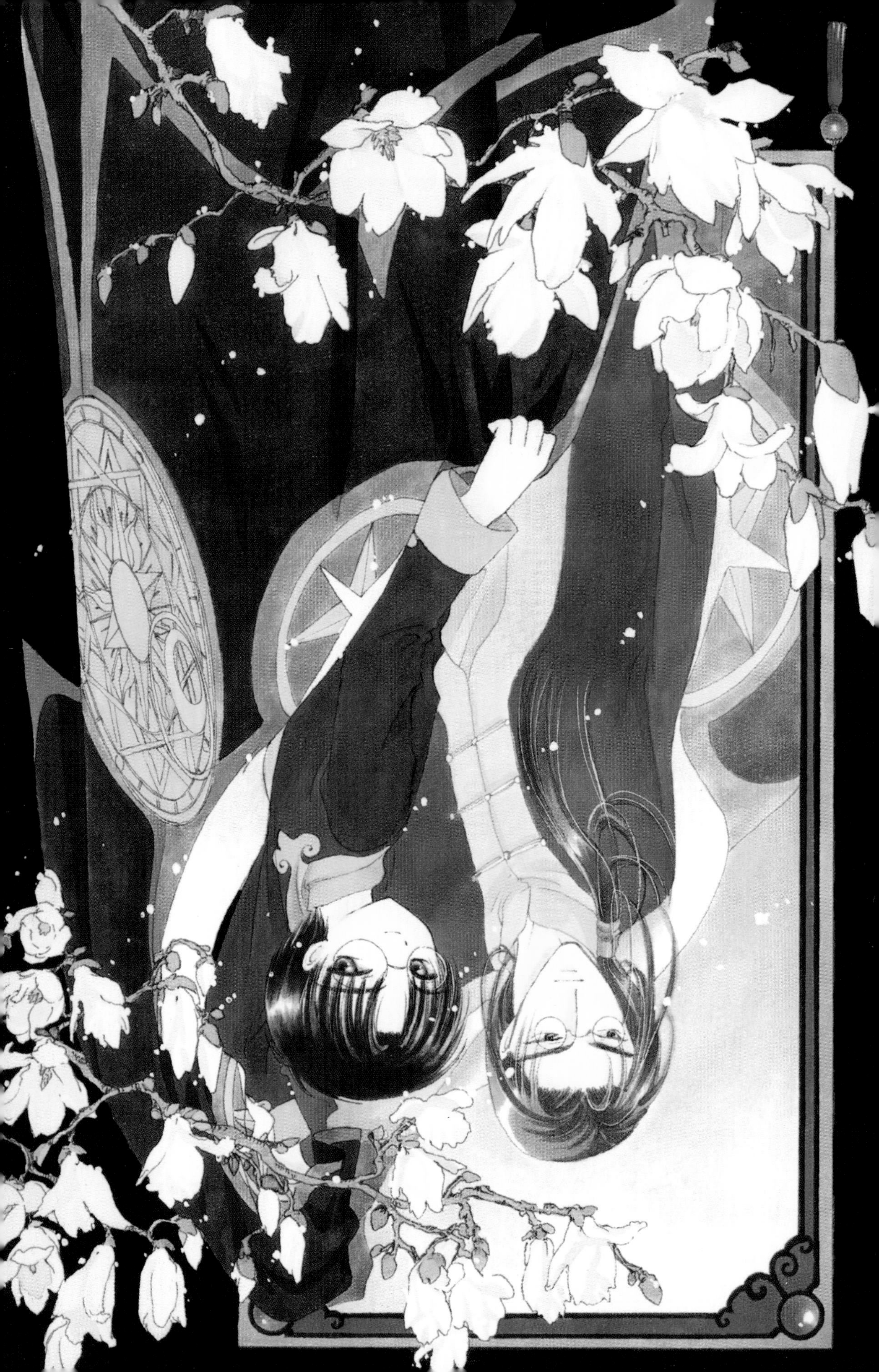

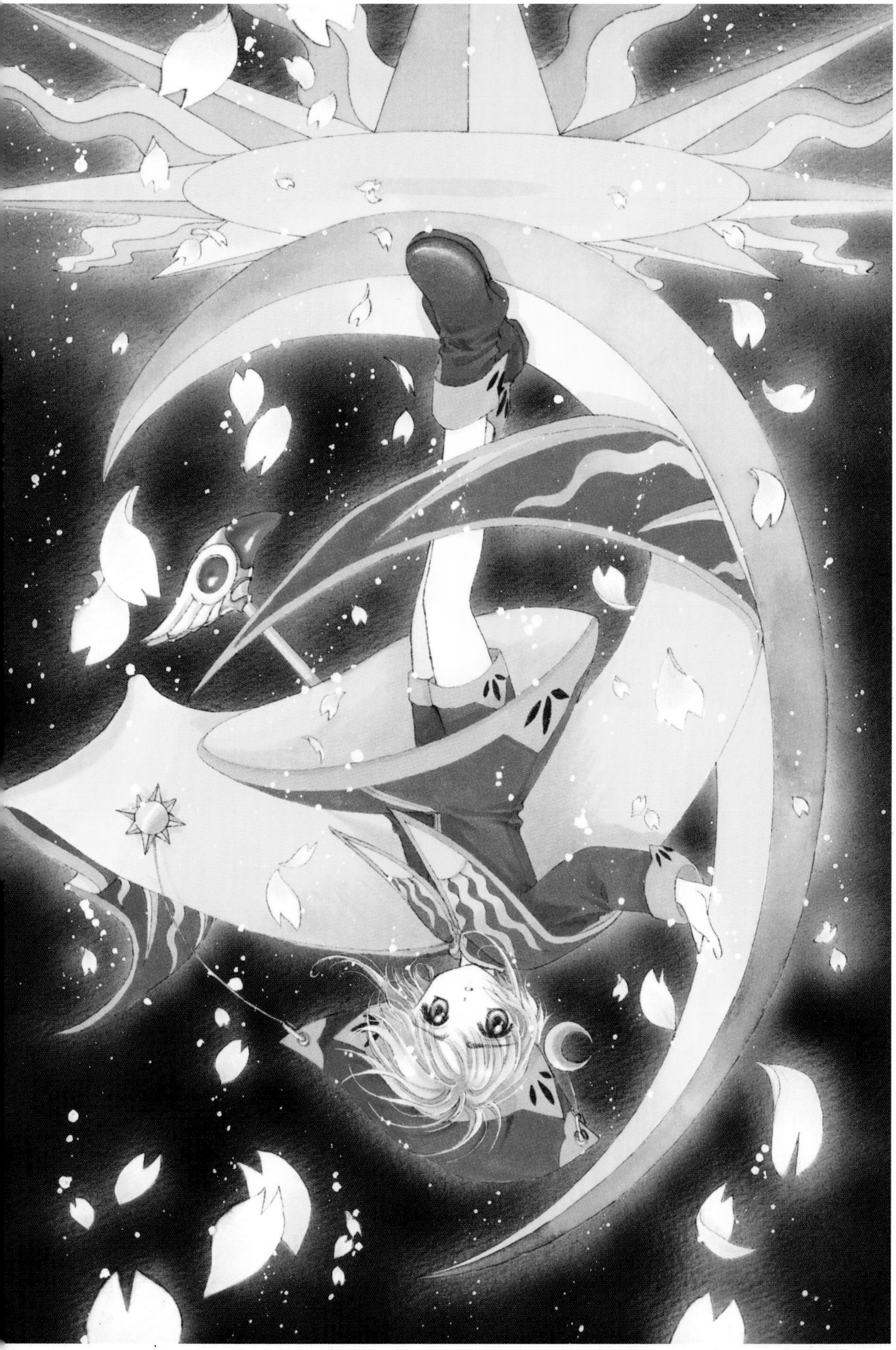

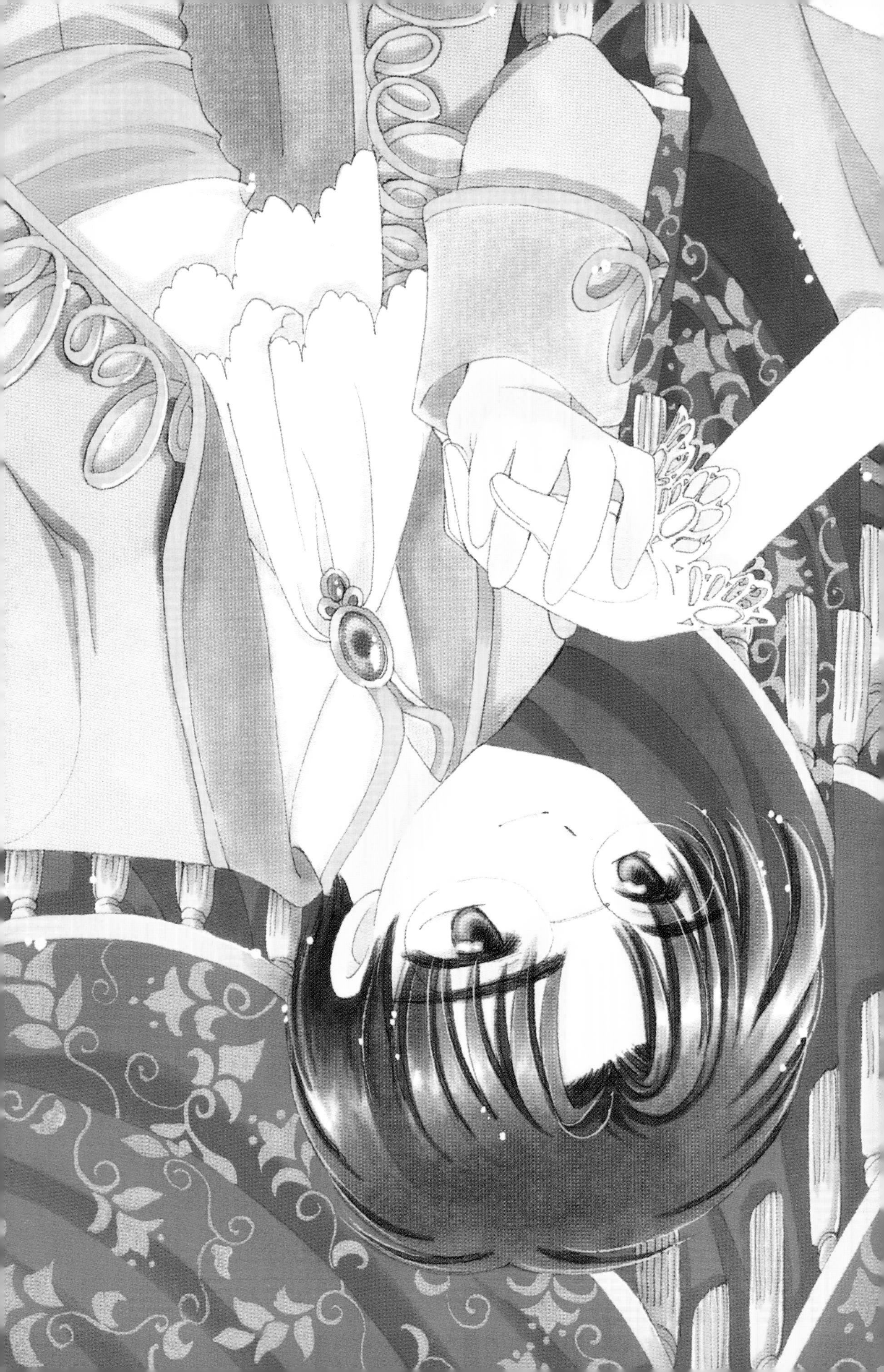

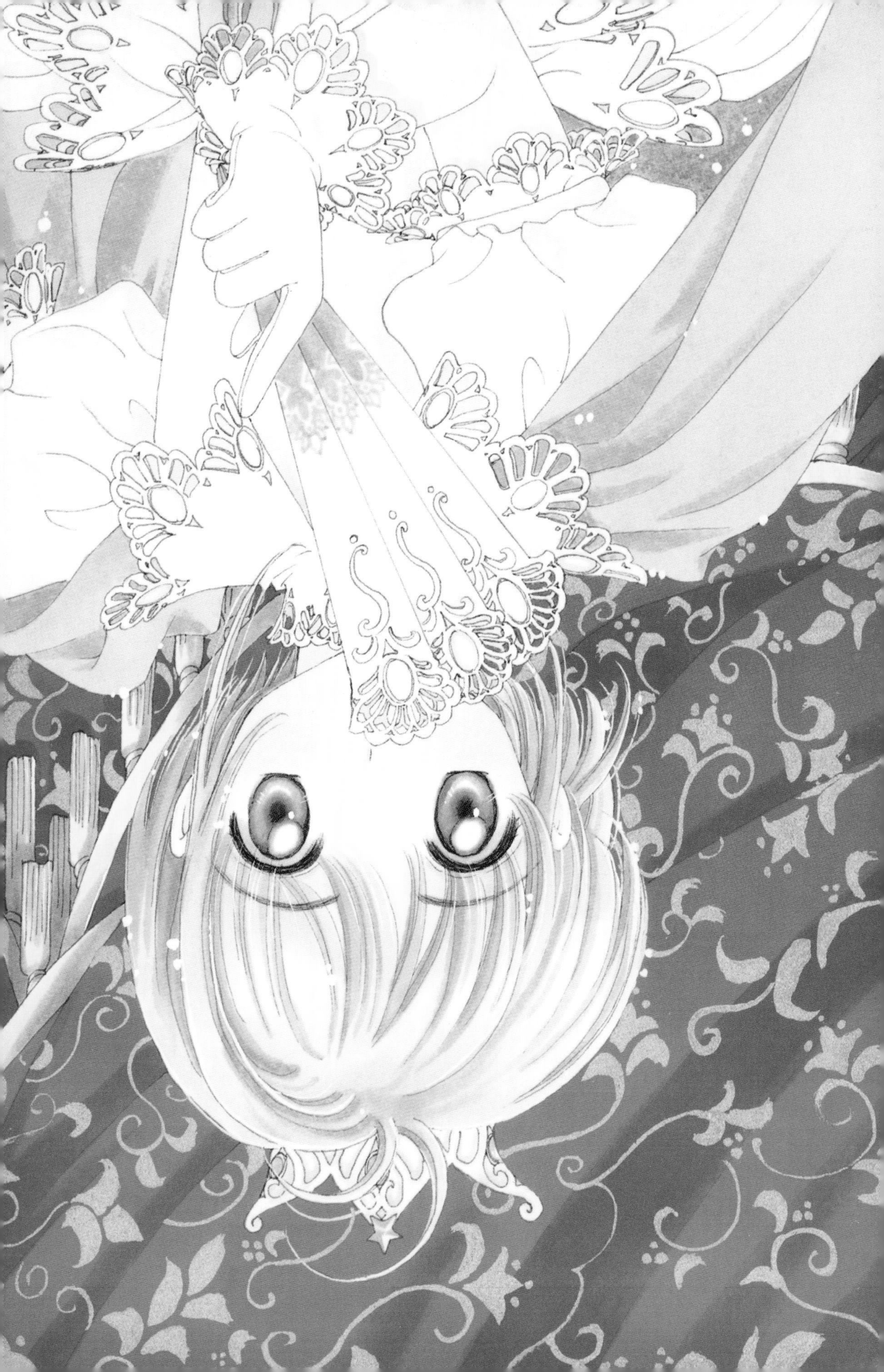

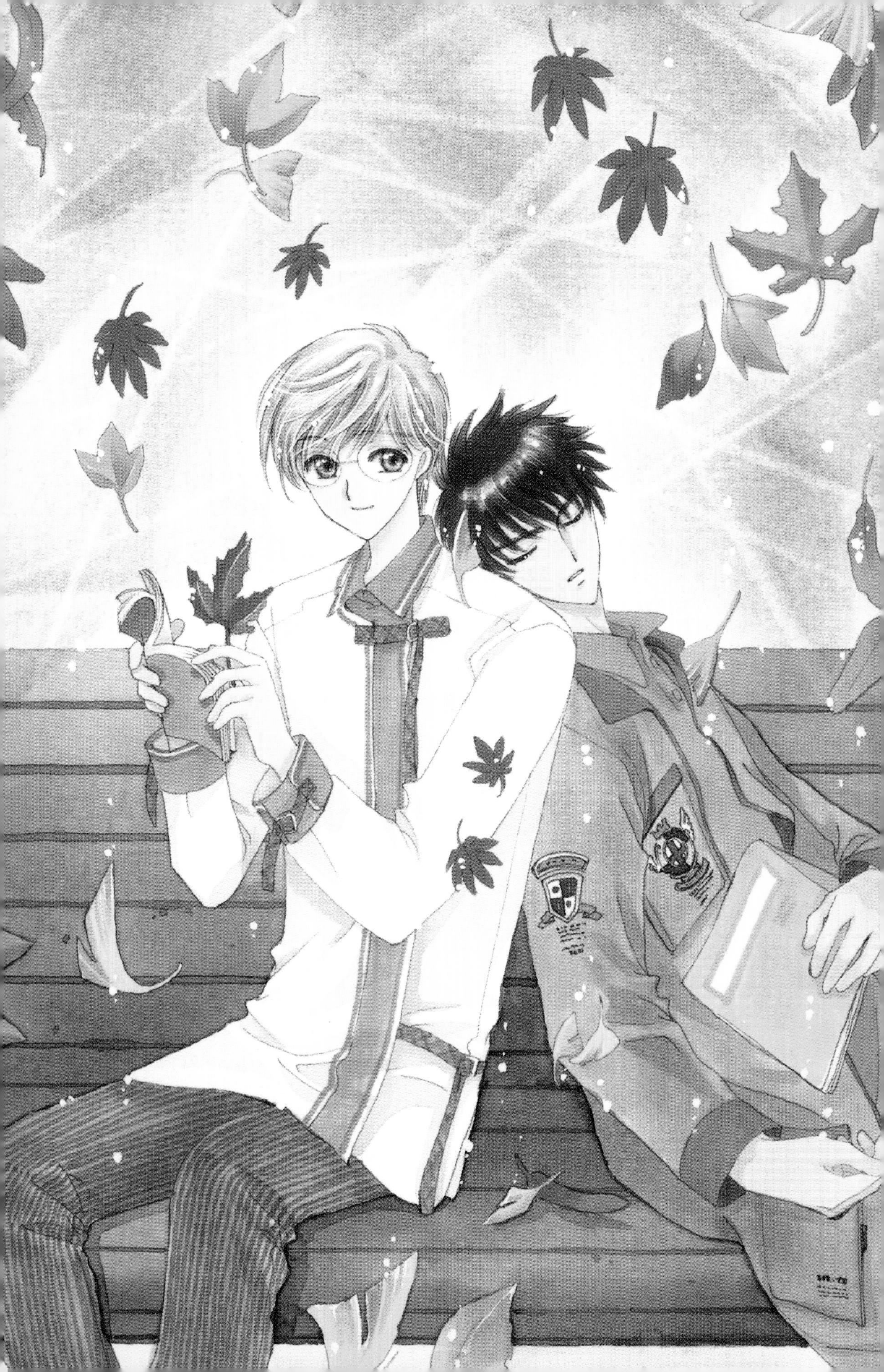

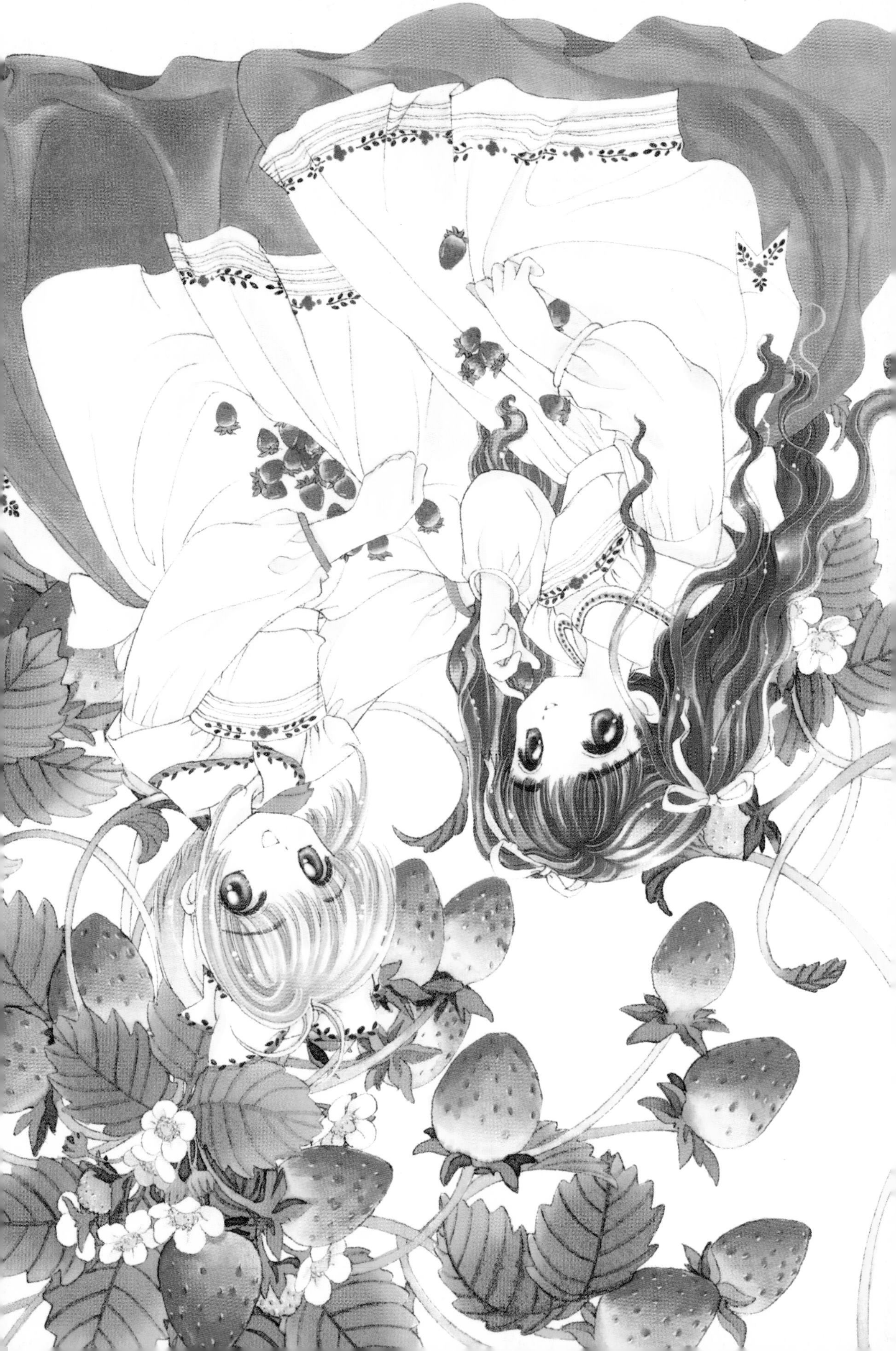

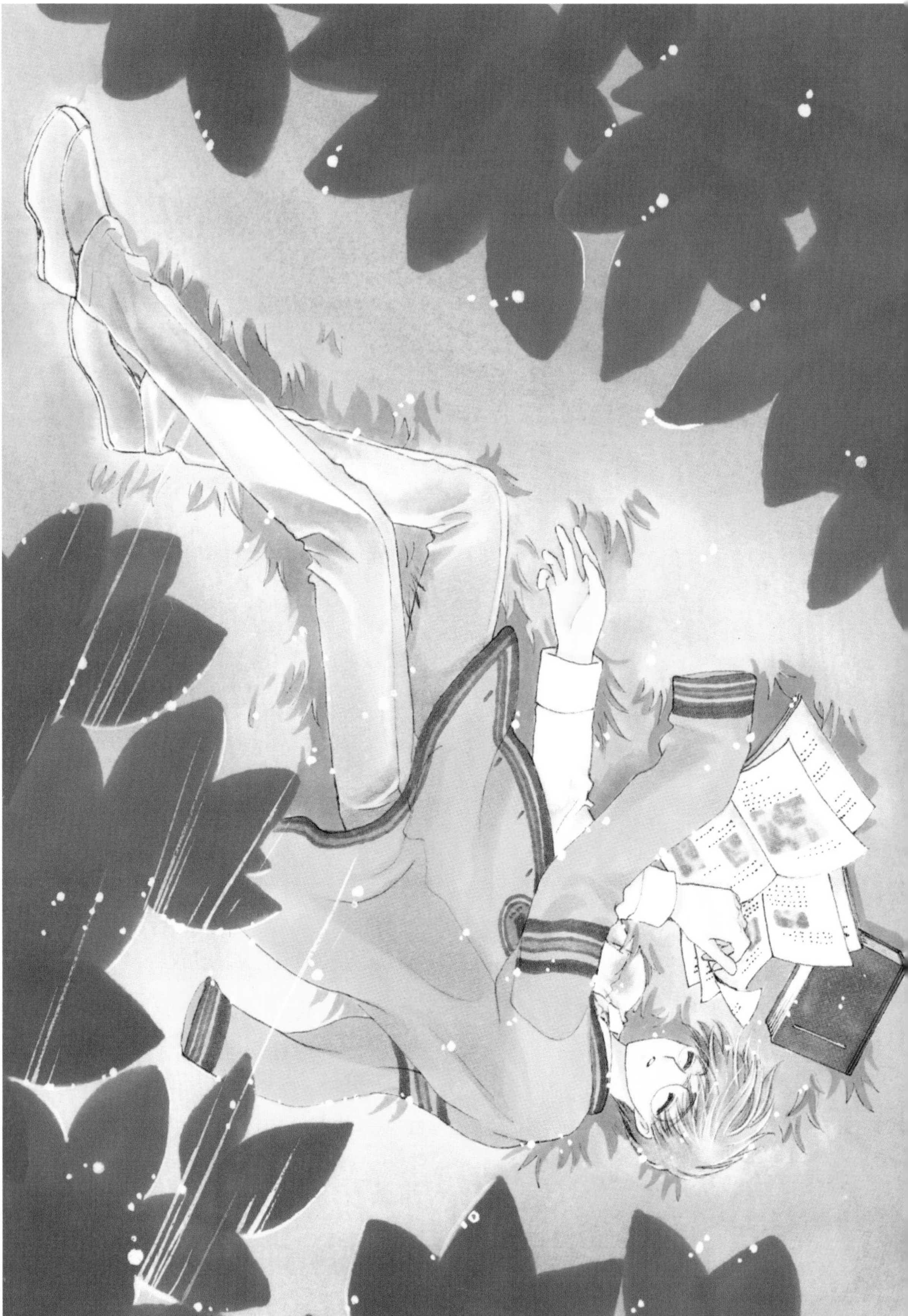

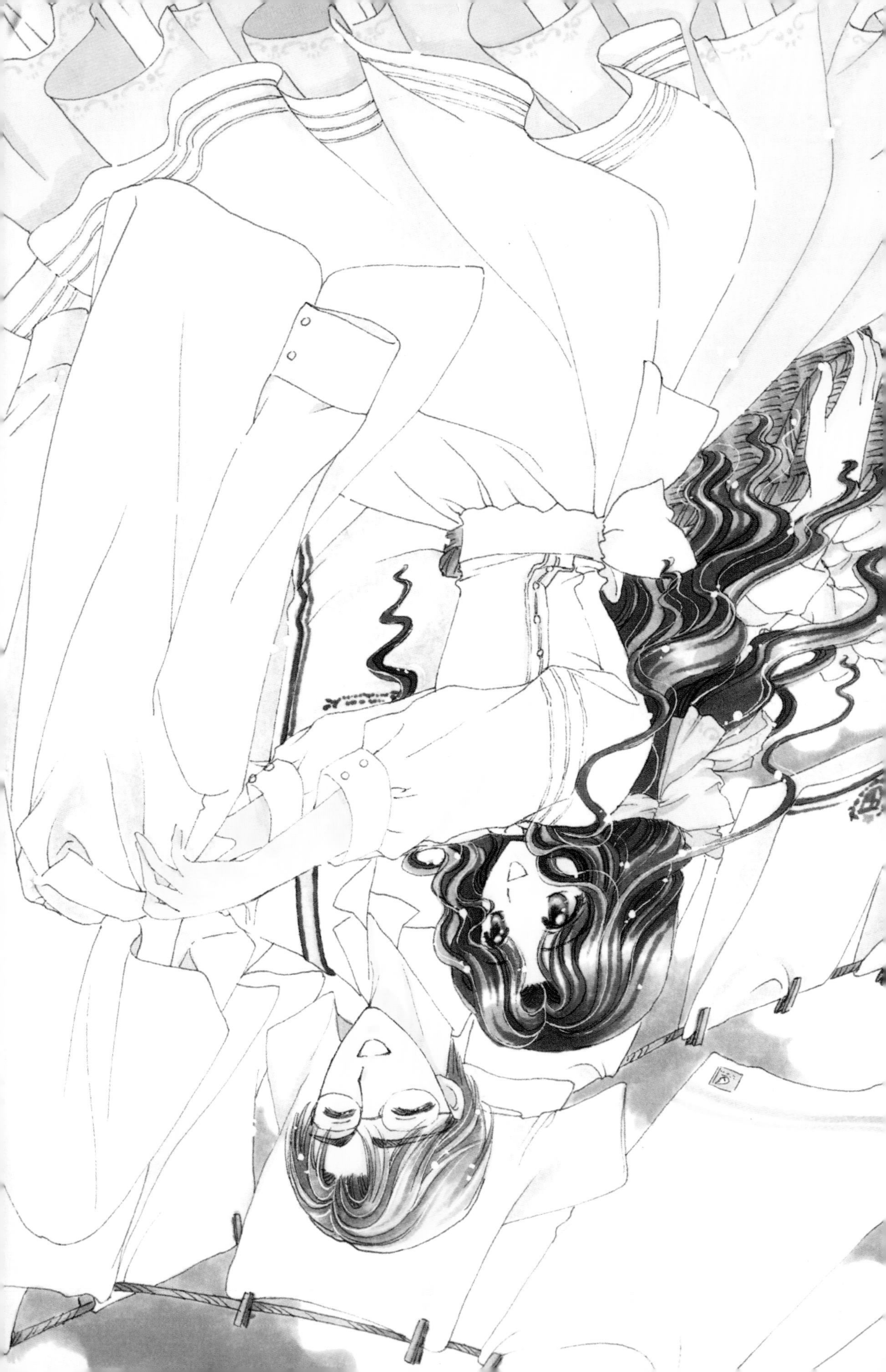

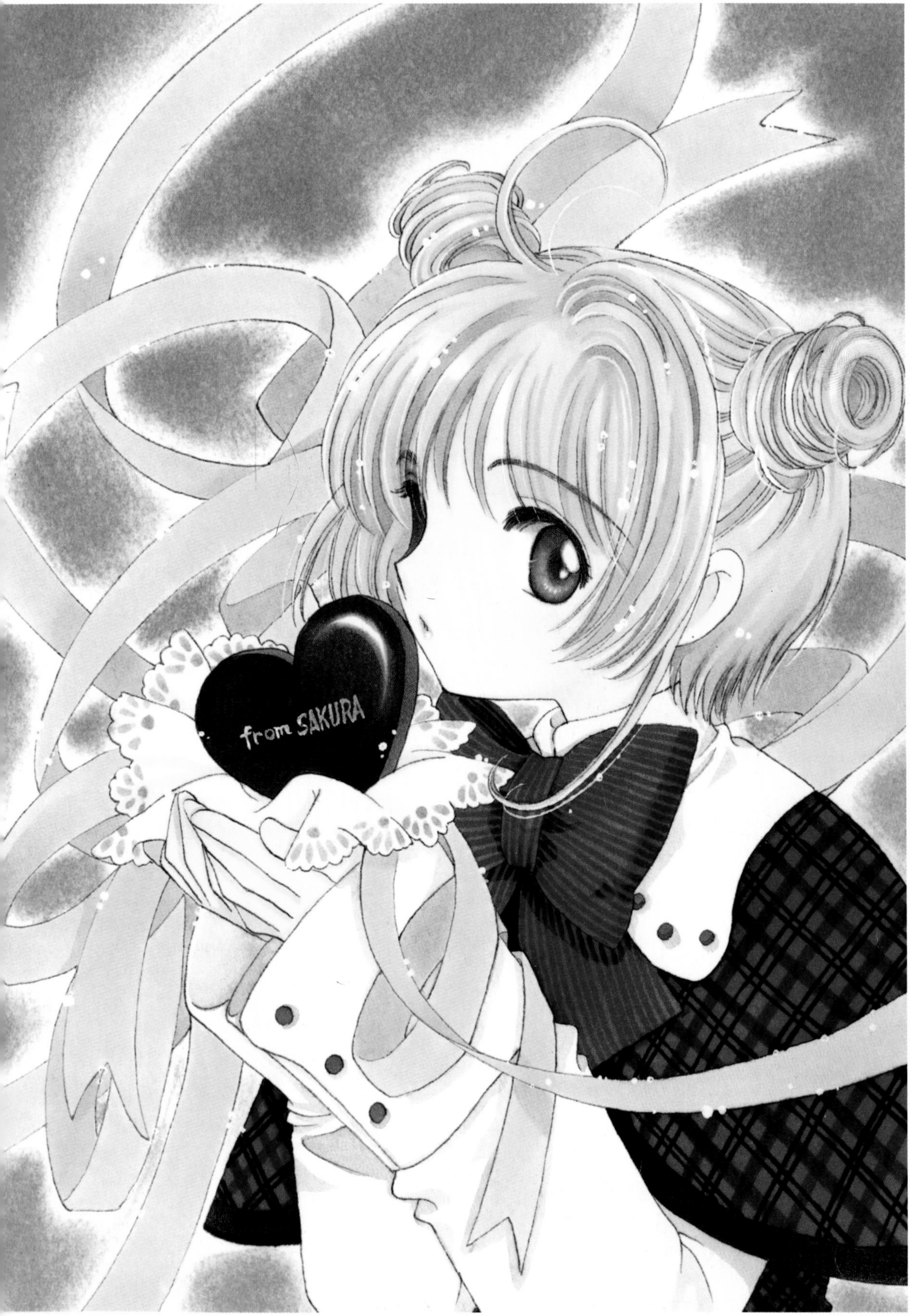
from SAKURA

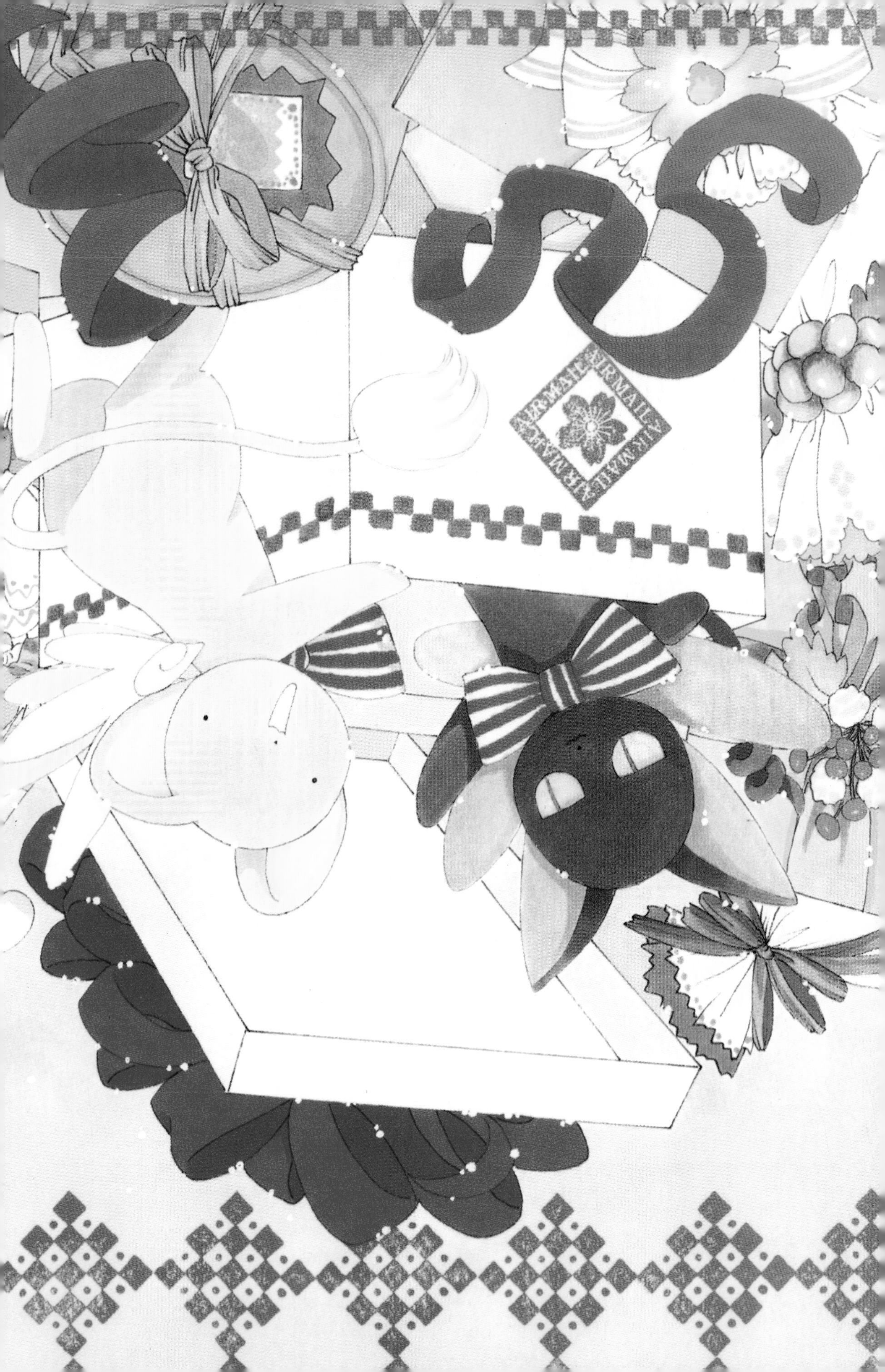
AIRMAIL

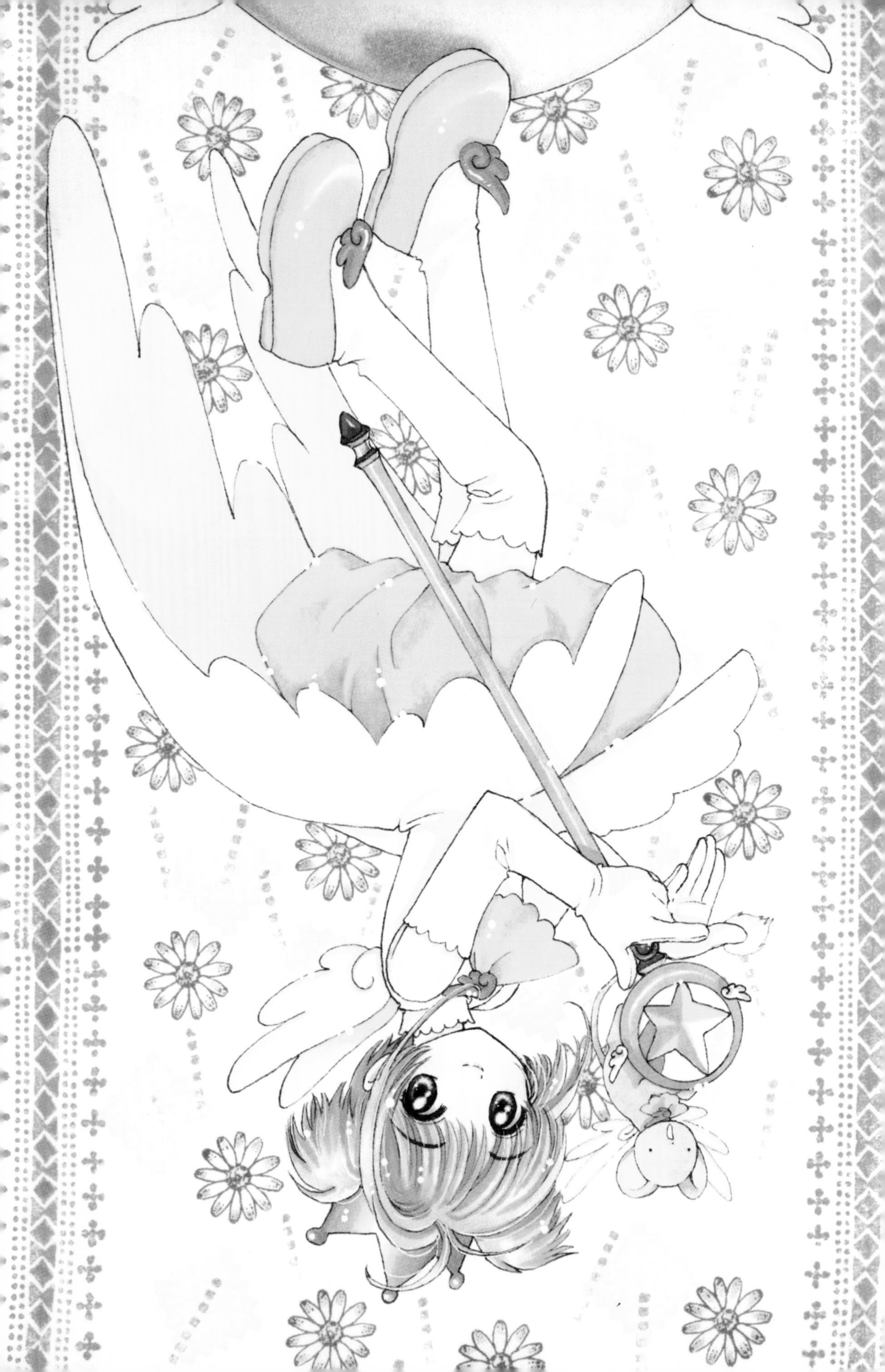

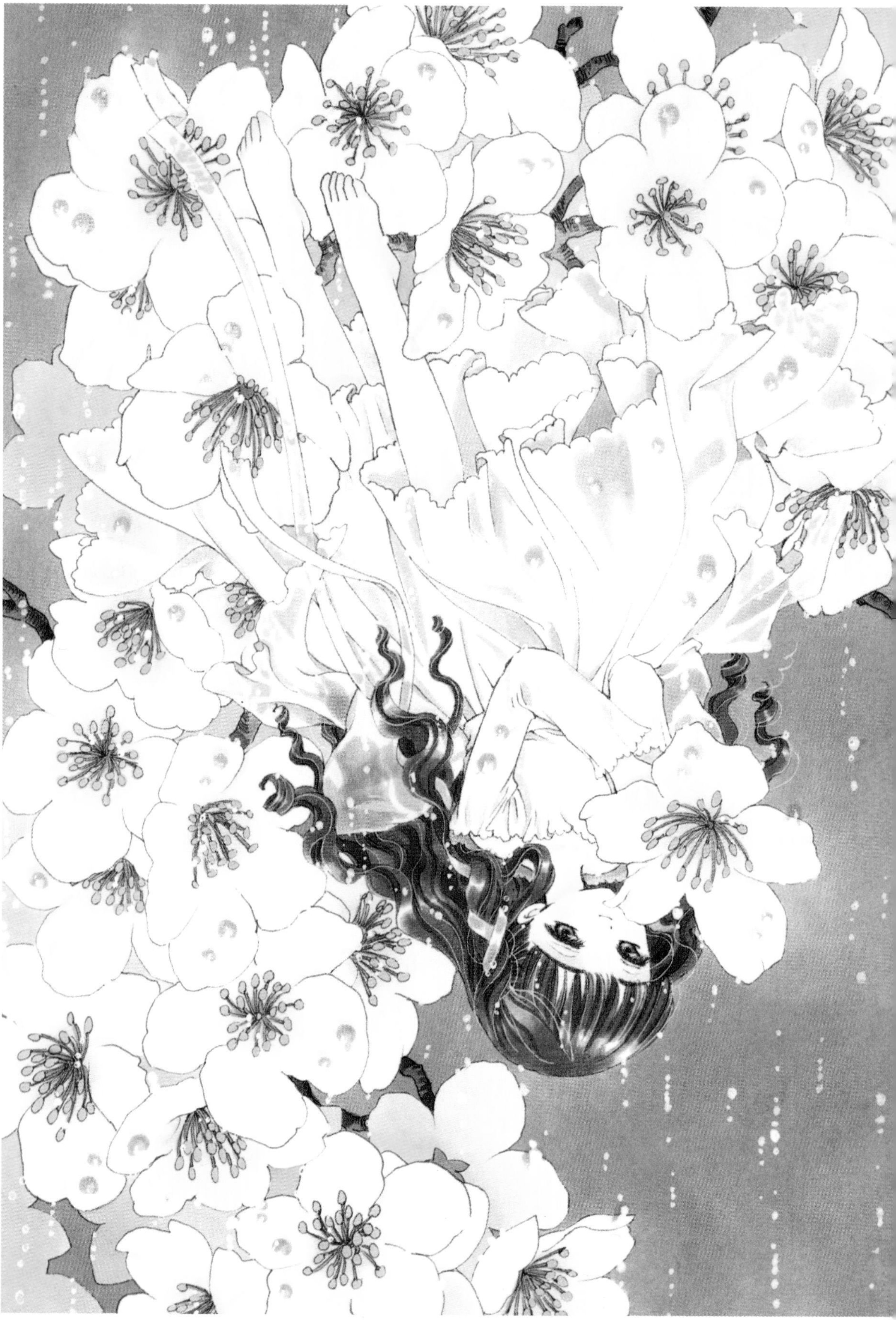

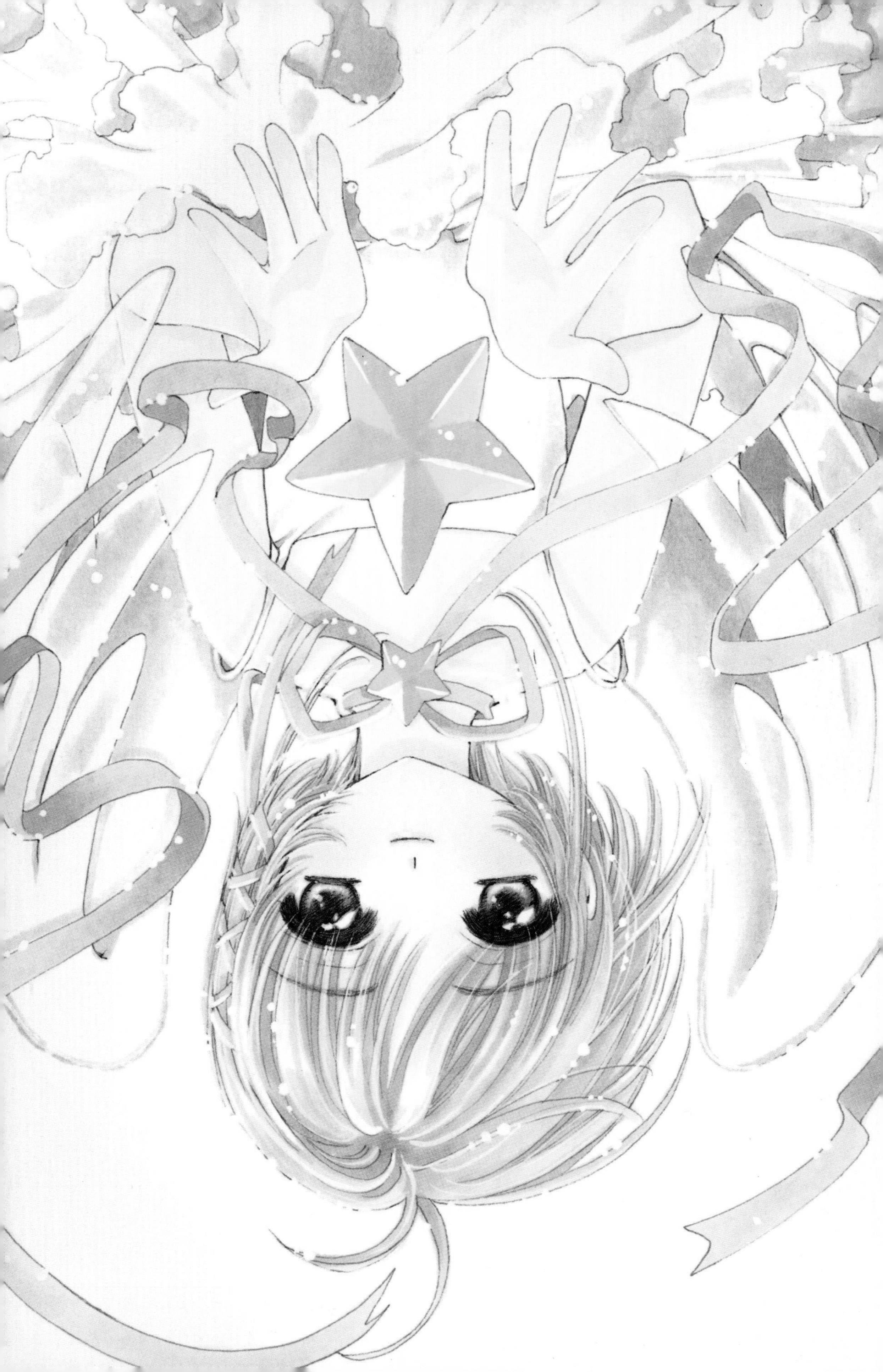

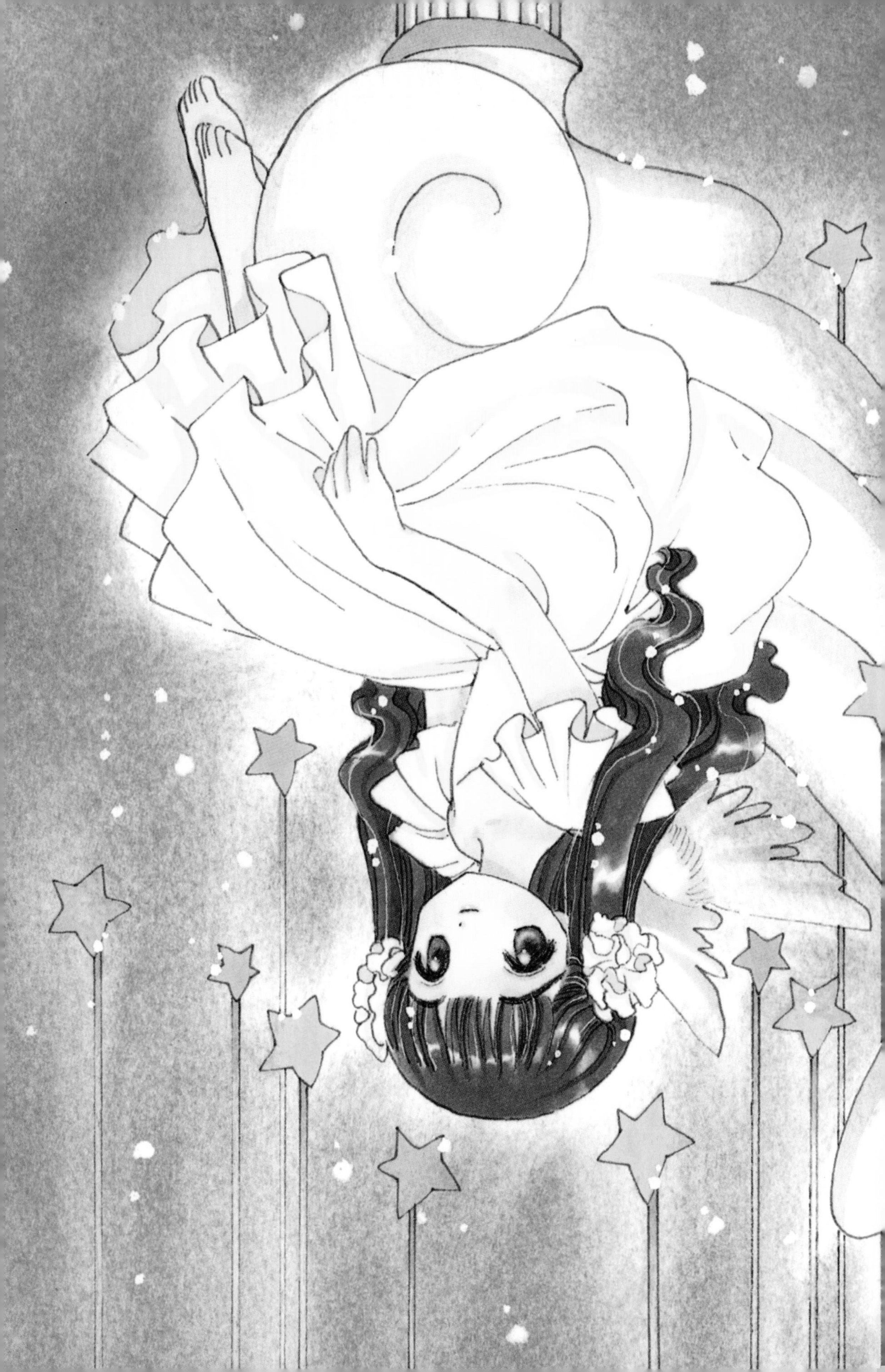

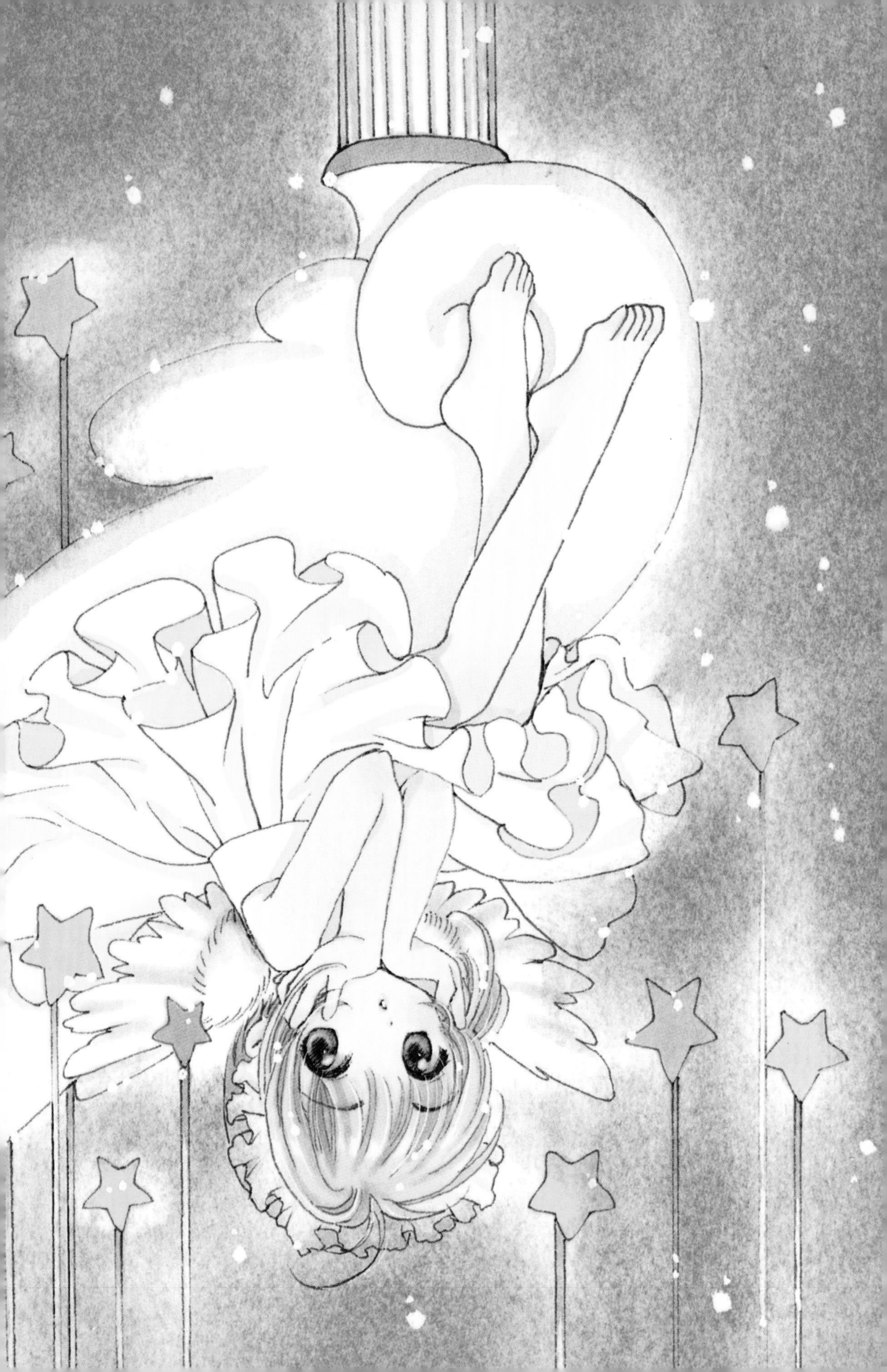

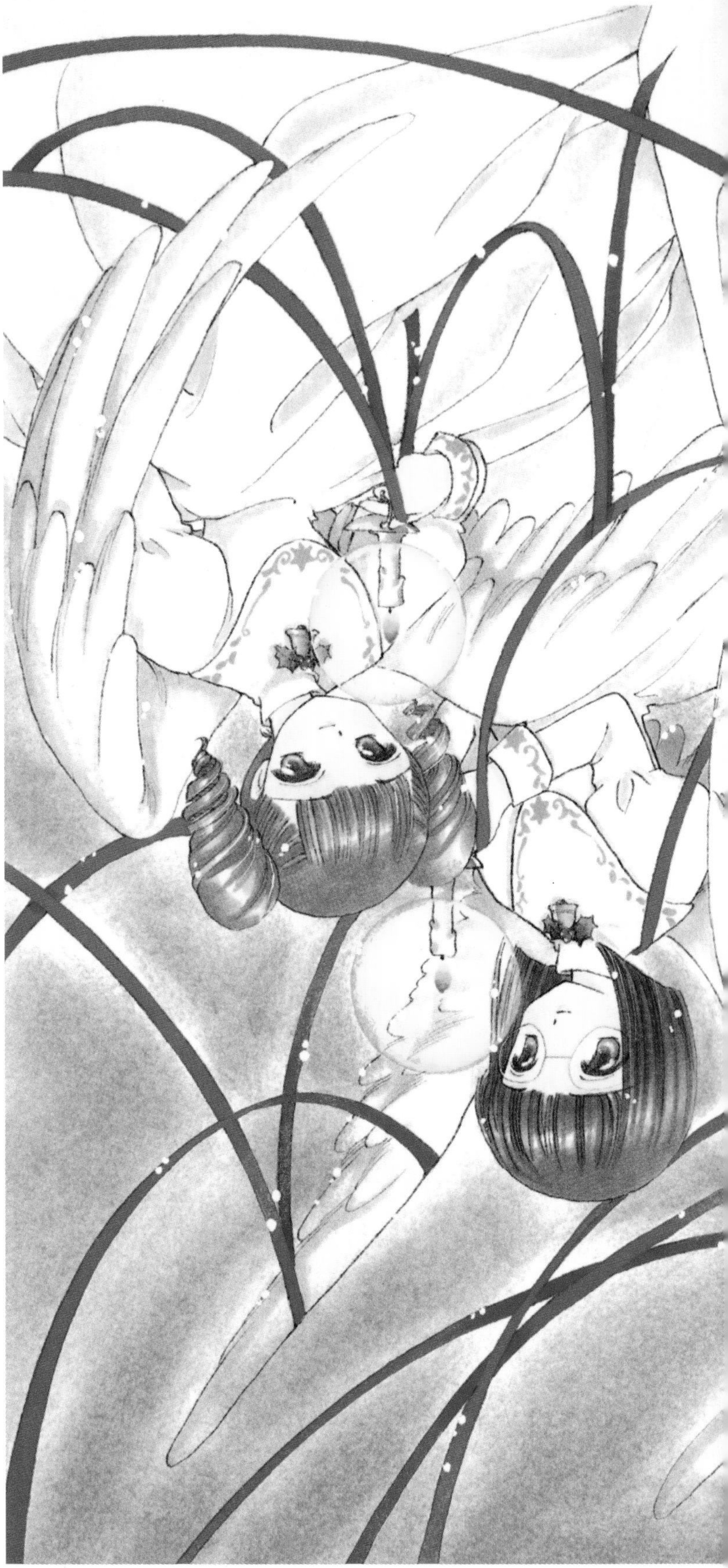

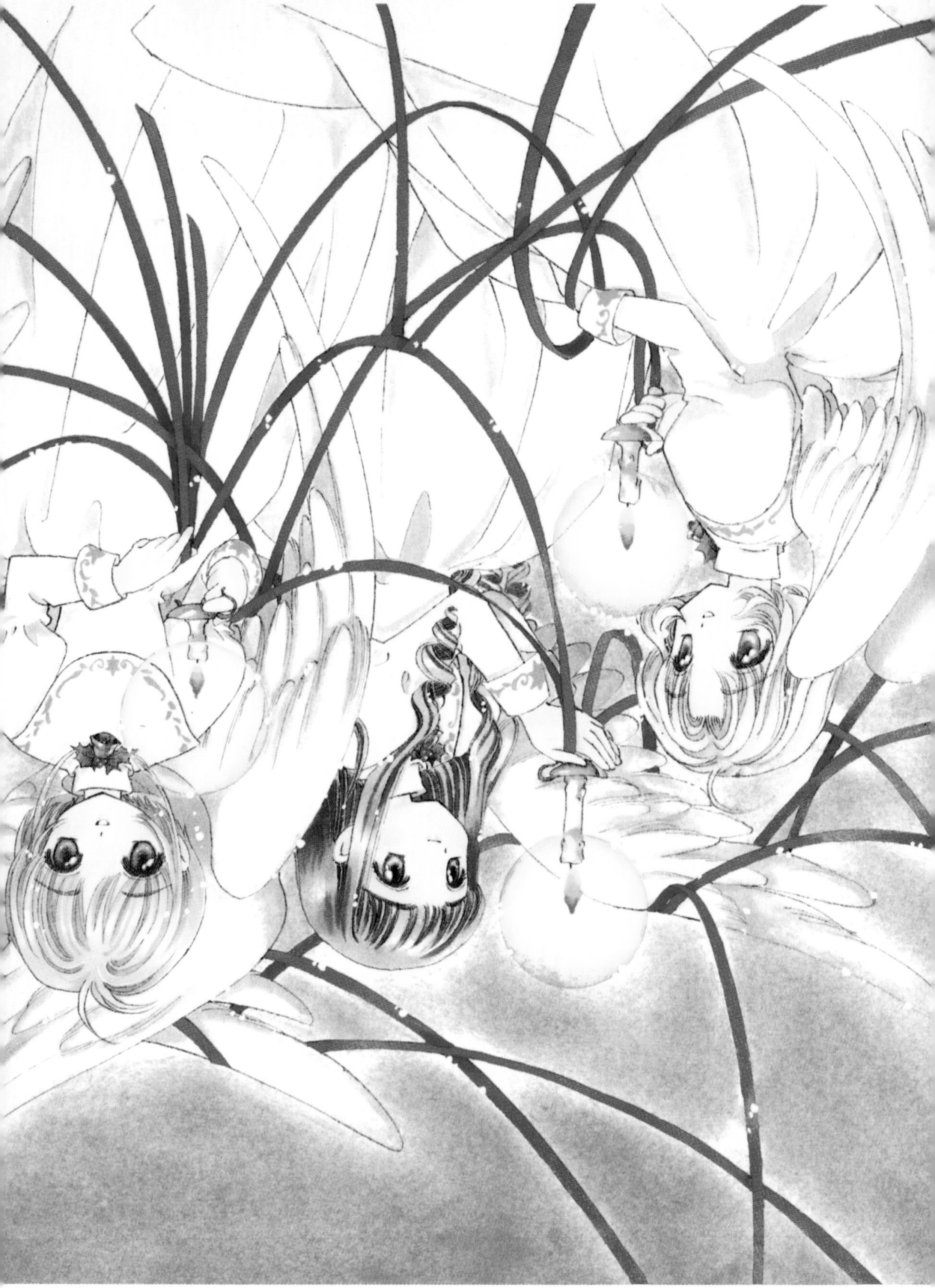

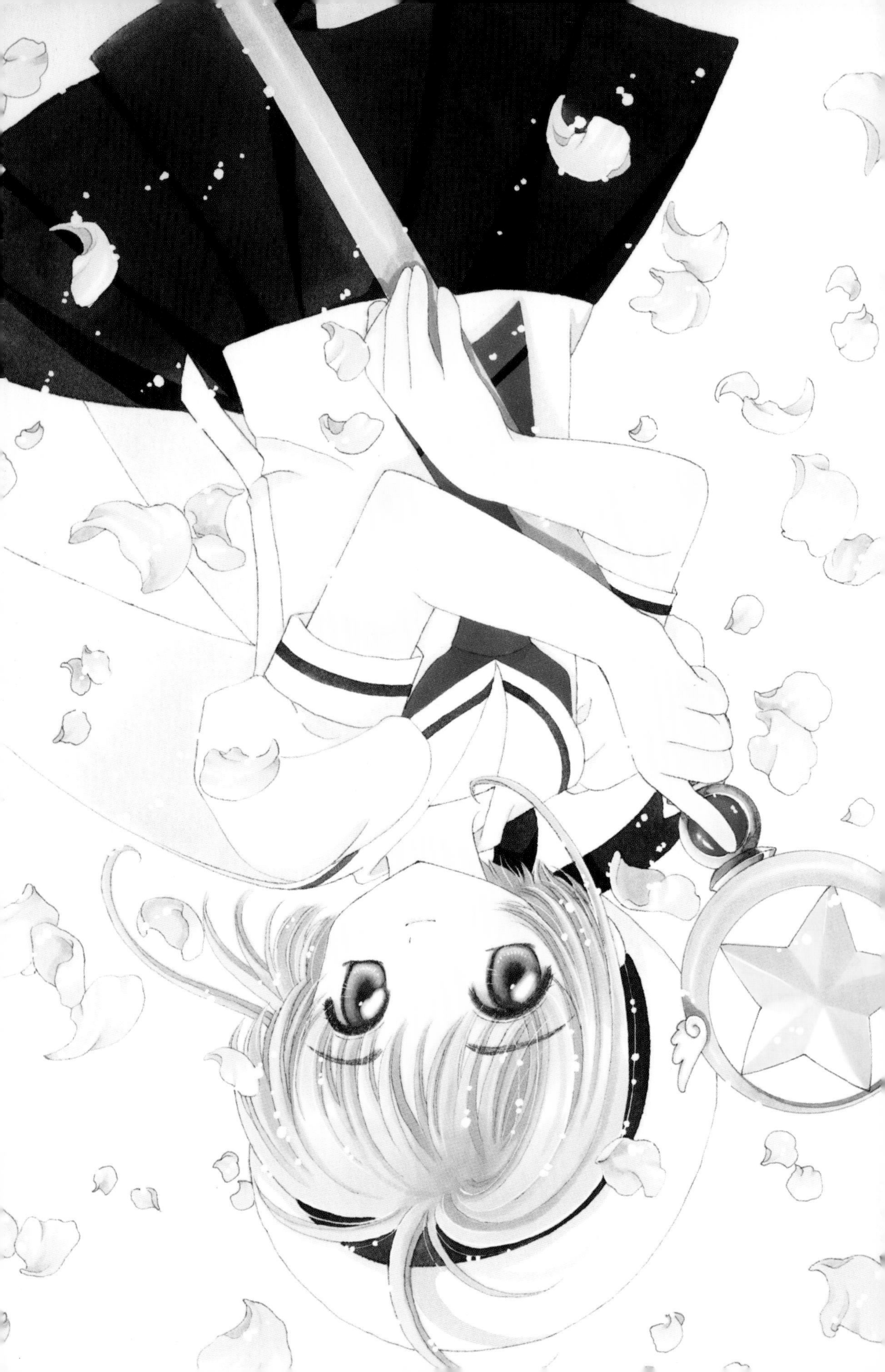

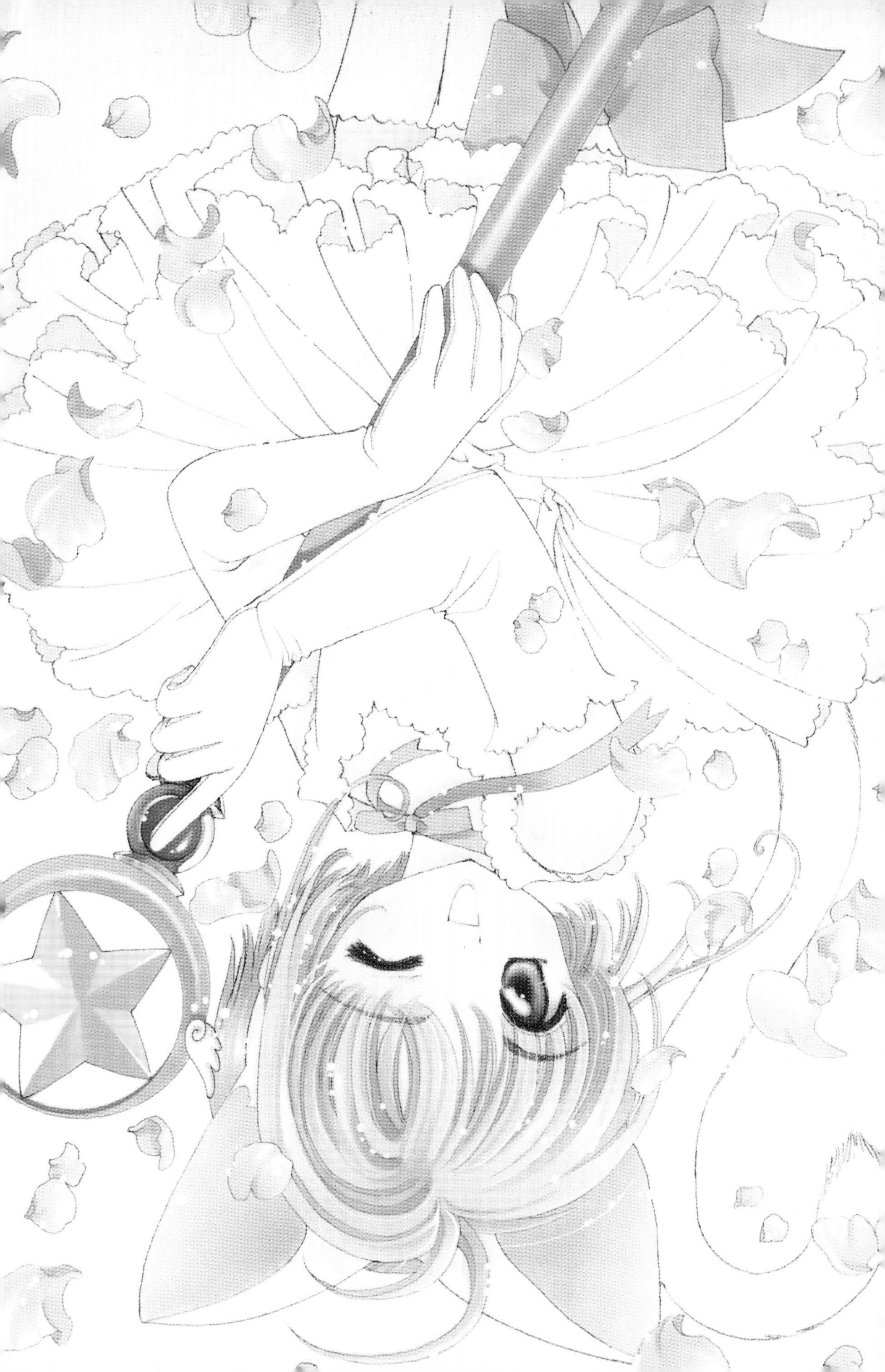

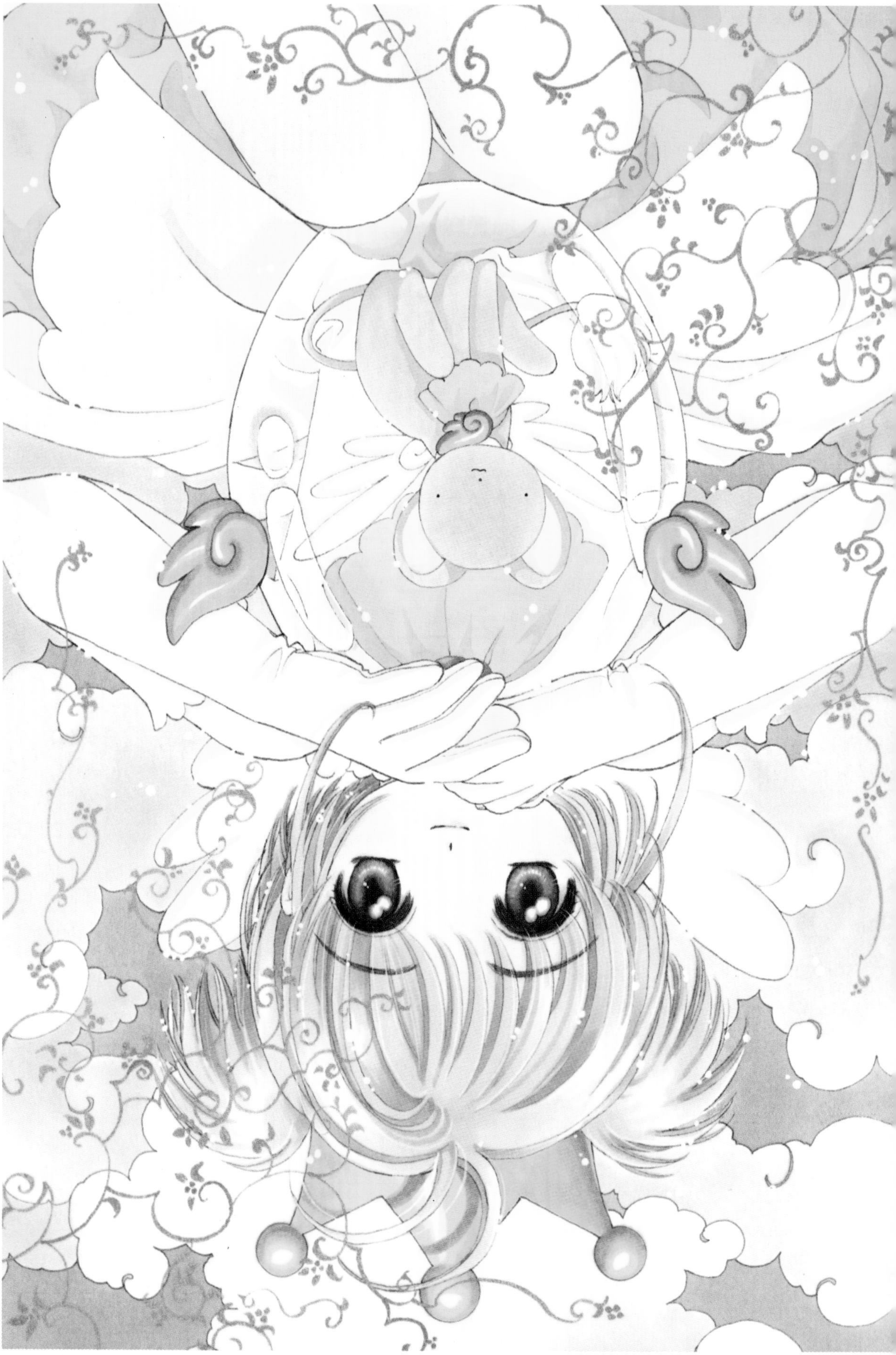

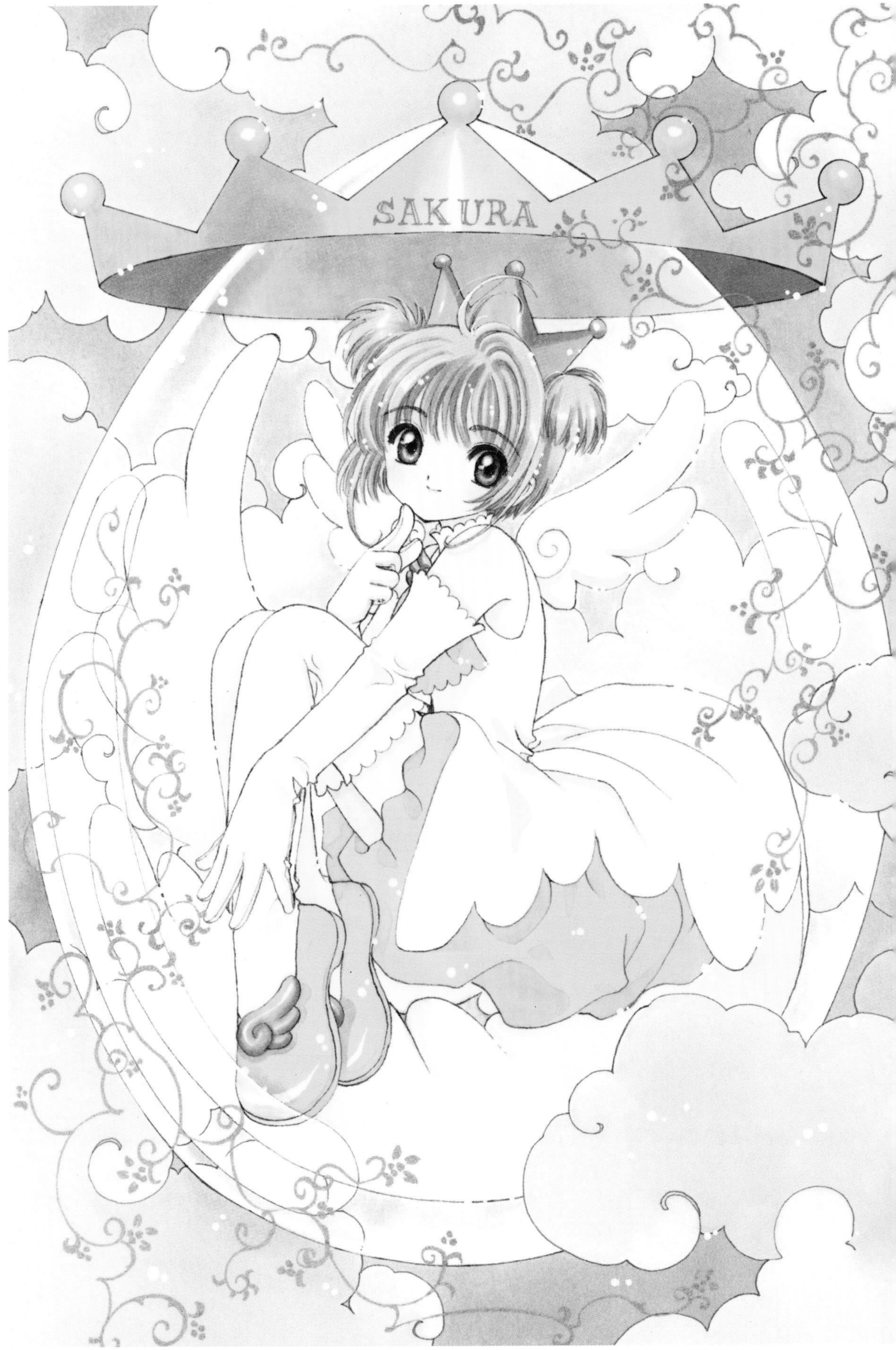
SAKURA

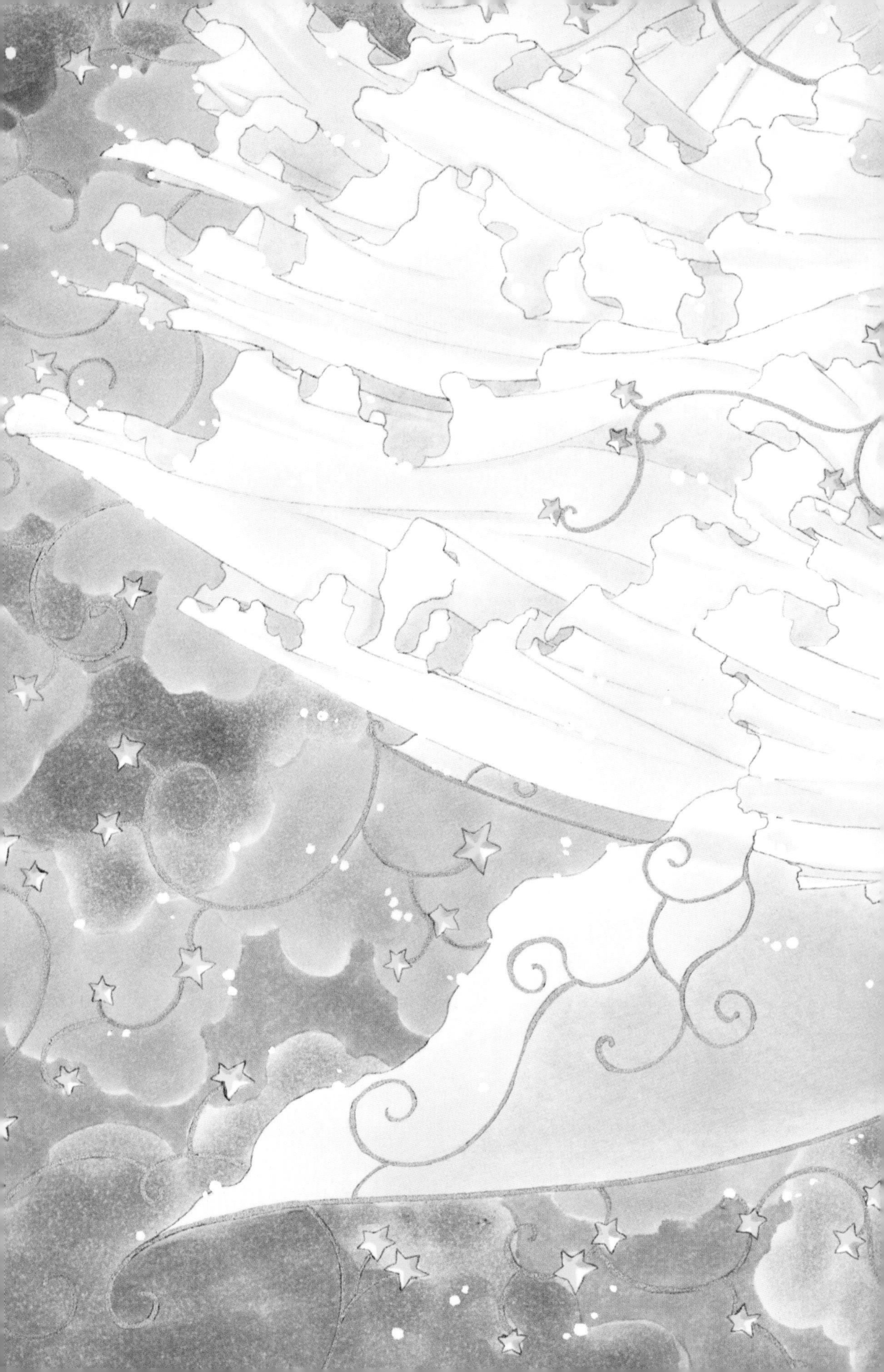

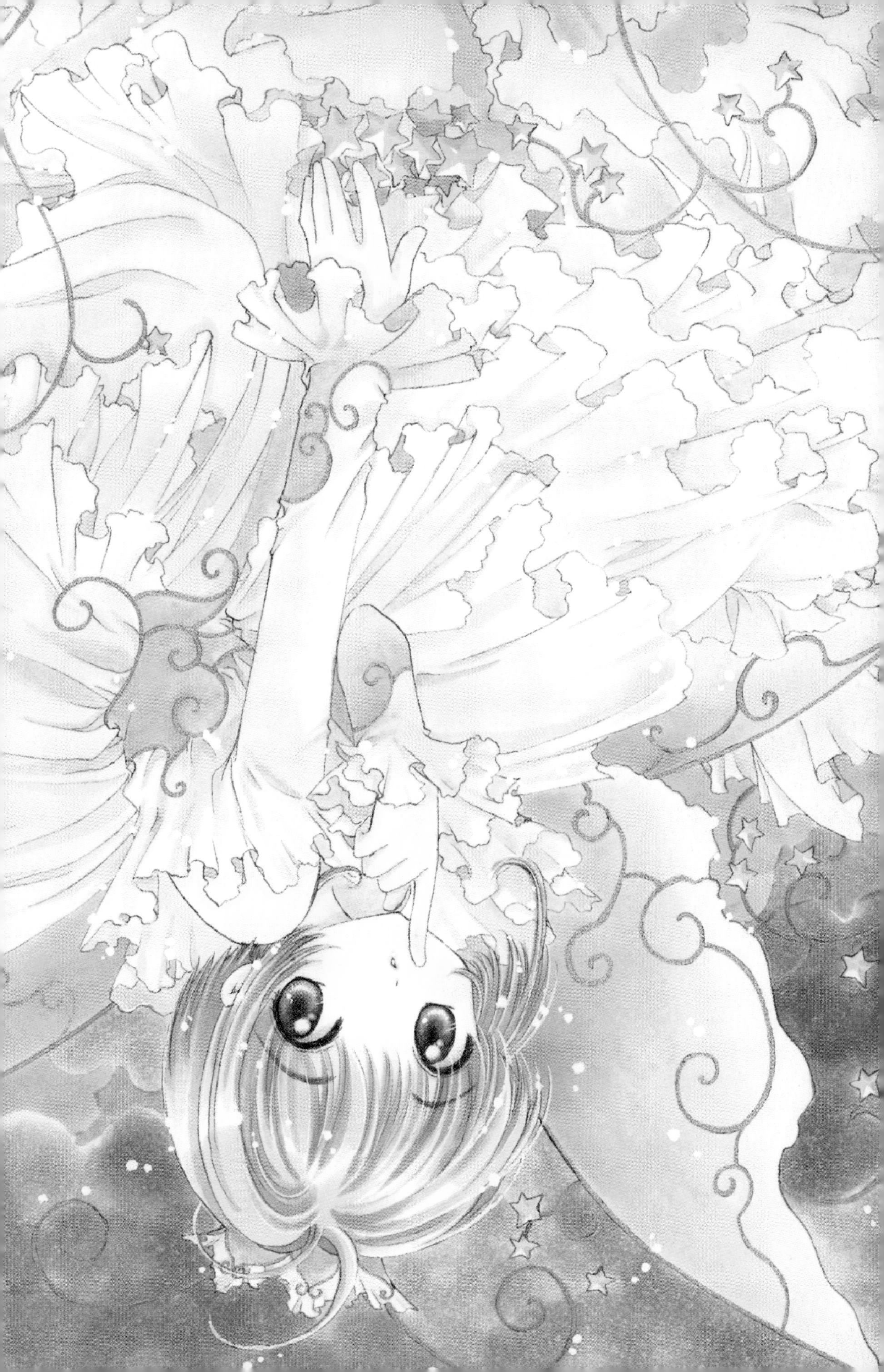

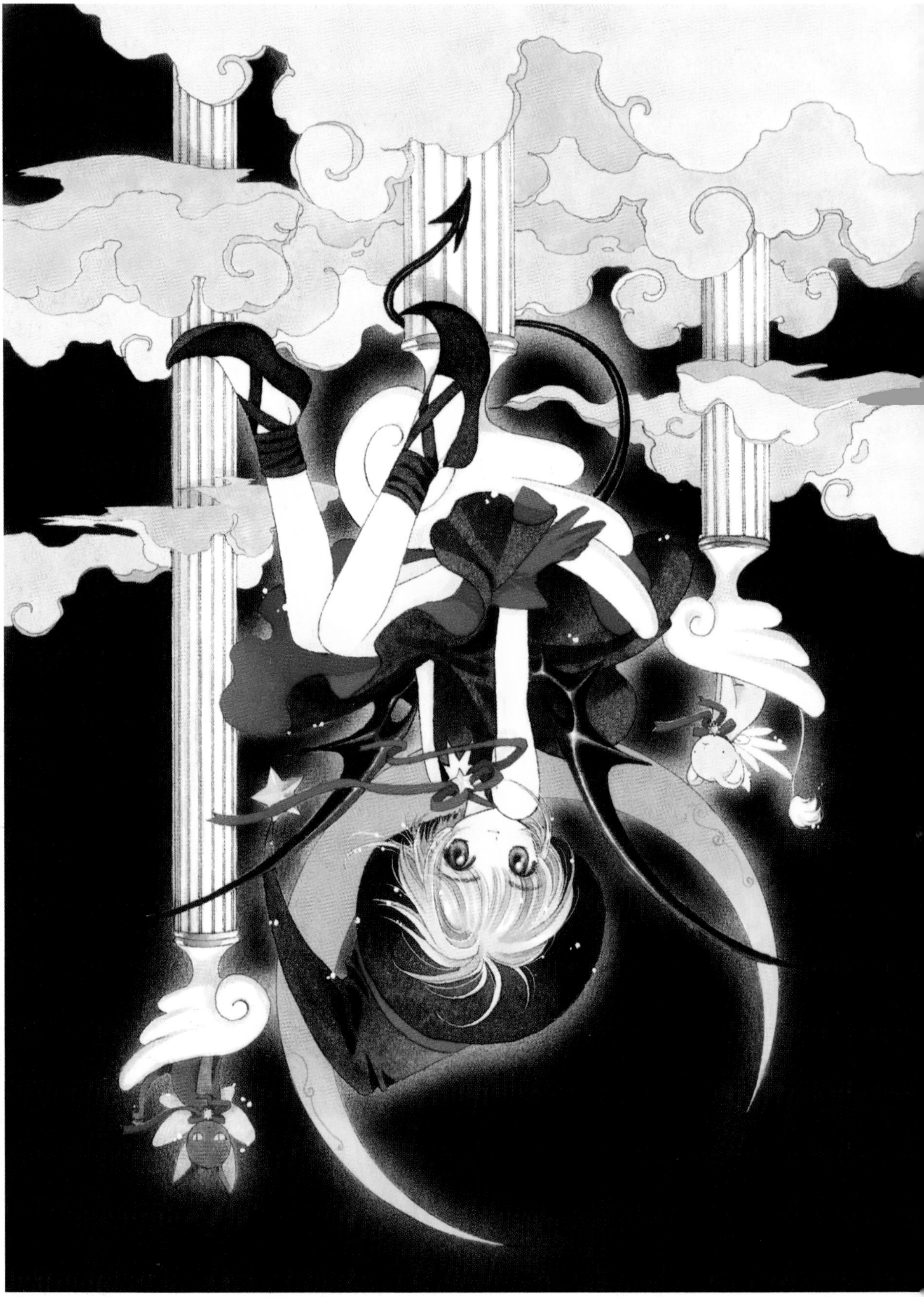

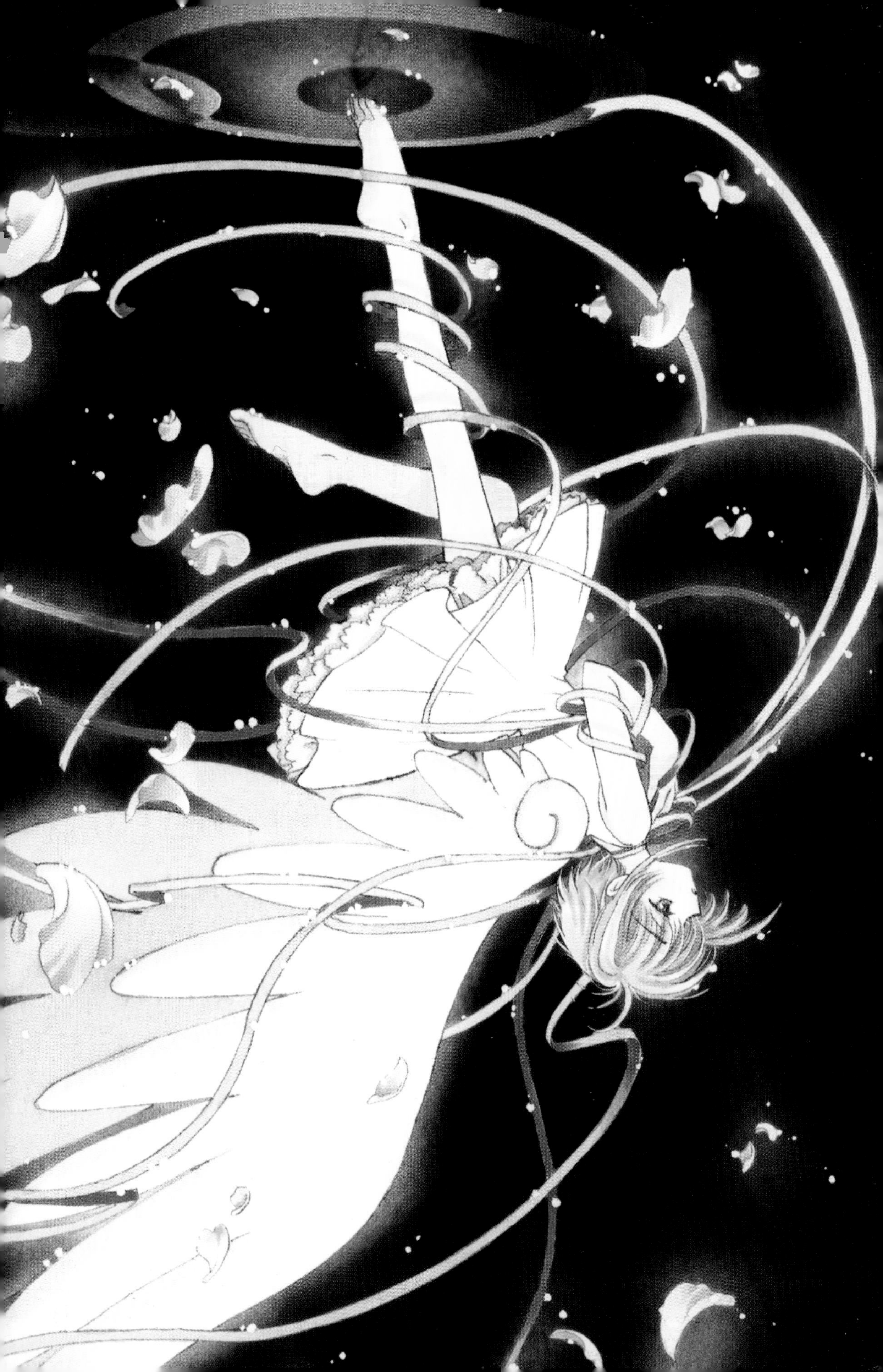

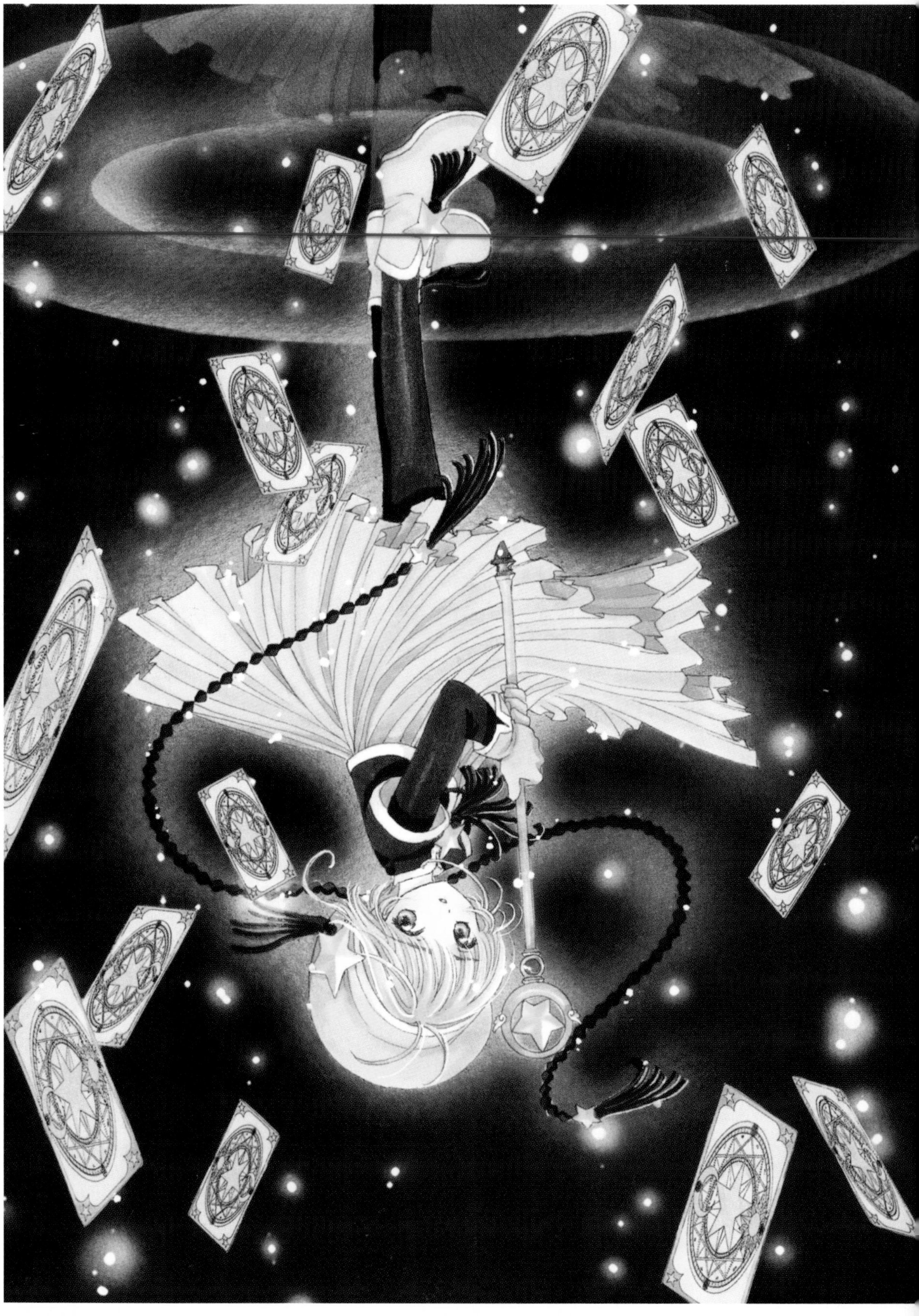

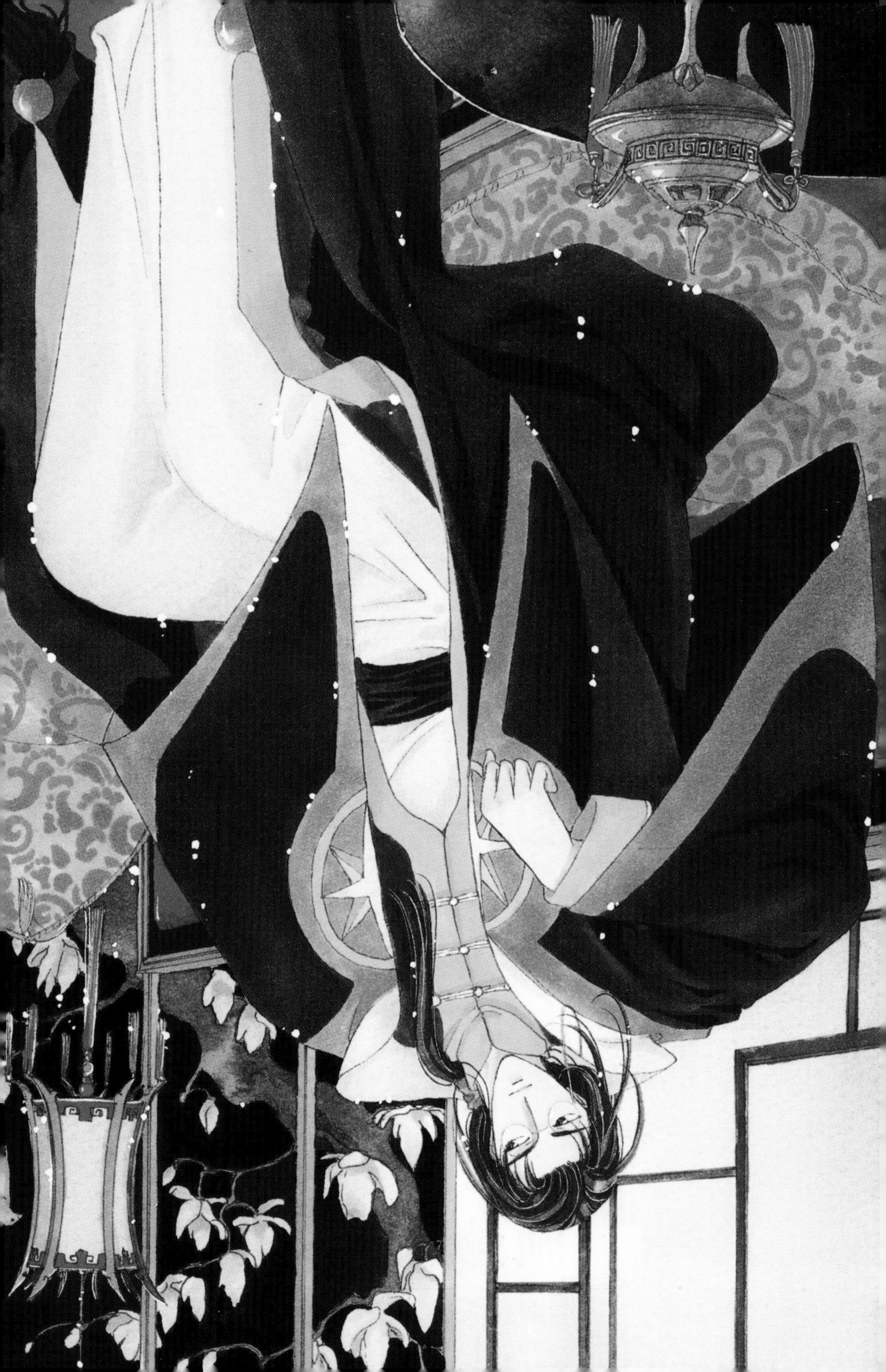

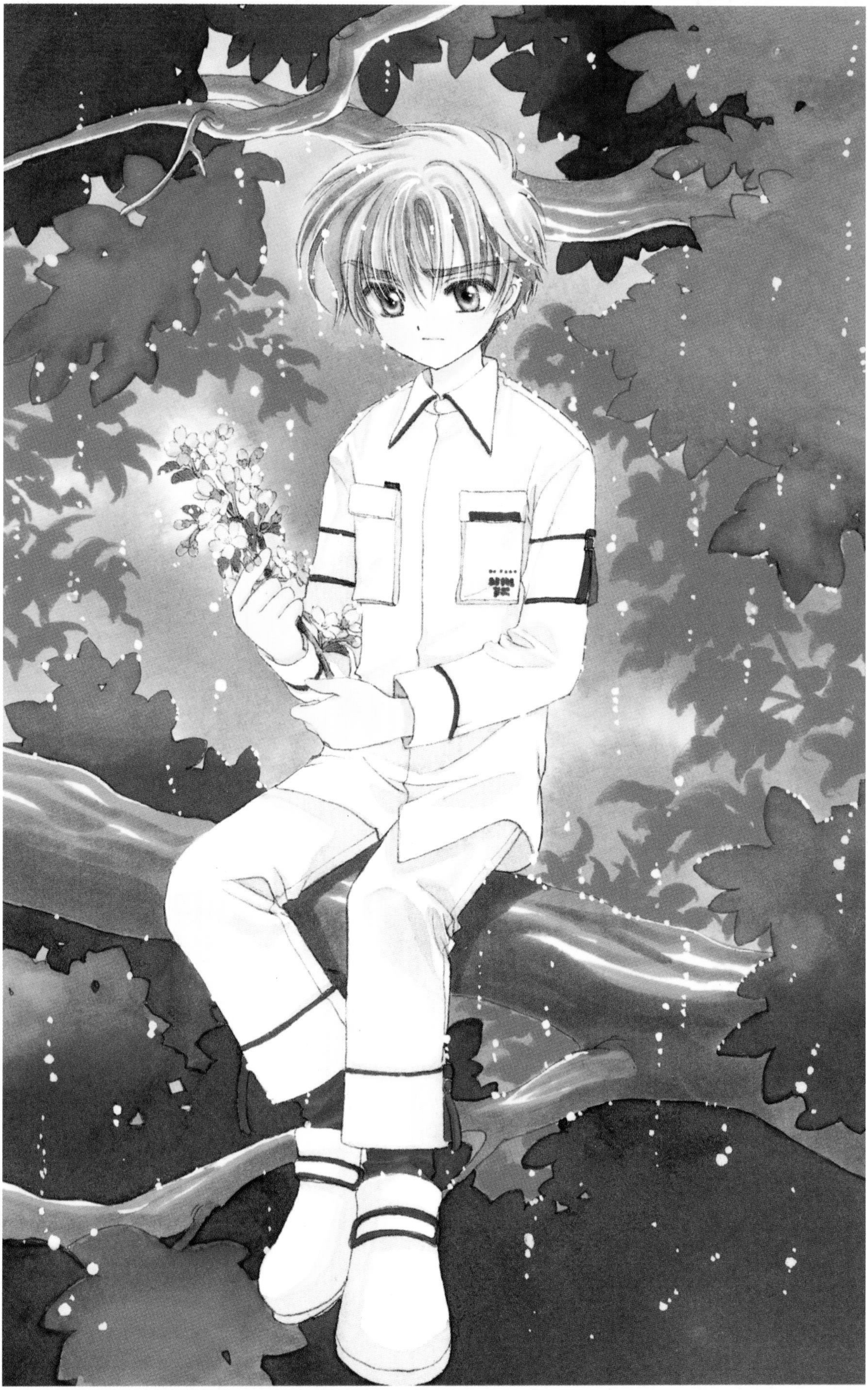

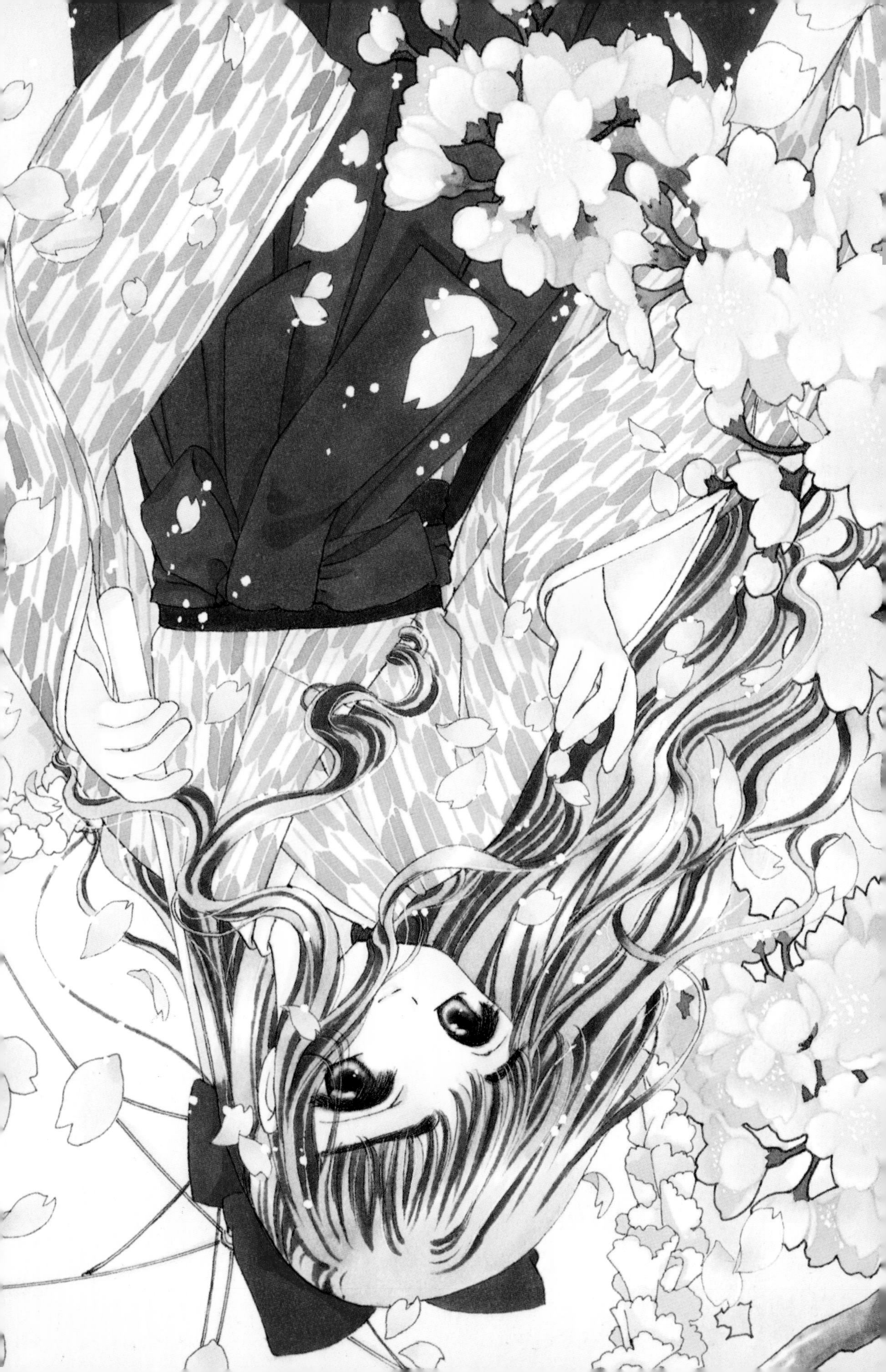

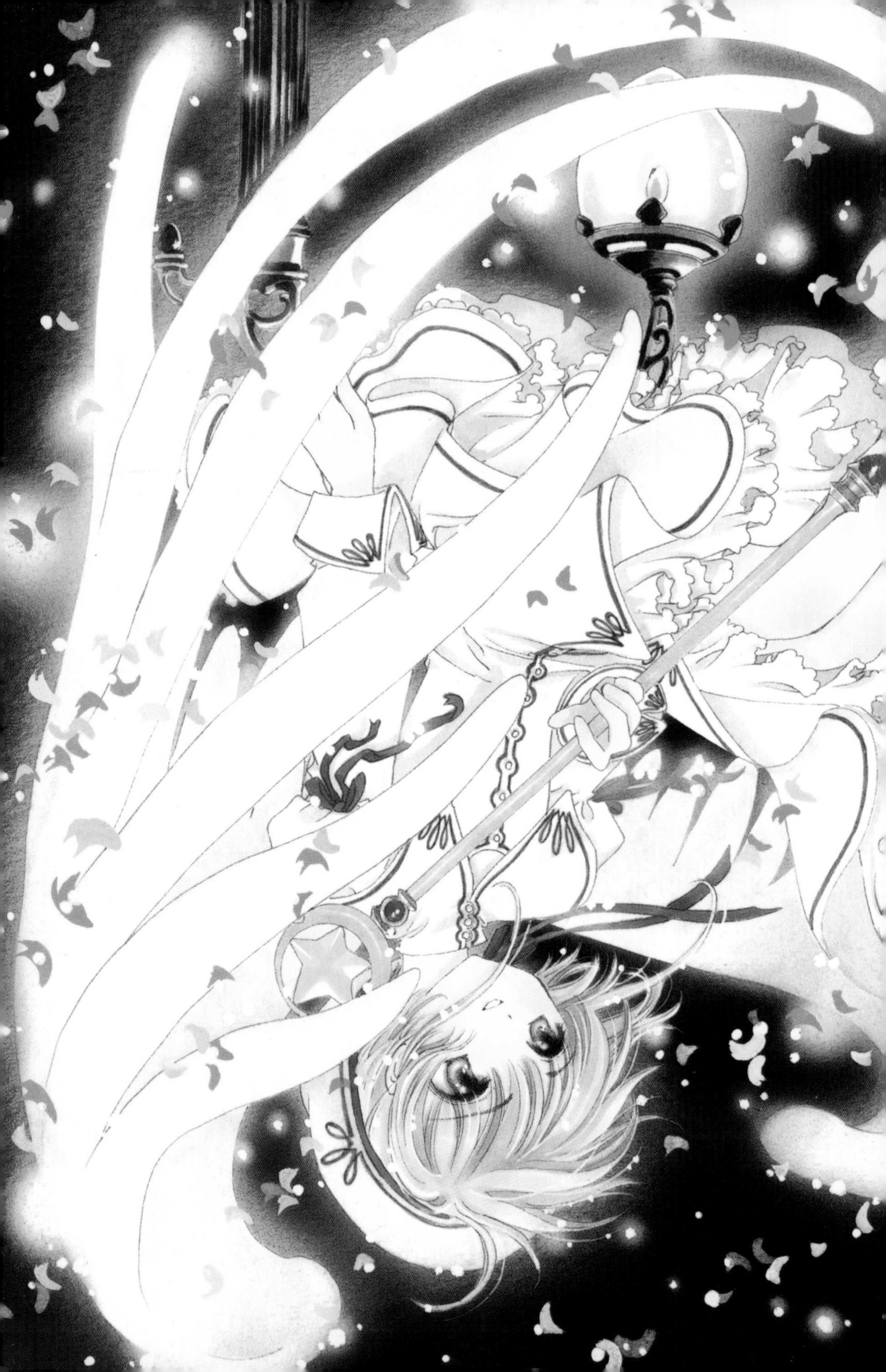

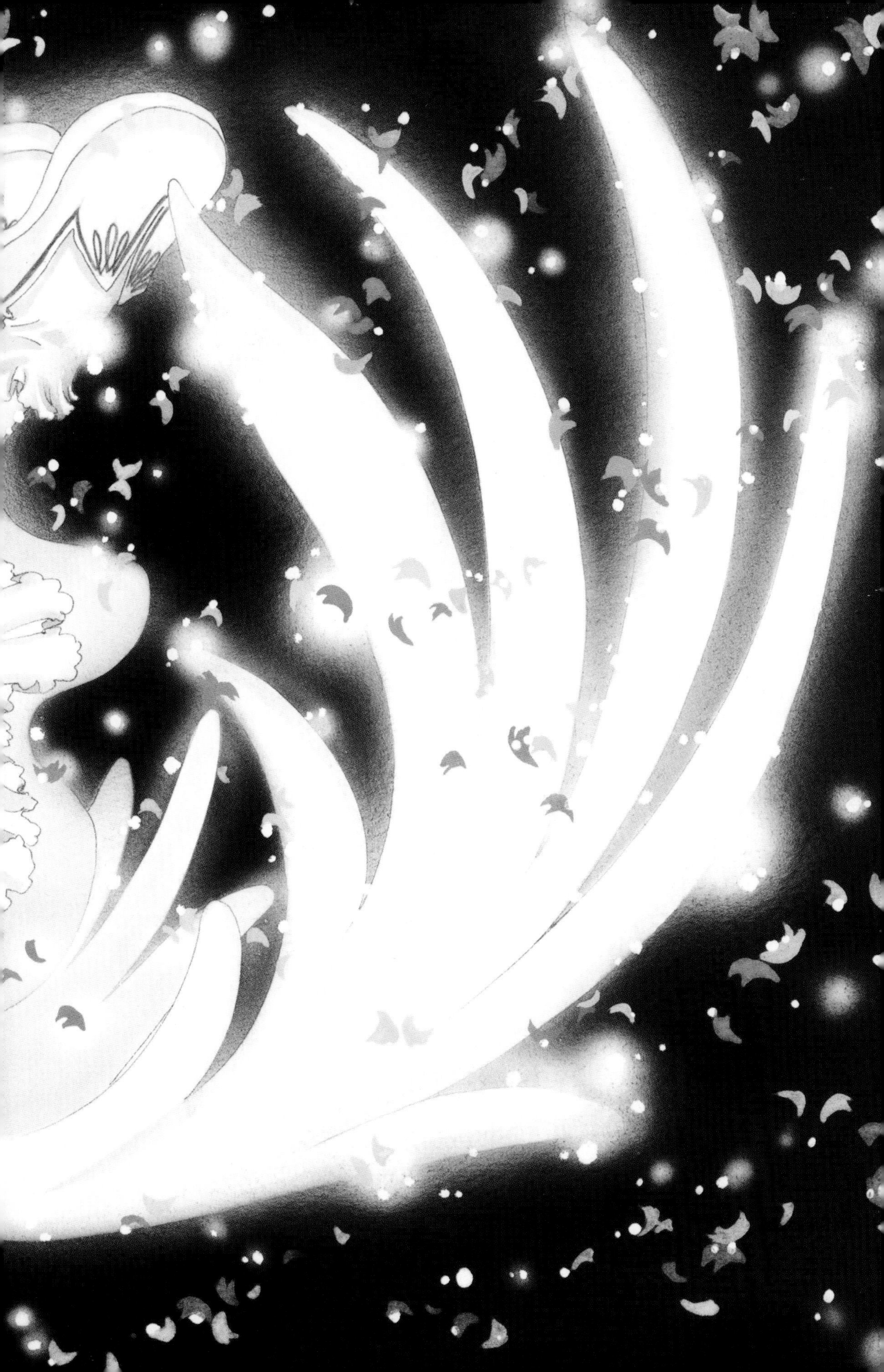

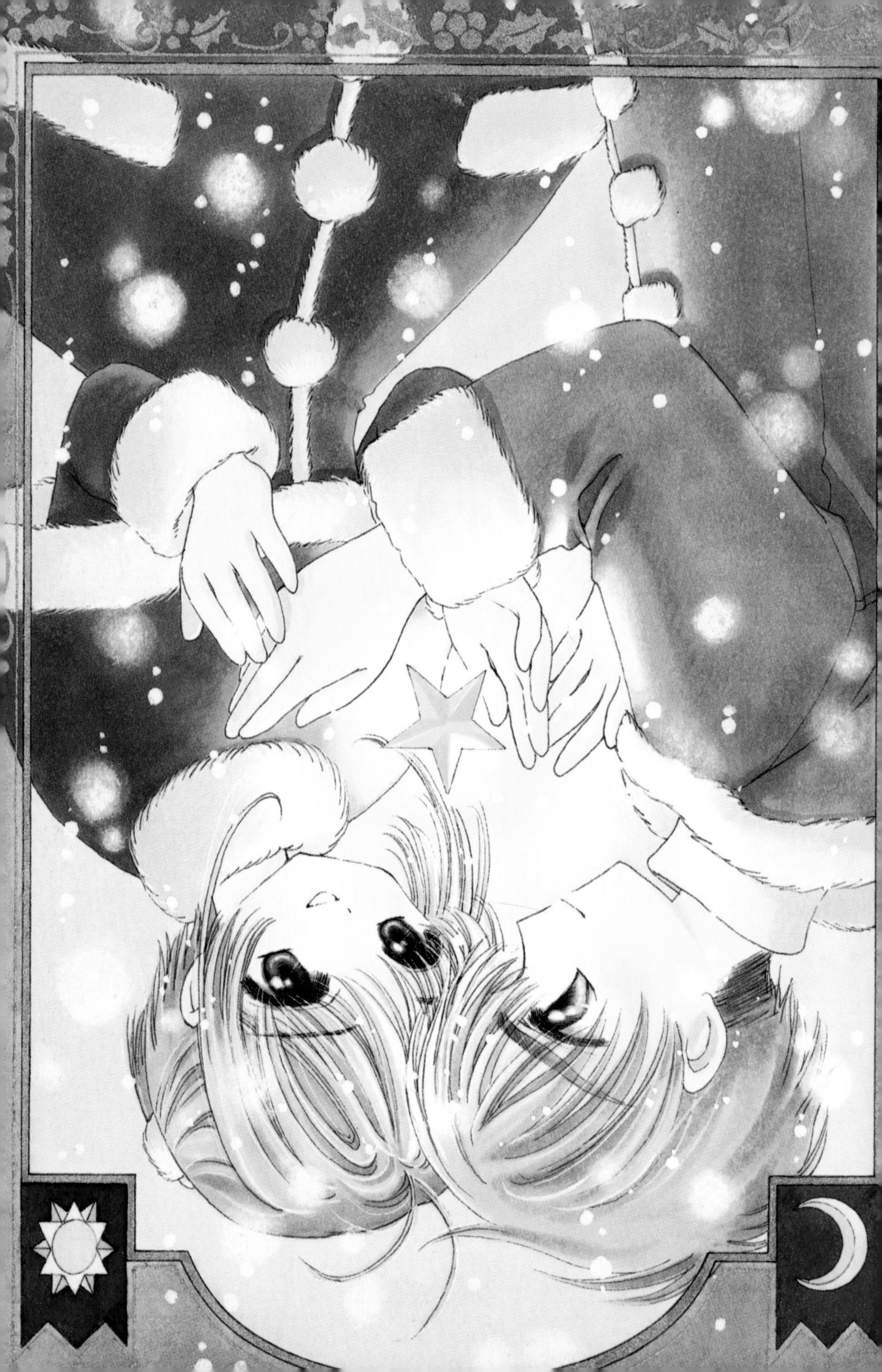

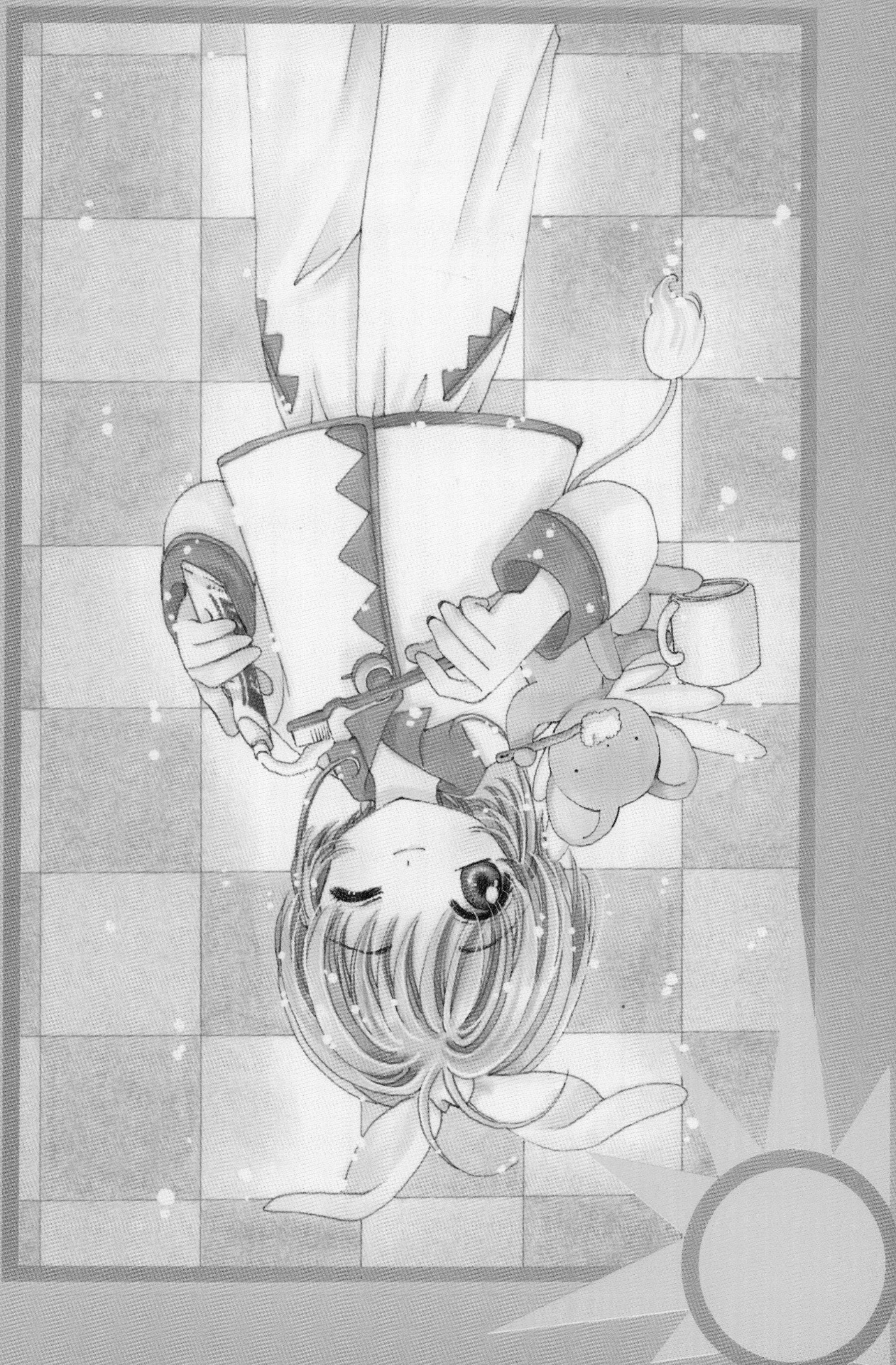

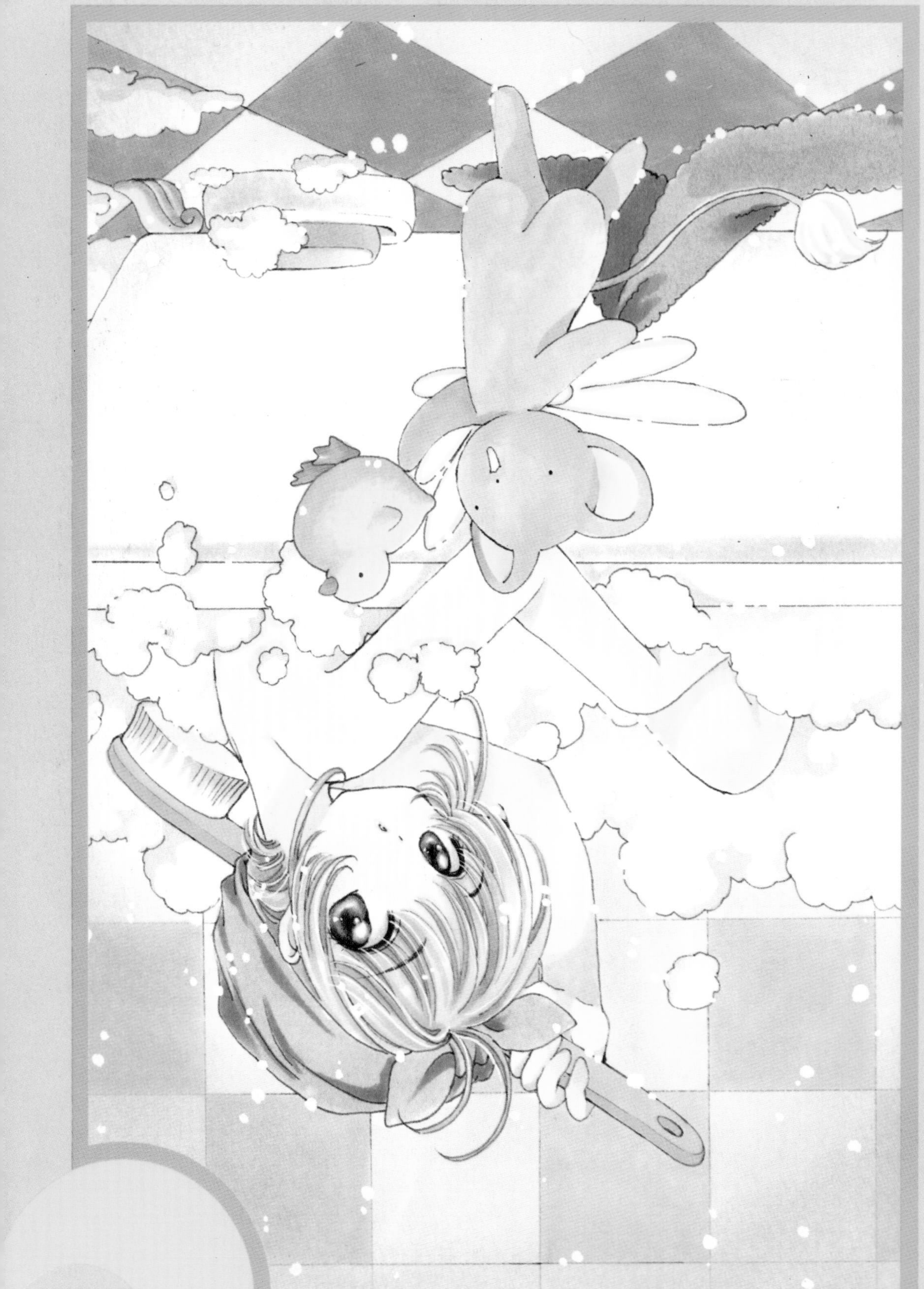

CARDCAPTOR SAKURA
ILLUSTRATIONS COLLECTION 2

🌸 ARTISTS' NOTES 🌸

NAKAYOSHI – NOVEMBER 1999 TITLE PAGE

Ever since Sakura upgraded to the Star Staff, the star motif appears a lot more frequently in her costumes.

NAKAYOSHI – FEBRUARY 2000 TITLE PAGE

It's Sakura holding a bouquet of her namesake flower, cherry blossoms. To give it a springtime feeling, the colors are sunny and vibrant. Those translucent wings were really hard to pull off! (no pun intended!)

NAKAYOSHI - FEBRUARY 1999 COVER

I drew this cover in honor of the Chinese New Year. The streamers and confetti usher in a happy and prosperous new year. I really enjoyed drawing this one because I like Chinese dresses.

NAKAYOSHI - MAY 1999 ISSUE OMAKE*

These illustrations were used on the covers of an omake notebook. I tried to give it a springtime feel. Looking back, I'm not so sure this look works on Eriol... (laugh)

*omake: bonus trinket included with some manga anthologies in Japan (also called furoku)

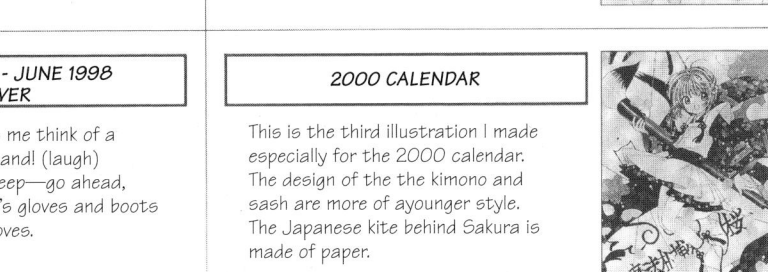

NAKAYOSHI - MAY 1998 ISSUE OMAKE

For the May issue appendix, I created these new illustrations of Tomoyo and Sakura showing off their Japanese style teddy bears, made from kimono fabric. The kimono patterns come from CLAMP members.

NAKAYOSHI - MAY 1999 TITLE PAGE

I always see balloons shaped like rabbits and other animals, so I thought, "why don't I make balloons shaped like Kero and Souppy?"

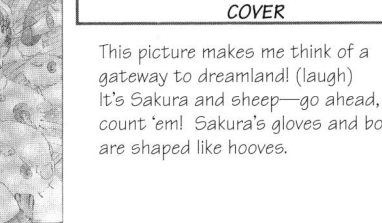

NAKAYOSHI - JUNE 1998 COVER

This picture makes me think of a gateway to dreamland! (laugh) It's Sakura and sheep—go ahead, count 'em! Sakura's gloves and boots are shaped like hooves.

2000 CALENDAR

This is the third illustration I made especially for the 2000 calendar. The design of the the kimono and sash are more of a younger style. The Japanese kite behind Sakura is made of paper.

CARDCAPTOR SAKURA

ILLUSTRATIONS COLLECTION 2

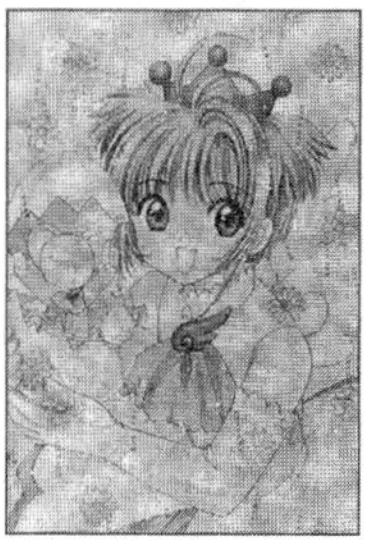

NAKAYOSHI – APRIL 1999
COVER

This outfit is from the second version of the anime opening. I added the stamps to make this image more exciting.

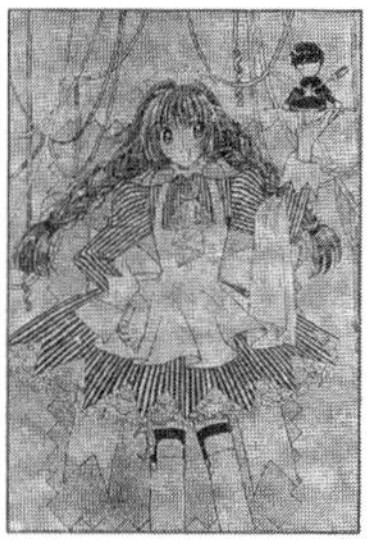

NAKAYOSHI – FEBRUARY 1999
TITLE PAGE

Nakuru dressed like a waitress carrying Toya on a platter. I wish there was more opportunity to paint Nakuru in color, but he/she rarely appears in the color pages.

NAKAYOSHI – JANUARY 1999
COVER

In this picture Sakura's wearing a battle costume from the Clow Card story arc, but she's carrying her Star Staff. It's a pretty unusual picture, having the two arcs mixed.

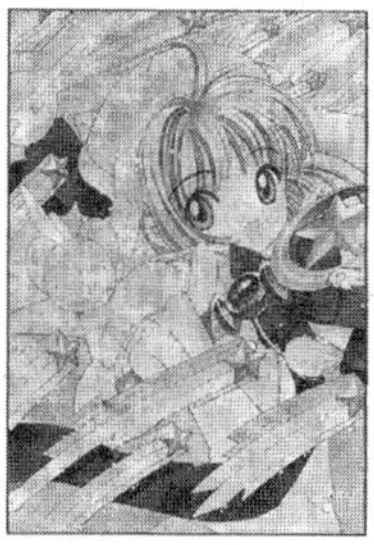

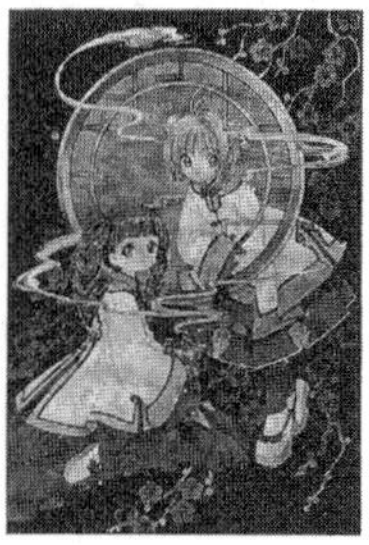

NAKAYOSHI – JUNE 1999
TITLE PAGE

The girl version of this Chinese-themed pair has a pink scheme. The four characters in the two pictures have different styles of clothes. Notice how the clouds in the round window are drawn like the ones you might see in a Chinese painting.

1999 CALENDAR

This is another illustration made for the 199 calendar. The Chinese designs on the cloth may be different, but the colors and cut of the clothing match.

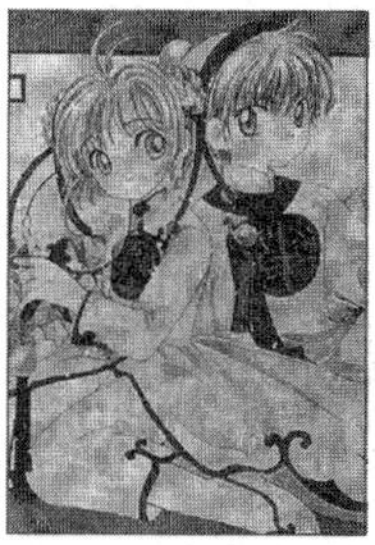

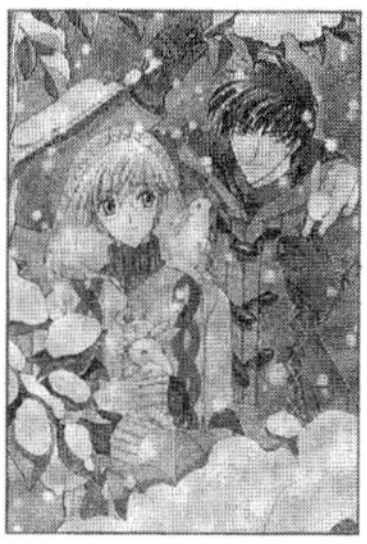

1999 CALENDAR

This iillustration is exclusive to the 199 calendar. It's winter, so I put Yukito, Toya and some rabbits in the snow. It gets so quiet when it's snowing, doesn't it? I tried to capture that tranquility in this picture.

NAKAYOSHI – JUNE 1999
TITLE PAGE

This was one of several boy/girl matching pictures that we've made for this series. I just love drawing the Chinese-style clothes!

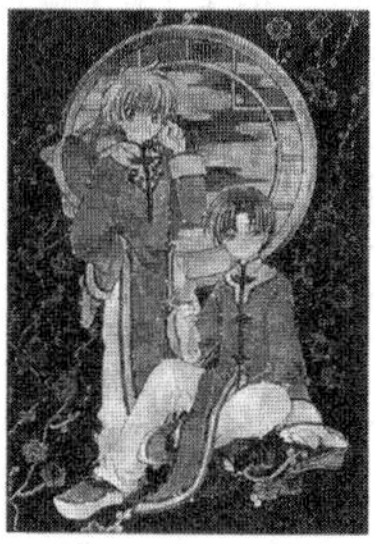

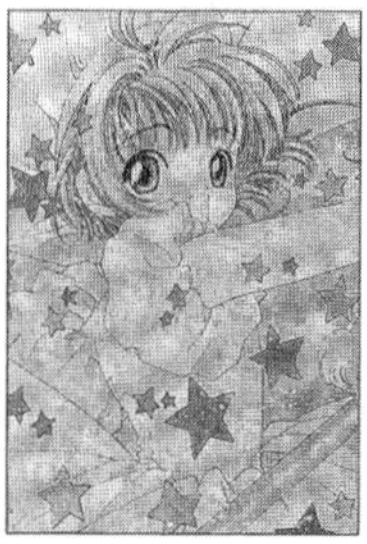

NAKAYOSHI – AUGUST 1998
TITLE PAGE

This title page is for the chapter in which Sakura first gets her Star Staff, so i packed as many stars in the picture as possible! (laugh)

NAKAYOSHI – SEPTEMBER 1999
TITLE PAGE

This is the chapter in which Sakura declarares her love, so that's why she looks a little overly sentimental. I can't have her eyes closed on the cover, but for the title page I could.

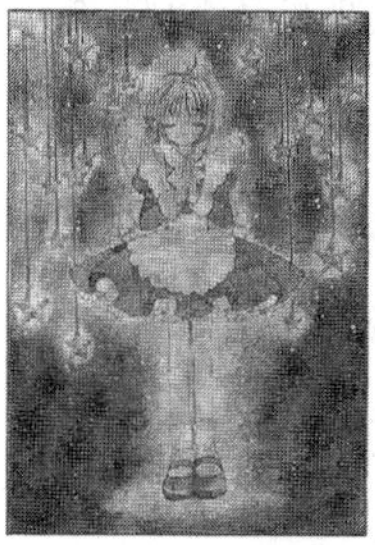

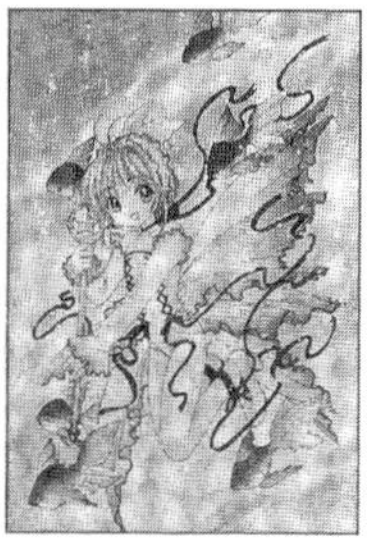

NAKAYOSHI - DECEMBER 1999
OMAKE

This illustration was used on a library card omake. In the summer spirit, I gave Sakura a goldfish-themed battle costume. Fluttering fins are a motif of this picture.

JULY 1999 - LIMITED EDITION
TELEPHONE CARD

This illustration was created in conjunction with the first *Cardcaptor Sakura* movie's release. In the movie, the girls wear Chinese outfits at Syaoran-kun's house. Even though you only see their tops, I designed the bottom of the girls' skirts.

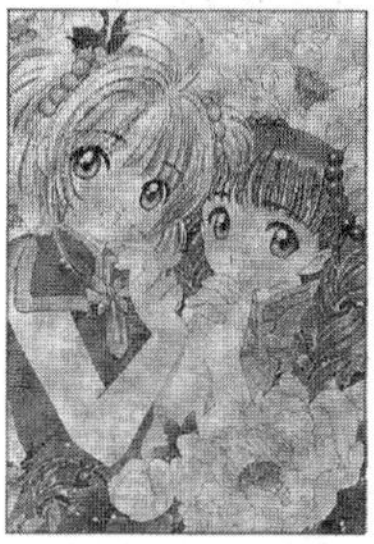

CARDCAPTOR SAKURA
ILLUSTRATIONS COLLECTION 2

NAKAYOSHI - AUGUST 1998
COVER

At the time I made this, I was really into beaded crowns. This is a picture of Queen Sakura-chan. The color scheme of the issue was blue, so that's why I added blue trim to the lace.

NAKAYOSHI - OCTOBER 1998
OMAKE

For the omake I made a front and back picture of Kero-chan. From the front or from the back, he doesn't look that different, does he? (laugh)

1998
TELEPHONE CARD

A new image made for a promotional telephone card. Sakura-chan and Kero must be using the Little card.

NAKAYOSHI - JANUARY 2000
COVER

This is a flower-motif battle costume. Sakura's battle costumes only appear in color on covers. This is another fine outfit under the Tomoyo-chan label…(laugh)

1999 TELEPHONE CARD

This is another drawing in Sakura's "Flowers of the World" series. (OK, I just made that up - laugh!) This is Sakura-chan on a lily. In order to make Sakura really stand out, the background is done with done as a gradation, going from light to dark.

NAKAYOSHI - SEPTEMBER 1998
TITLE PAGE

Another boy/girl illustration pair. Of course the boys get a blue color scheme.   Syaoran looks very upset, doesn't he? (laugh)

2000 CALENDAR

This is a picture of onichan (brother) and Yukito-san working a flower shop. In both the anime and the manga, brother Toya is always working part-time jobs.

1999 "SAKURA FESTIVAL"
CLEAR FILE

This illustration is intended to look like antique toy packaging. Kero is modeled after a tin toy carousel animal.

NAKAYOSHI - OCTOBER 1998
TITLE PAGE

For this boy/girl illustration pair, I dressed the kids as boy scouts and girl scouts. The girls' picture is pink, naturally.

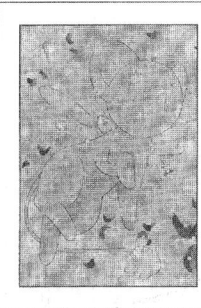

TANKOUBON* VOLUME 6
FRONTISPIECE (FRONT)

As with the first five volumes, the frontispieces feature a character posed the same way in a daytime version and night version. Since this is small Kero-chan, I was able to fit his whole body in frame. (laugh)

*Tankoubon- The collected edition of the manga, like a graphic novel.

DECEMBER 1998
TITLE PAGE

I wanted to create a European castle-style banner featuring Kero-chan and Souppy. To distinguish their alignments at the top, Kero's sun is orange and Souppy's is peppermint-colored.

CARDCAPTOR SAKURA
ILLUSTRATIONS COLLECTION 2

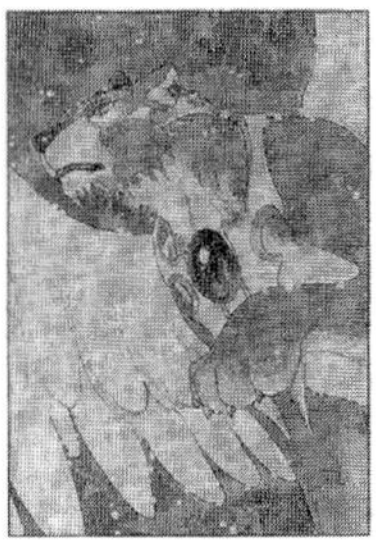

TANKOUBON VOLUME 6 FRONTISPIECE (BACK)

The younger readers aren't as fond of Kero-chan in his true form. Maybe, like Sakura, they're a little afraid of big Kero-chan. (laugh)

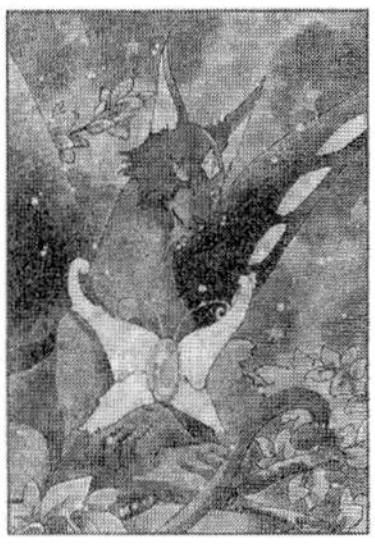

TANKUBOUN VOLUME 9 FRONTISPIECE (BACK)

This is a night version of Spinnel Sun with his arms crossed like the daytime version. Much to my dismay, he's just a little too big to fit on the page.

TANKOUBON VOLUME 9 FRONTISPIECE (FRONT)

This is a daytime version of Souppy. If you compare his size to that of the leaves, you can see that he's about the size of a kitten.

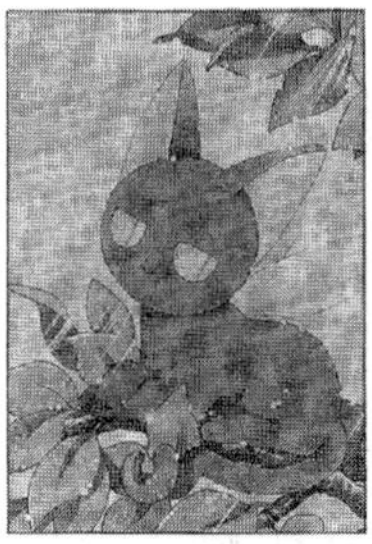

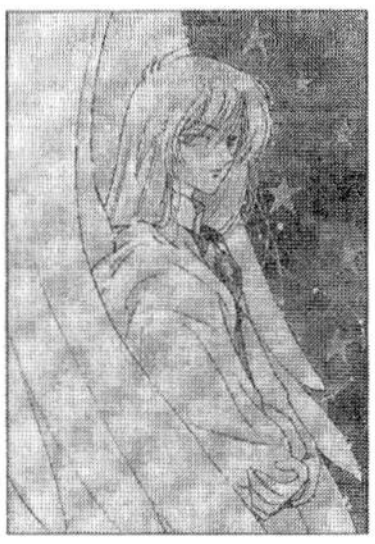

TANKOUBON VOLUME 7 FRONTISPIECE (BACK)

This is Yue drawn for the rear frontispiece. His whole body is very white. He probably only looks good at night when he stands out. (laugh)

TANKOUBON VOLUME 7 FRONTISPIECE (FRONT)

This is the daytime version of Yukito-san. I suppose Yue and Yukito are the same person, but I draw them as if they were different people.

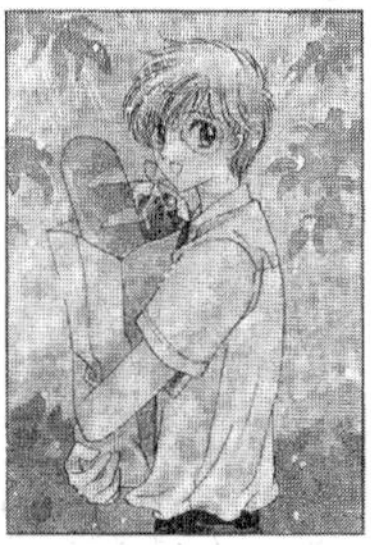

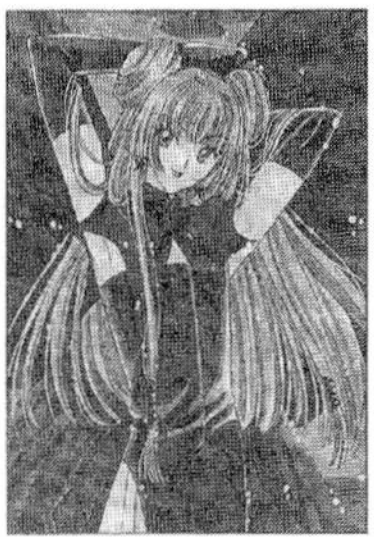

TANKOUBON VOLUME 8 FRONTISPIECE (BACK)

Nakuru's true form is that of Ruby Moon. The only differences in her physical appearance between forms are her hair and eye color. This outfit makes her seem older.

TANKOUBON VOLUME 8 FRONTISPIECE (FRONT)

This is a daytime version of Nakuru-san. She's posed as if she's just hanging out between classes. I love this character because I can draw her hair in so many ways.

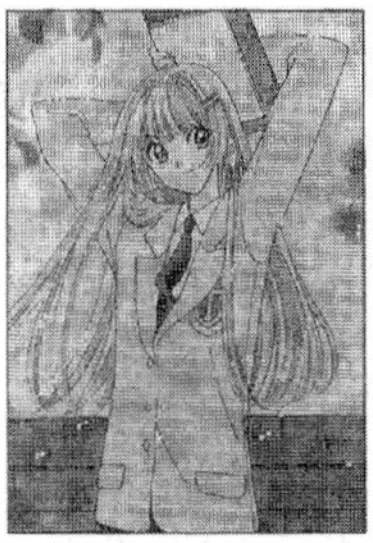

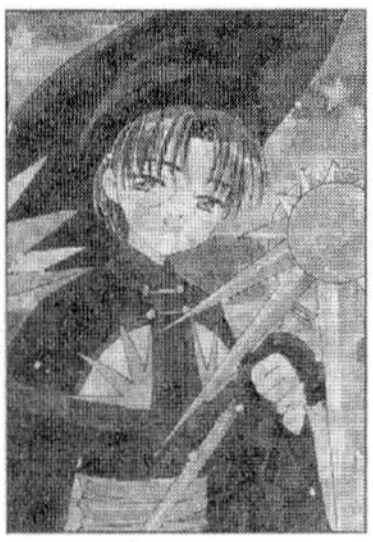

TANKOUBON VOLUME 10 FRONTISPIECE (BACK)

The night-version of Eriol features his cermonial robes. This design is kind of like a European witch. The other CLAMP members tell me his head looks like a shiitake-mushroom. (laugh)

TANKOUBON VOLUME 10 FRONTISPIECE (FRONT)

Eriol is wearing the dark red winter uniform. With the fall hues in the leaves behind him, the effect is very mellow and soothing.

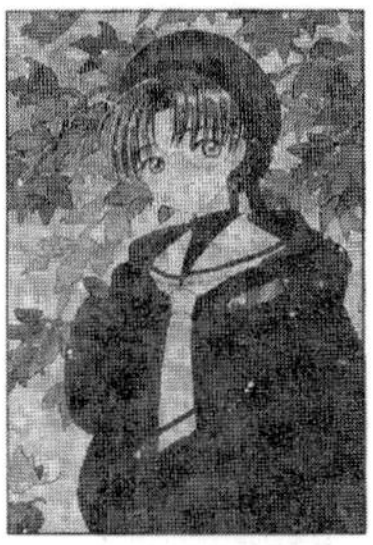

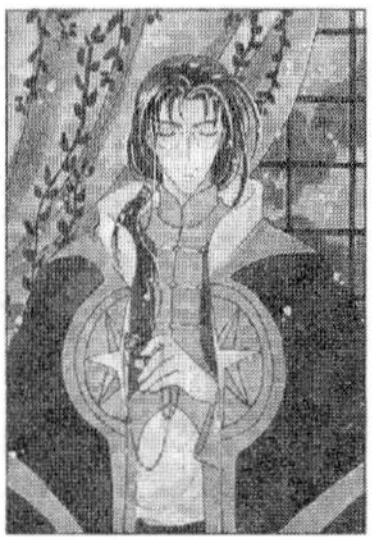

TANKOUBON VOLUME 11 FRONTISPIECE (BACK)

The nighttime version of Clow Reed is dressed in ceremonial Chinese Robes.

TANKOUBON VOLUME 11 FRONTISPIECE (FRONT)

This is the daytime version of Clow Reed. He is half-Chinese and half-British so I drew him in Western clothes here, and in Chinese clothes in the back.

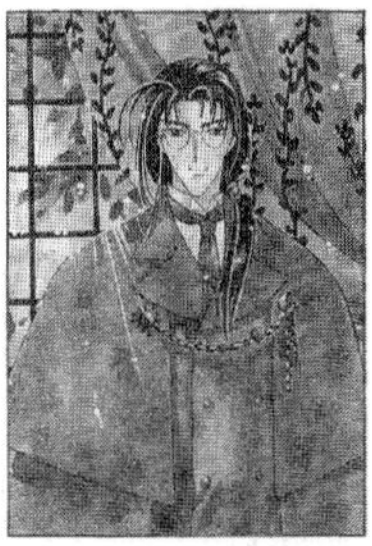

CARDCAPTOR SAKURA
ILLUSTRATIONS COLLECTION 2

NAKAYOSHI - JUNE 1998
TITLE PAGE

This is the first illustration of Yue in color. I added the silver ornamentaion to match with the picture of Kero from last month's title page.

NAKAYOSHI - NOVEMBER 1998
TITLE PAGE

The printed version of this illustration is only one page, but I drew the original as a two-page spread. In order to make the wings look mysterious, I drew them over a black background.

NAKAYOSHI - MAY 1998
TITLE PAGE

This is the first color illustration of Kero-chan in his true form. This time the ornamentation is gold.

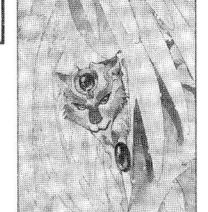

NAKAYOSHI - APRIL 1999
OMAKE

This was also used on the stationery omake. . Sakura-chan sits on a clock at night. I tried using all three motifs, the sun, moon and star, on the clock, but... I don't know.

NAKAYOSHI - APRIL 1999
OMAKE

This picture of Sakura-chan is featured in a stationery omake. Since she's the main character, I figured it was time she had an outfit featuring the classic sun and moon motif. Her star is featured in the background. She looks very resolute, doesn't she?

NAKAYOSHI - APRIL 1999
OMAKE

One more illustration for the stationery supplement. This is a rare shot of Kero and Spinnel in their true forms. The background features the sun, the symbol of power for Kero and Spinnel.

NAKAYOSHI - APRIL 1999
OMAKE

Another illustration for the stationary omake. White Yue and red and black Ruby Moon make a nice looking pair, don't they? (It's too bad they never actually get to be alone together in the manga). In the background is their shared symbol of power: the moon.

NAKAYOSHI - JULY 1998
TITLE PAGE

This illustration was made for Sakura's final battle in the Clow Card saga. Because it is night, the background is black and elements of the sun and moon are worked into Sakura's costume.

NAKAYOSHI - AUGUST 1998
TITLE PAGE

This title page illstration features Eriol and Clow wearing matching clothes. The idea behind this picture is that Eriol's true form is revealed in the mirror.

NAKAYOSHI - NOVEMBER 1998
TITLE PAGE

I drew this illustration for the fall issue. Yukito and Toya are taking a break in the park. In the actual story, it's Yukito-san who's always sleeping, but here it's Toya who's in sleep mode.

NAKAYOSHI - JANUARY 1999
TITLE PAGE

The theme of this picture is a royal ball. I liked making this costume because it is slightly different from the actual battle costume.

CARDCAPTOR SAKURA
ILLUSTRATIONS COLLECTION 2

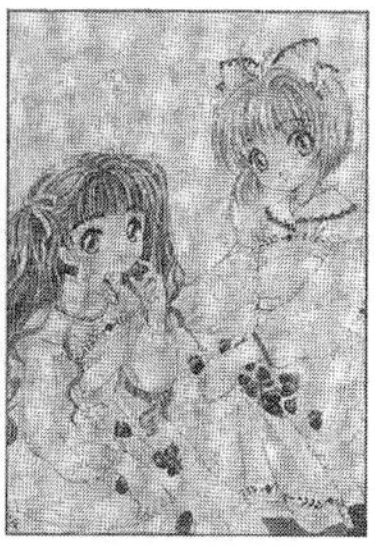

NAKAYOSHI - NOVEMBER 1998
COVER

It's rare in *Sakura* illustrations that characters and backgrounds are drawn separately like this. I went after a country style, like something out of *Anne of Green Gables*.

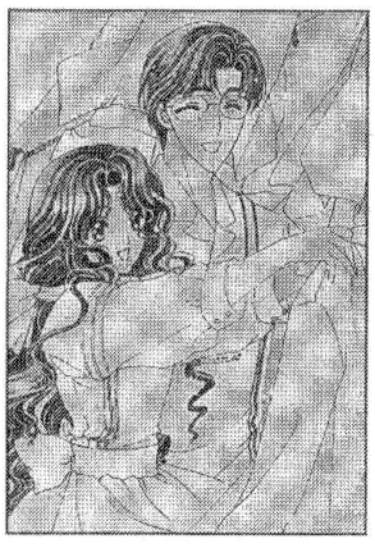

NAKAYOSHI - DECEMBER 1999
TITLE PAGE

It's Sakura's parents, Nadeshiko and Fujitaka. I tried to bring out the fact that they enjoy doing everything together, even housekeeping.

NAKAYOSHI - JUNE 1999
TITLE PAGE

It's Yukito taking a nap. In the actual story he's not just napping, but fell into a magical coma. You can see that in this picture he's starting to disappear.

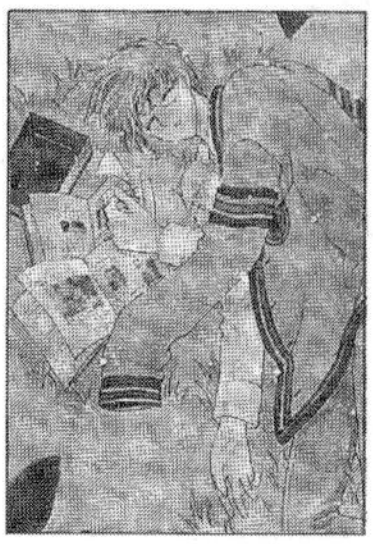

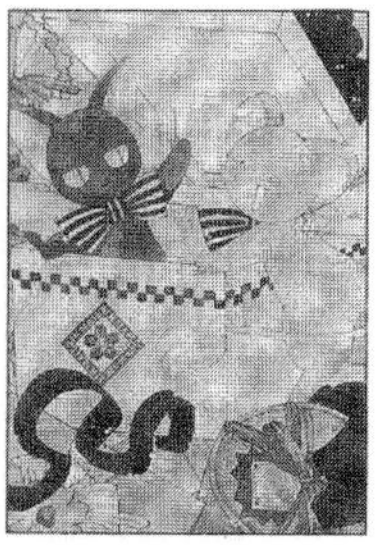

NAKAYOSHI - APRIL 1999
TITLE PAGE

This is another Valentine's Day-themed piece. It took a lot of work, but I enjoyed thinking up all of the gift wrapping designs. I used stamps and lots of other techniques to pull off this simple-looking picture. (laugh)

NAKAYOSHI - MARCH 1999
TITLE PAGE

Since this story is about Valentine's Day, I drew Sakura with chocolate and a ribbon. There have been several Valentine's Day illustrations for Sakura, and in all of them, the hardest part of drawing them is getting the chocolate just right! (laugh)

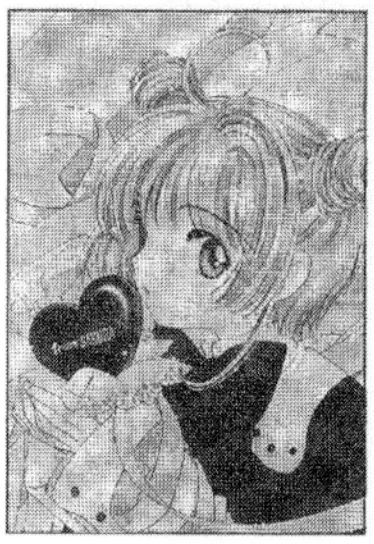

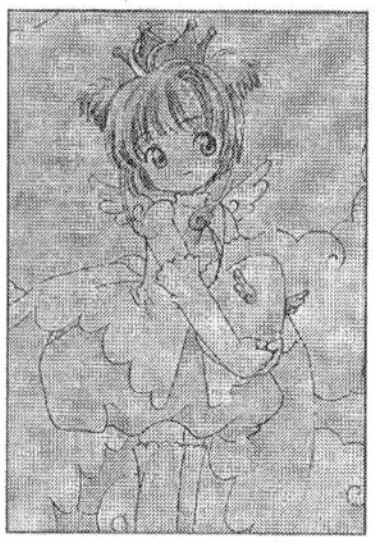

NAKAYOSHI - APRIL 1999
OMAKE

This illustration was used on the omake. Sakura looks a little bit like a chibi-character. Sakura emerges from an egg holding an egg! Now, that's what I call an egg-themed picture!

SAKURA MATSURI - 1999
LIFE-SIZE CUT-OUT

This picture was used for a life-size cut-out. The pattern in the background is done with stamps.

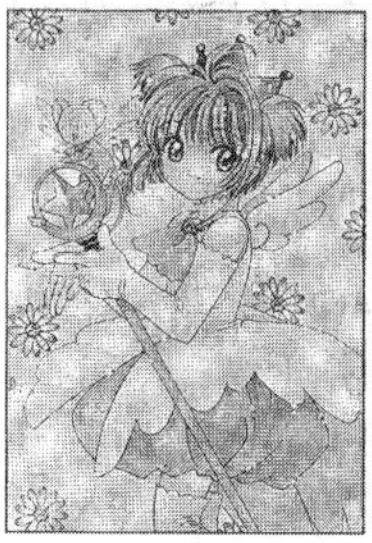

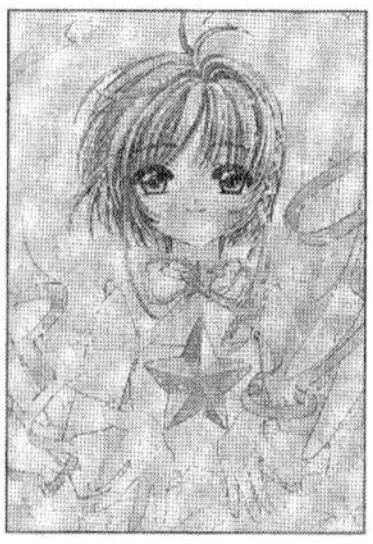

NAKAYOSHI - SEPTEMBER 1999
TITLE PAGE

This angel-like costume is inspired by a ballerina's tu-tu. How do you like it?

NAKAYOSHI - JULY 1999
TITLE PAGE

I never did a full-fleged series (laugh) but I did make several fairy-like illustrations. This is fairy-Tomoyo in the morning dew.

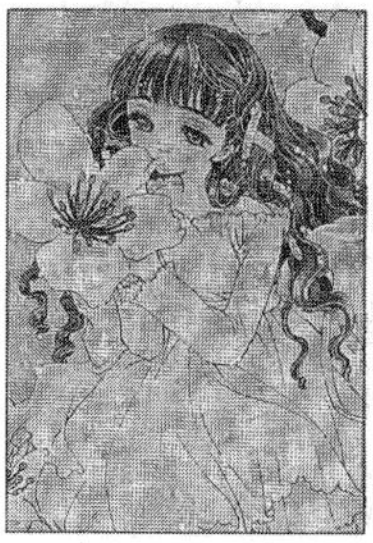

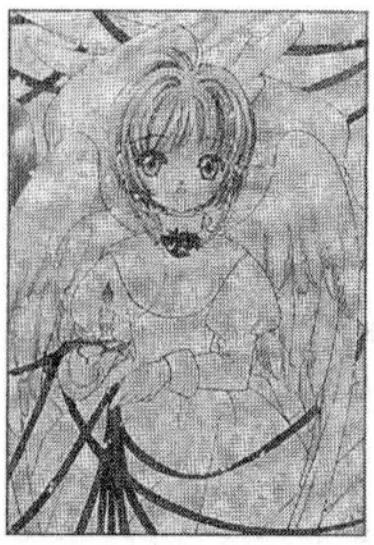

1999 CALENDAR

This illustration is for the calendar's December page, of course! The theme is "Silent Night, Holy Night." It's nice to get together with friends at the holidays. For this picture, I tried to make the girls look a little older.

NAKAYOSHI - SEPTEMBER 1999
TITLE PAGE

Tomoyo and Sakura often wear costumes of different shapes but matching colors. This picture uses a "wing" theme. The girls are dressed like angels.

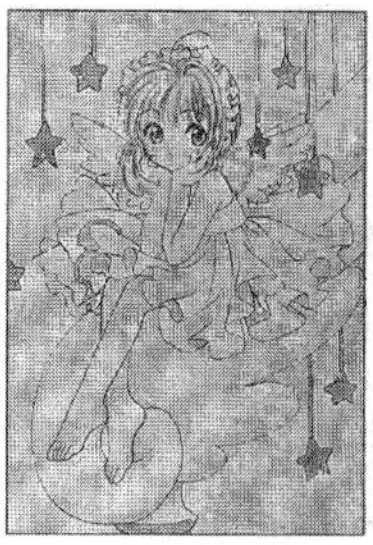

CARDCAPTOR SAKURA
ILLUSTRATIONS COLLECTION 2

1998 SAKURA FESTIVAL SOUVENIR BAG

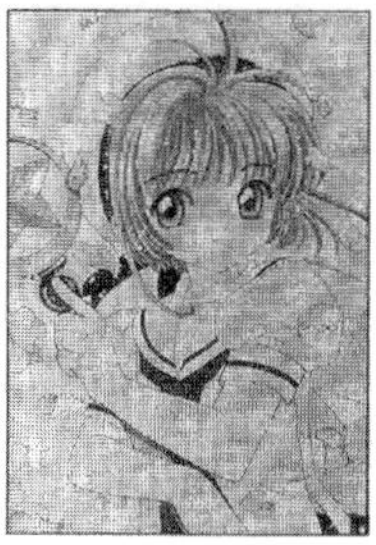

I made this illustration for the bag that was given away for the 1998 Sakura festival. The front and back feature Sakura in mirror image poses. Because the festival was held in summer, she's wearing her summer uniform.

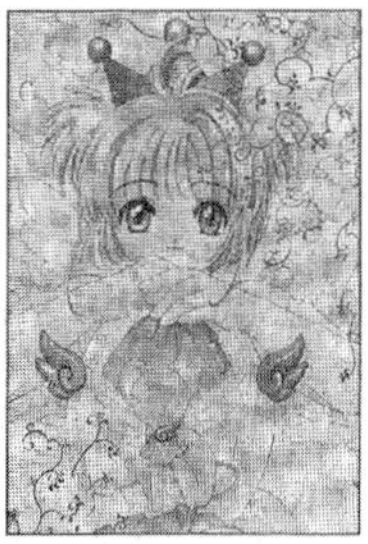

1999 SAKURA FESTIVAL SOUVENIR BAG

The winged egg theme is a CLAMP signature design. On this side of the bag, Kero-chan is inside an egg.

1998 SAKURA FESTIVAL SOUVENIR BAG

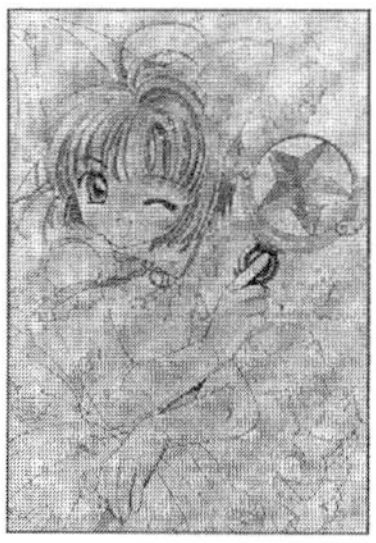

The back of the bag. I'd already drawn Sakura as a black cat, so for this picture, I dressed her as a white cat! Color is dominated by white and pink.

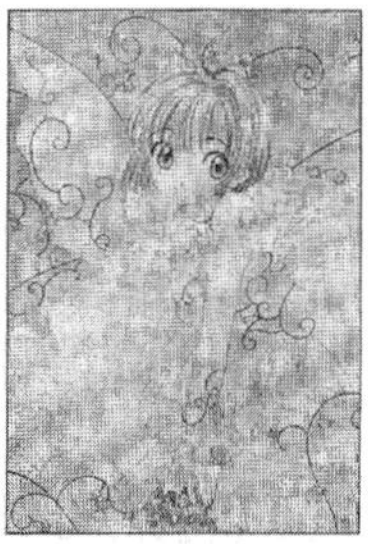

NAKAYOSHI - SEPTEMBER 1998 TITLE PAGE

It's unusual to see Sakura dressed in purple like this. The idea of this picture is that Sakura is a butterfly resting on a flower.

1999 SAKURA FESTIVAL SOUVENIR BAG

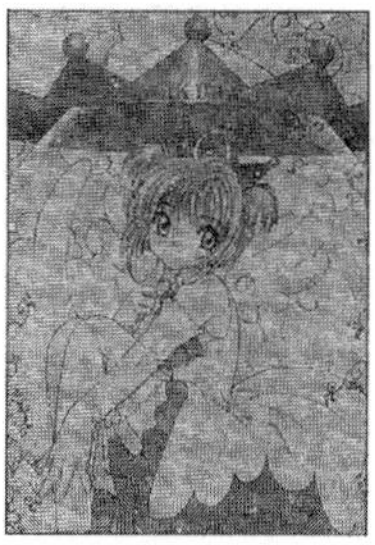

The reverse side of the souvenir bag. This time Sakura's in the egg. Her costume is one of the ones from the anime's second season opening.

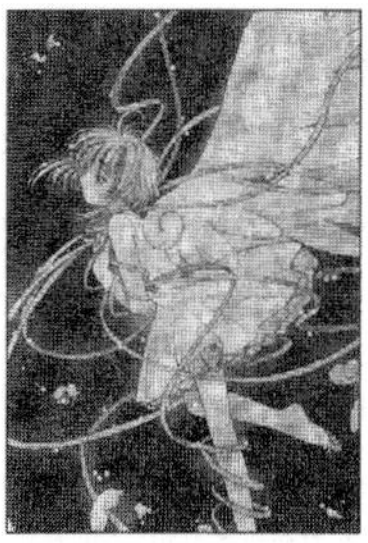

NAKAYOSHI - JANUARY 1998 TITLE PAGE

This is the first illustration featuring the new Fly card in color. It's rare that I use an airbrush on title pages, as I did here.

1999 CALENDAR CLEAR FILE

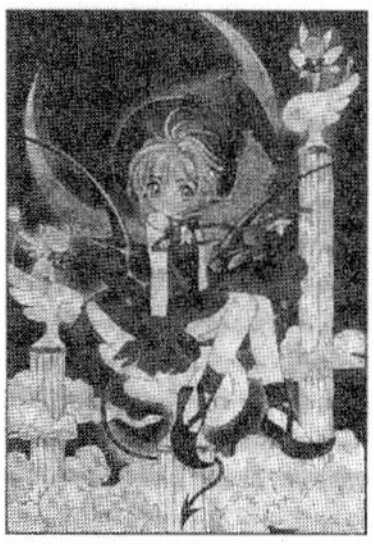

It's a demon-like Sakura with her messengers, Kero-chan and Souppy (color pictures of him are few and far between). The background is painted with an airbrush.

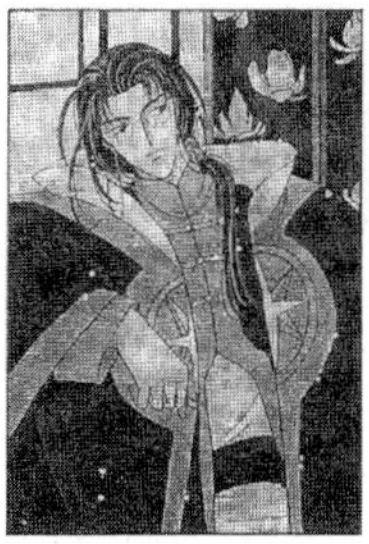

NAKAYOSHI - AUGUST 1998 TITLE PAGE

It's Clow Reed in a Chinese-style room. To make it like an old picture, I used sepia tones.

NAKAYOSHI - JANUARY 1998 TITLE PAGE

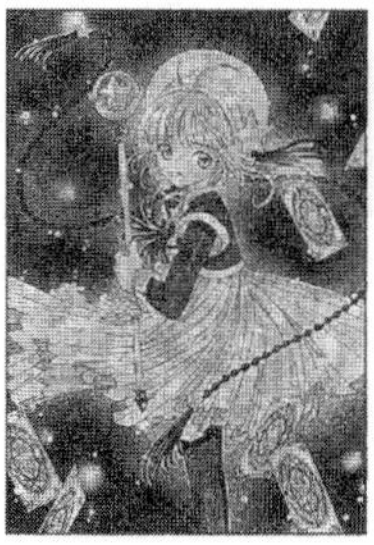

Sakura looks nervous as she awaits her final battle. The hardest part of making this picture was drawing the Sakura Cards because they're so tiny!

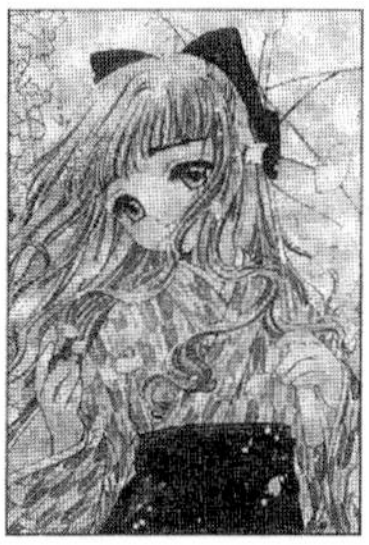

1999 CALENDAR

For this exclusive calendar illustration, I drew Tomoyo-chan in a traditional student-type kimono. With the hakama (pleated skirt) and western style parasol, it looks very old-fashioned. I tried to make her expression more grown-up with a touch of ennui.

NAKAYOSHI - OCTOBER 1999 TITLE PAGE

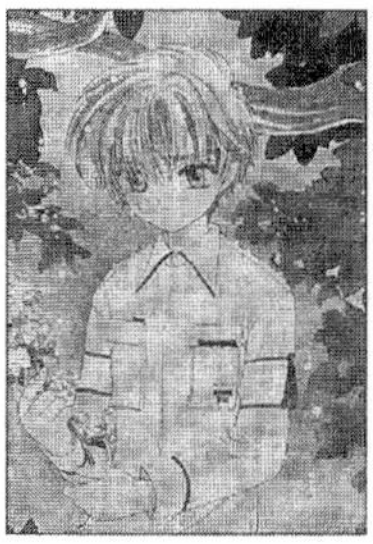

Syaoran-kun sits in the rain, holding a sprig of cherry blossoms. I tried to make his expression look as if his heart aches as he thinks about Sakura.

2000 CALENDAR

An original illustration for the 2000 calendar. I tried to slip in the images of the sun, moon and star. I hope I did it right so that it keeps the soft, relaxing feeling that I intended.

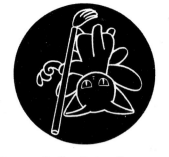

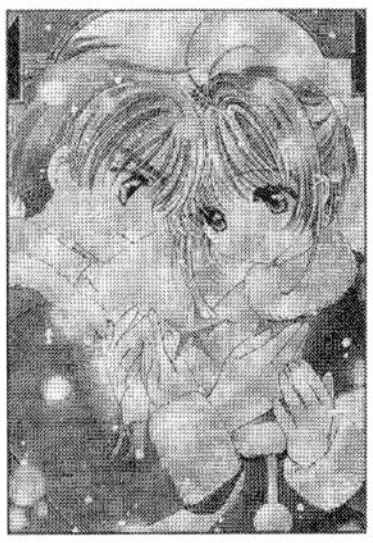

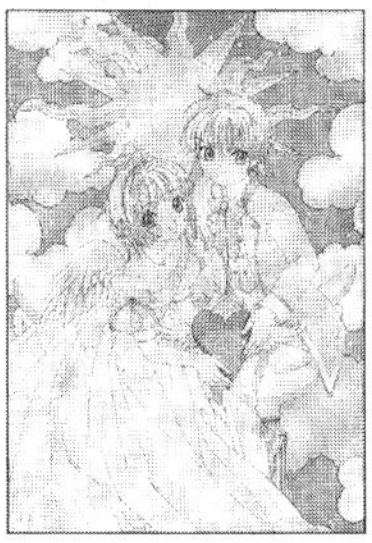

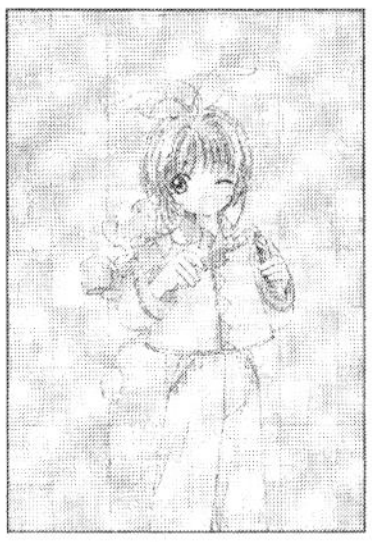

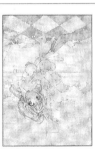

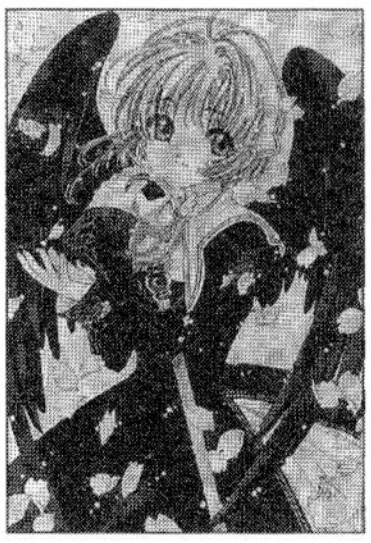

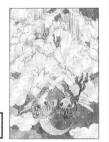

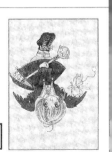

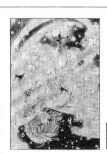

NAKAYOSHI - JANUARY 2000 TITLE PAGE

One spring night, Sakura drifts down like an angel to rest on a street lamp. At least, that's the image I had in mind here. I hope she looks glimmering with the white cloth and white wings.

BACK COVER FOR THE ART BOOK

I used the same stamping technique as on the back covers of the tankoubons. I am glad that I could show you the entire figure of the costume from the front cover (even if it is only in chibi-mode).

COVER FOR THE ART BOOK

In order to differentiate from the Collection 1, and in order to emphasize how Sakura has grown up through the"Master of the Clow" (Sakura Card) saga, I gave her the black costume with the black wings. The gold line on the costume is done with Poster Color.

ART BOOK FRONTISPIECE

It's Sakura-chan at night. In the first collection , there was "Goodnight Sakura", so this time it's "Sakura taking a bath."

ART BOOK FRONTISPIECE

Just like tankoubons' color frontispieces, it consists of morning and night. I did "Good morning Sakura" in the first art book, so here it's "Sakura brushing her teeth."

ART BOOK POSTER

The reverse side of the Art Book's poster. This time the poster comes with a "Sakura and Syaoran" version and "Sakura and Tomoyo" version. This is Sakura and Tomoyo. Their dresses are shaped differently, but the style and colors match.

ART BOOK POSTER

This picture was created especially for the Art Book's poster. It's Shaolan and Sakura. Don't their costumes make them look like they're at a wedding? (laugh)

CARDCAPTOR SAKURA

ILLUSTRATIONS COLLECTION 2

ARTISTS' NOTES

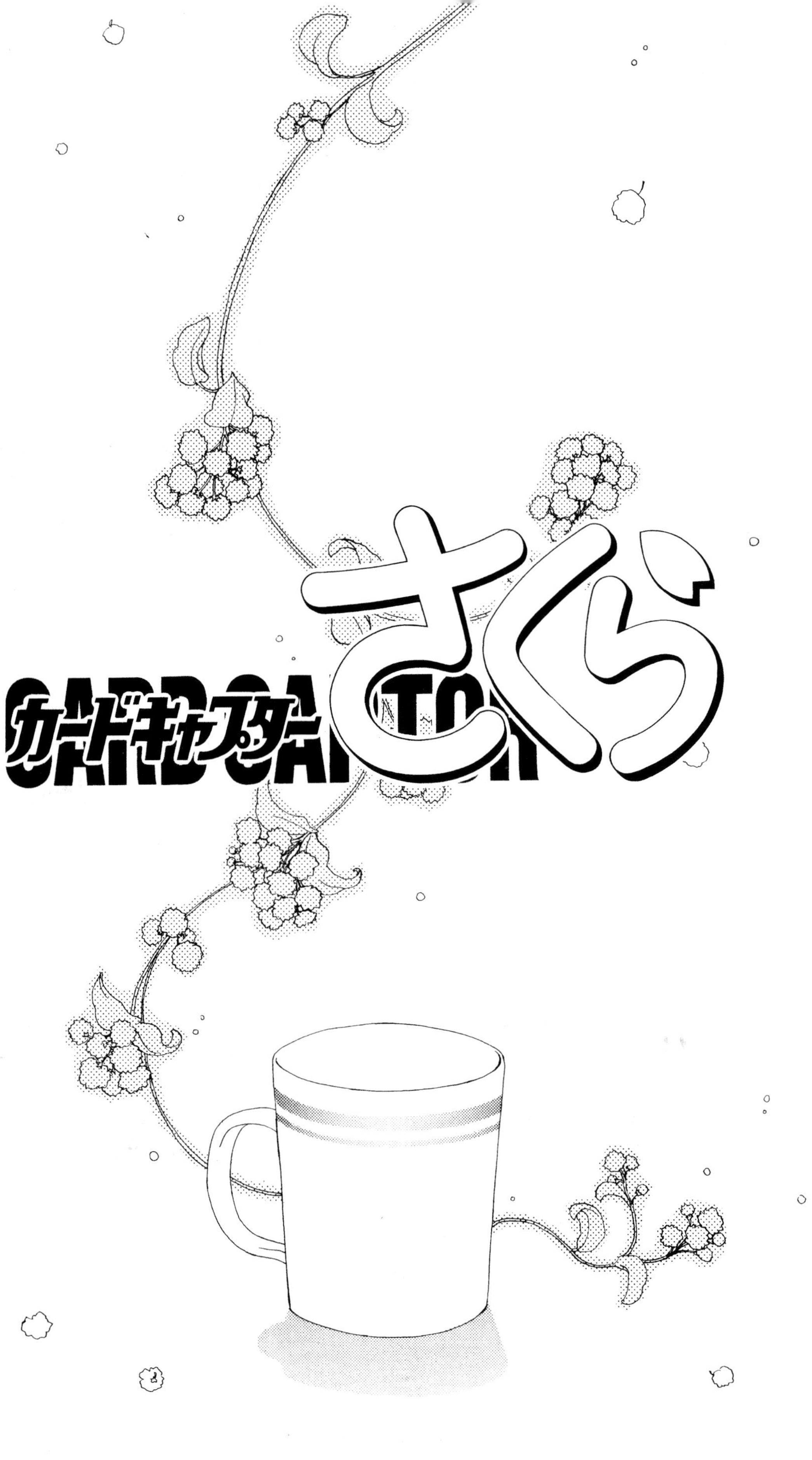
カードキャプターさくら
CARDCAPTOR

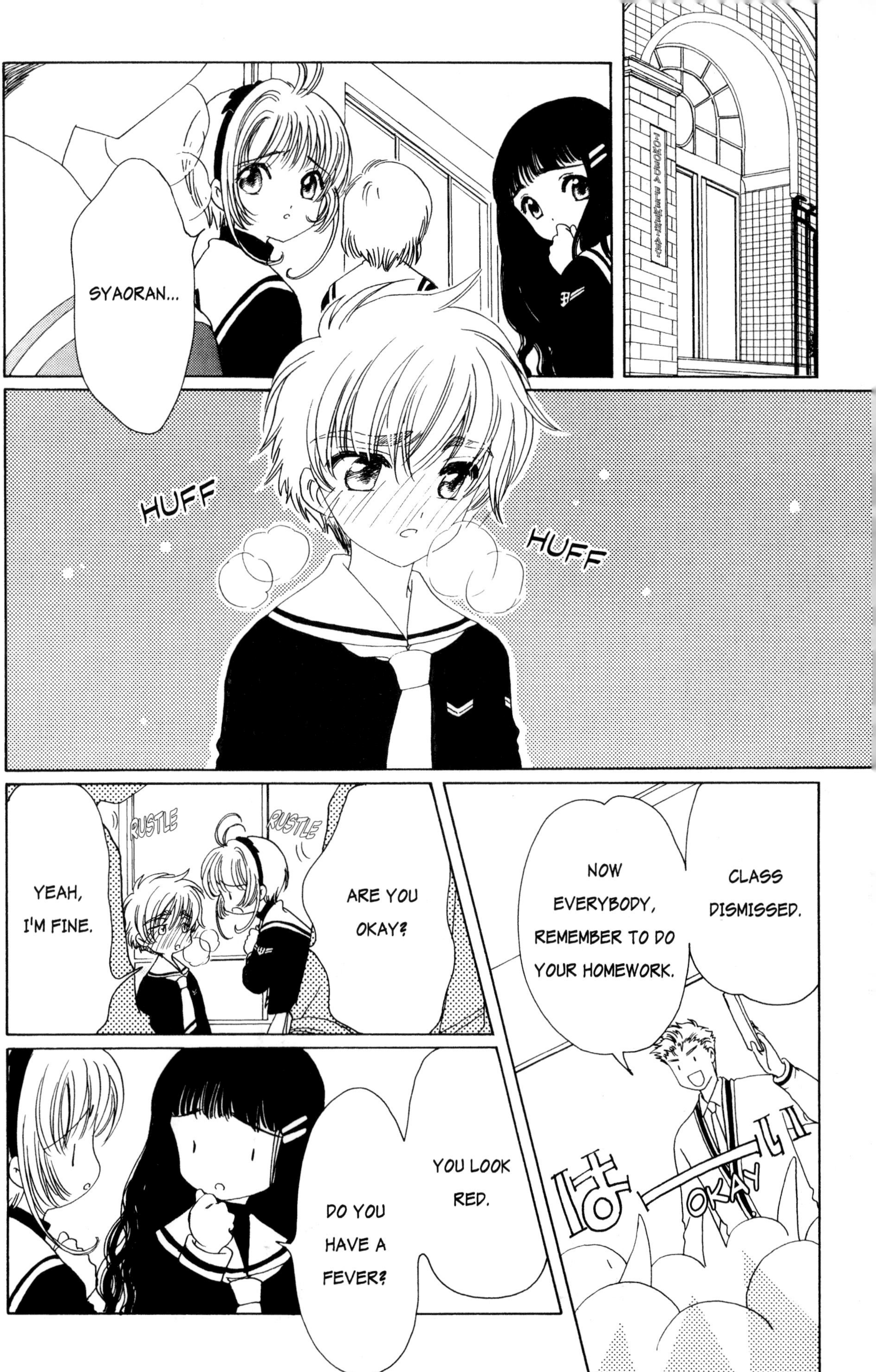
TOMOEDA ELEMENTARY
SYAORAN...
HUFF
HUFF
NOW EVERYBODY, REMEMBER TO DO YOUR HOMEWORK.
CLASS DISMISSED.
はーい
OKAY
RUSTLE
RUSTLE
ARE YOU OKAY?
YEAH, I'M FINE.
YOU LOOK RED.
DO YOU HAVE A FEVER?

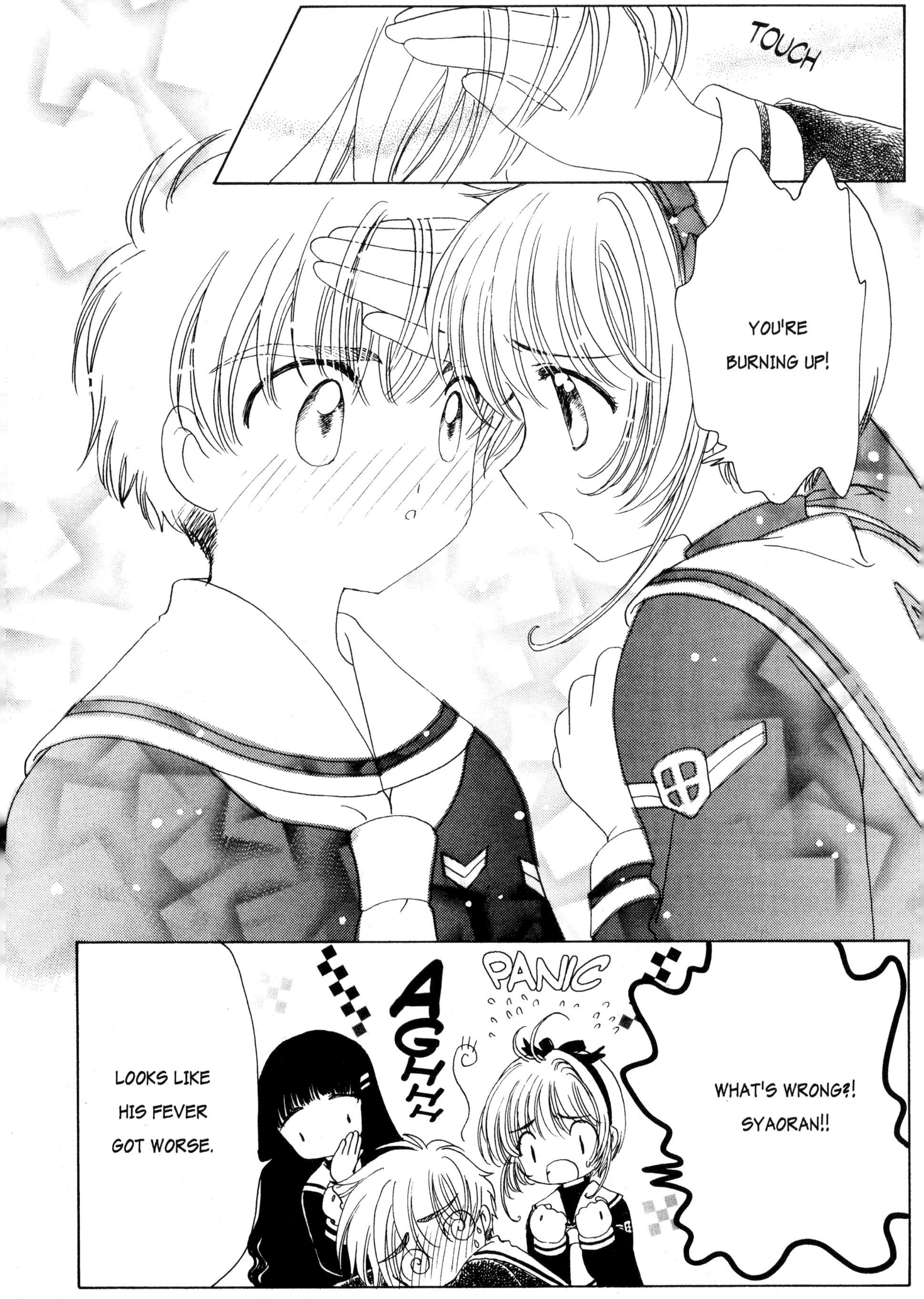
TOUCH
YOU'RE BURNING UP!
WHAT'S WRONG?! SYAORAN!!
PANIC
AGHHH
LOOKS LIKE HIS FEVER GOT WORSE.

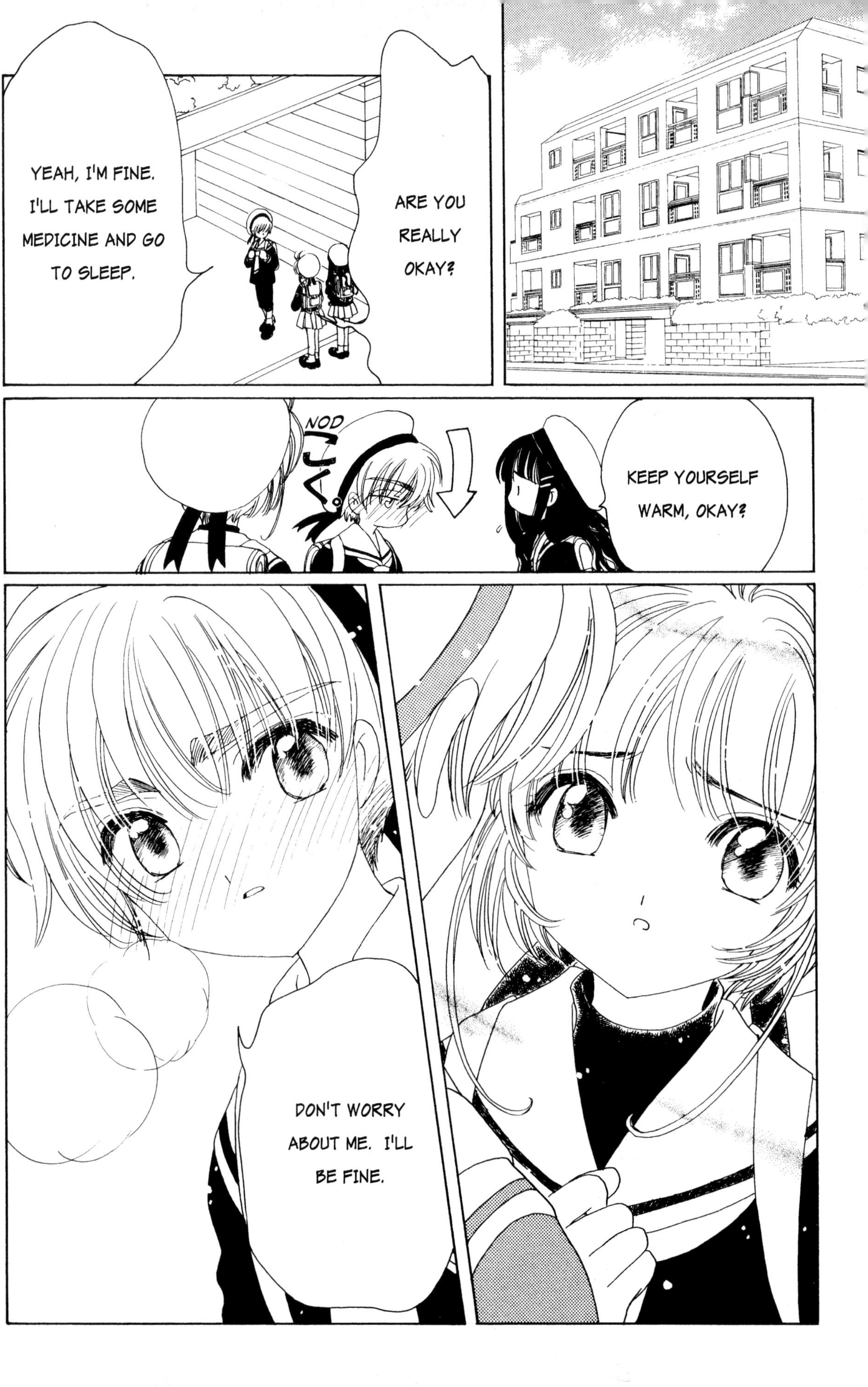
ARE YOU REALLY OKAY?
YEAH, I'M FINE. I'LL TAKE SOME MEDICINE AND GO TO SLEEP.
KEEP YOURSELF WARM, OKAY?
NOD
DON'T WORRY ABOUT ME. I'LL BE FINE.

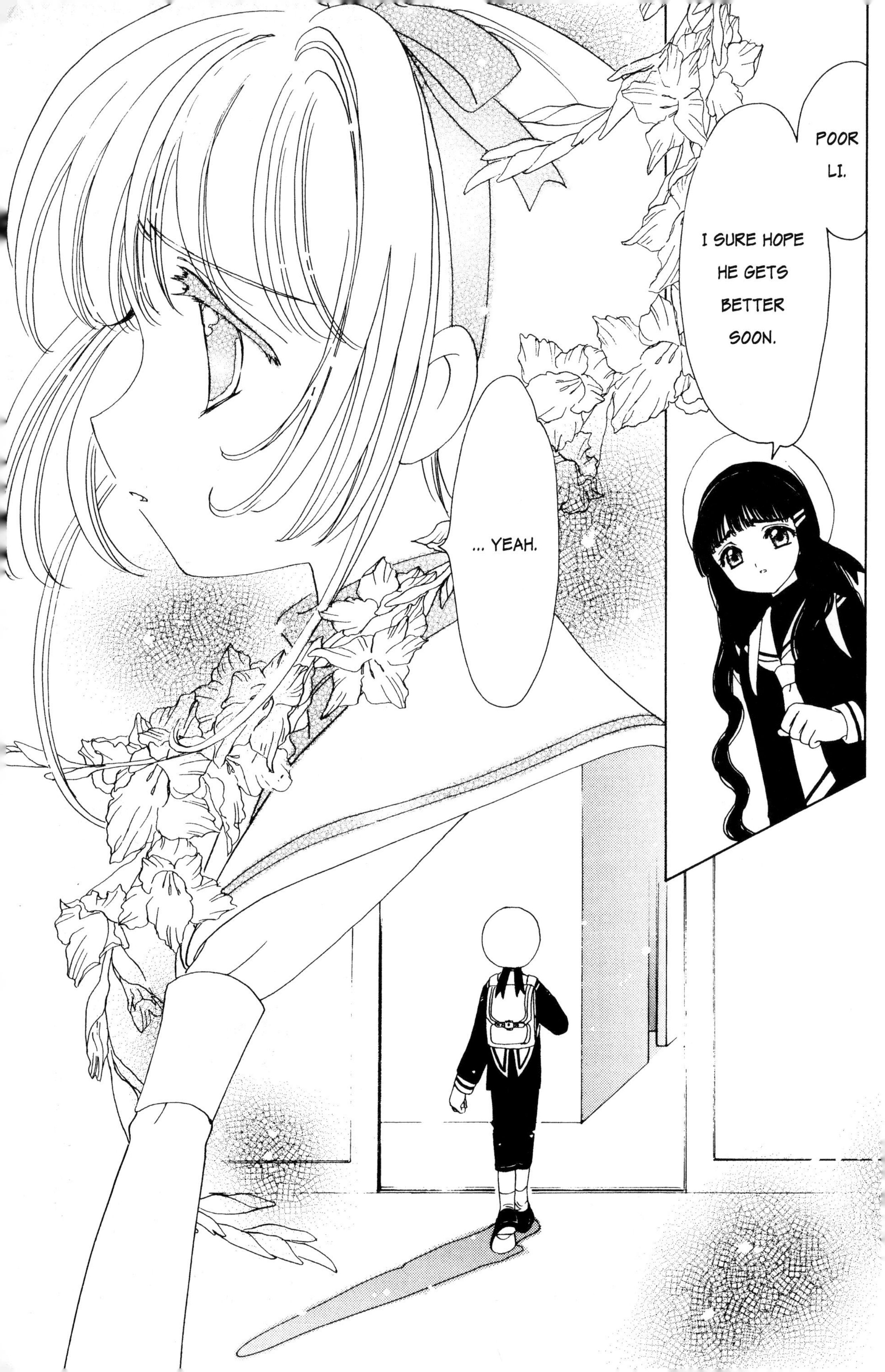
POOR LI.
I SURE HOPE HE GETS BETTER SOON.
... YEAH.

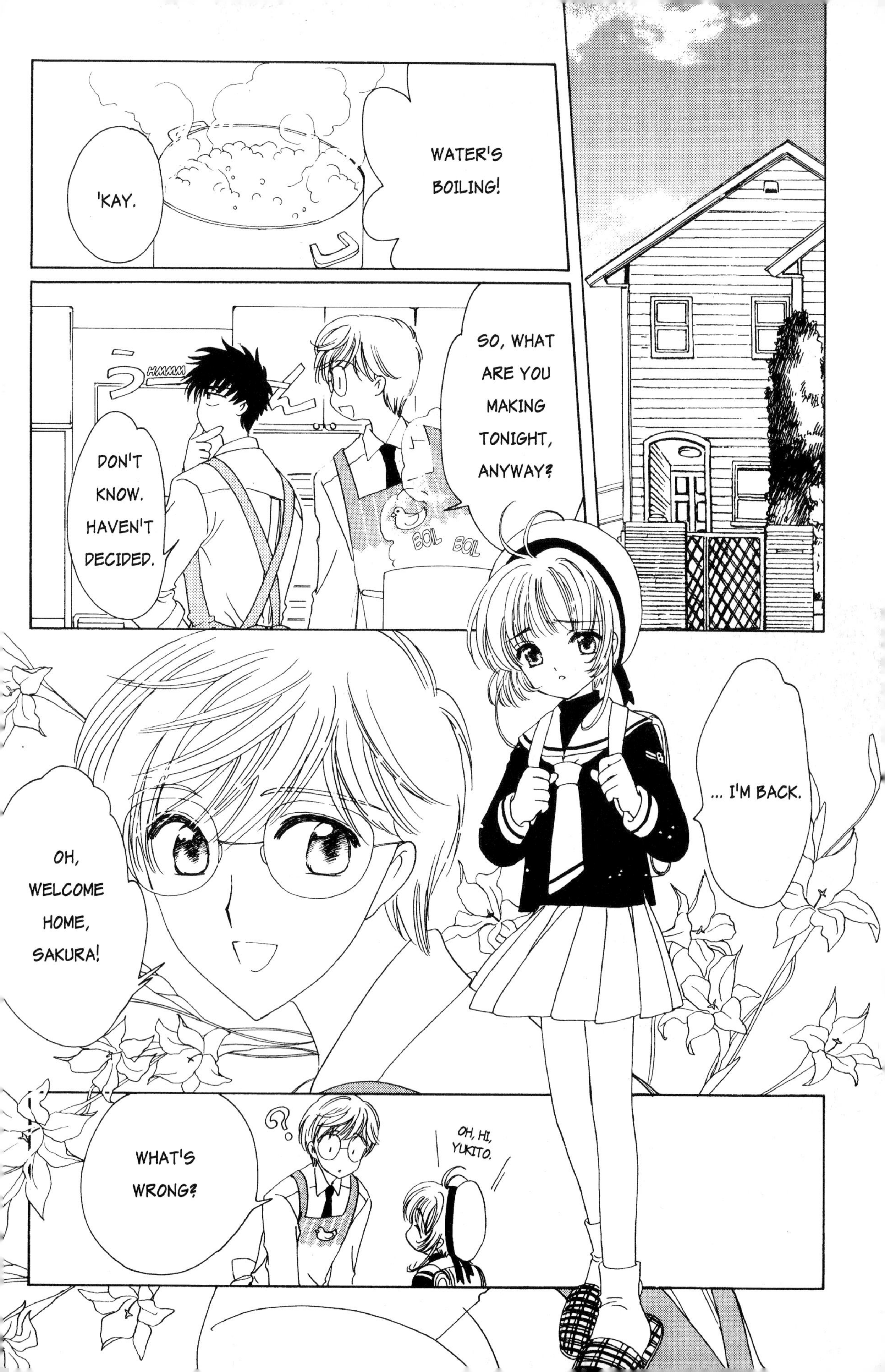
WATER'S BOILING!
'KAY.
SO, WHAT ARE YOU MAKING TONIGHT, ANYWAY?
BOIL BOIL
HMMM
DON'T KNOW. HAVEN'T DECIDED.
... I'M BACK.
OH, WELCOME HOME, SAKURA!
OH, HI, YUKITO.
WHAT'S WRONG?

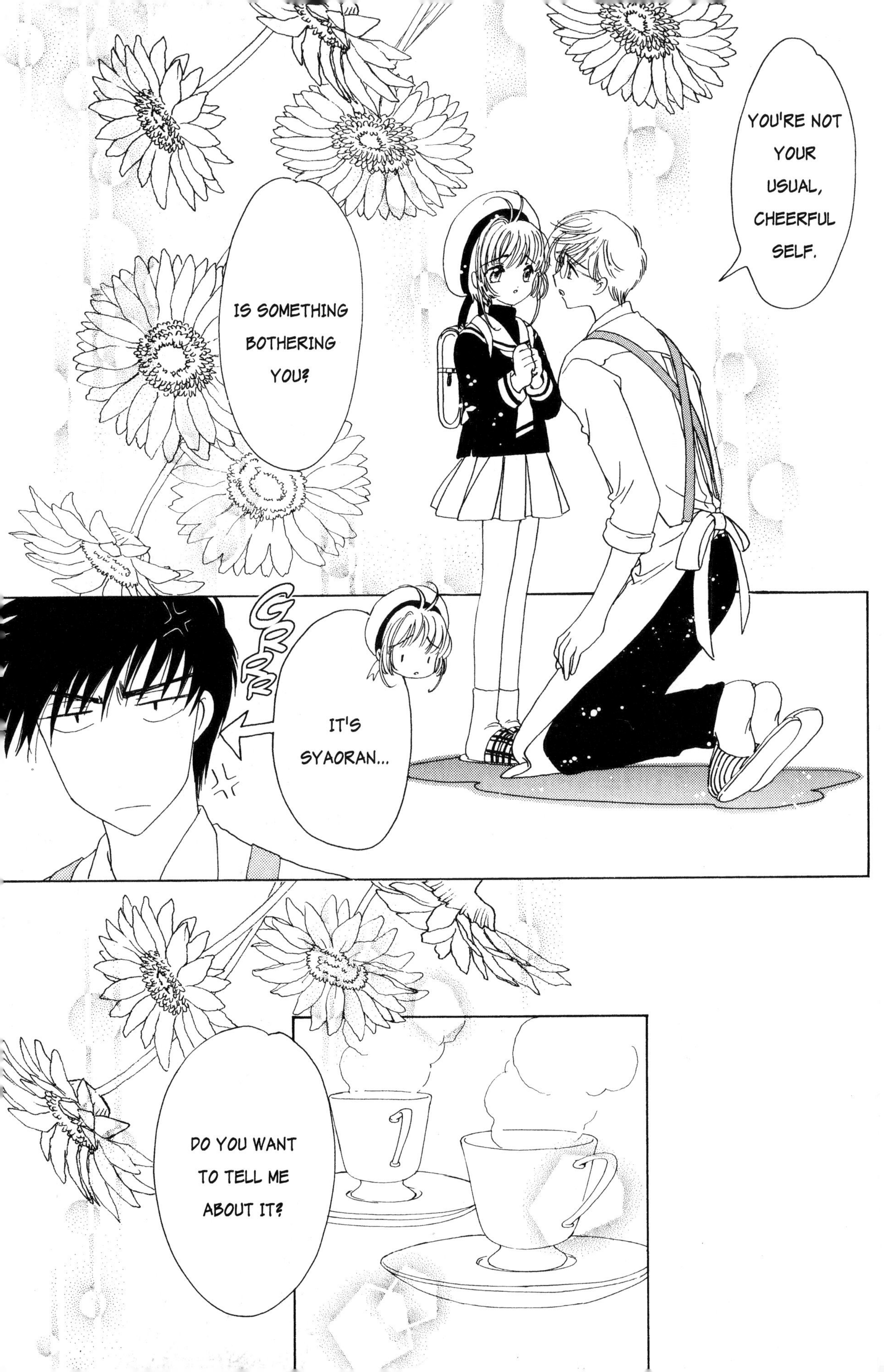
YOU'RE NOT YOUR USUAL, CHEERFUL SELF.
IS SOMETHING BOTHERING YOU?
IT'S SYAORAN...
GRRR
DO YOU WANT TO TELL ME ABOUT IT?

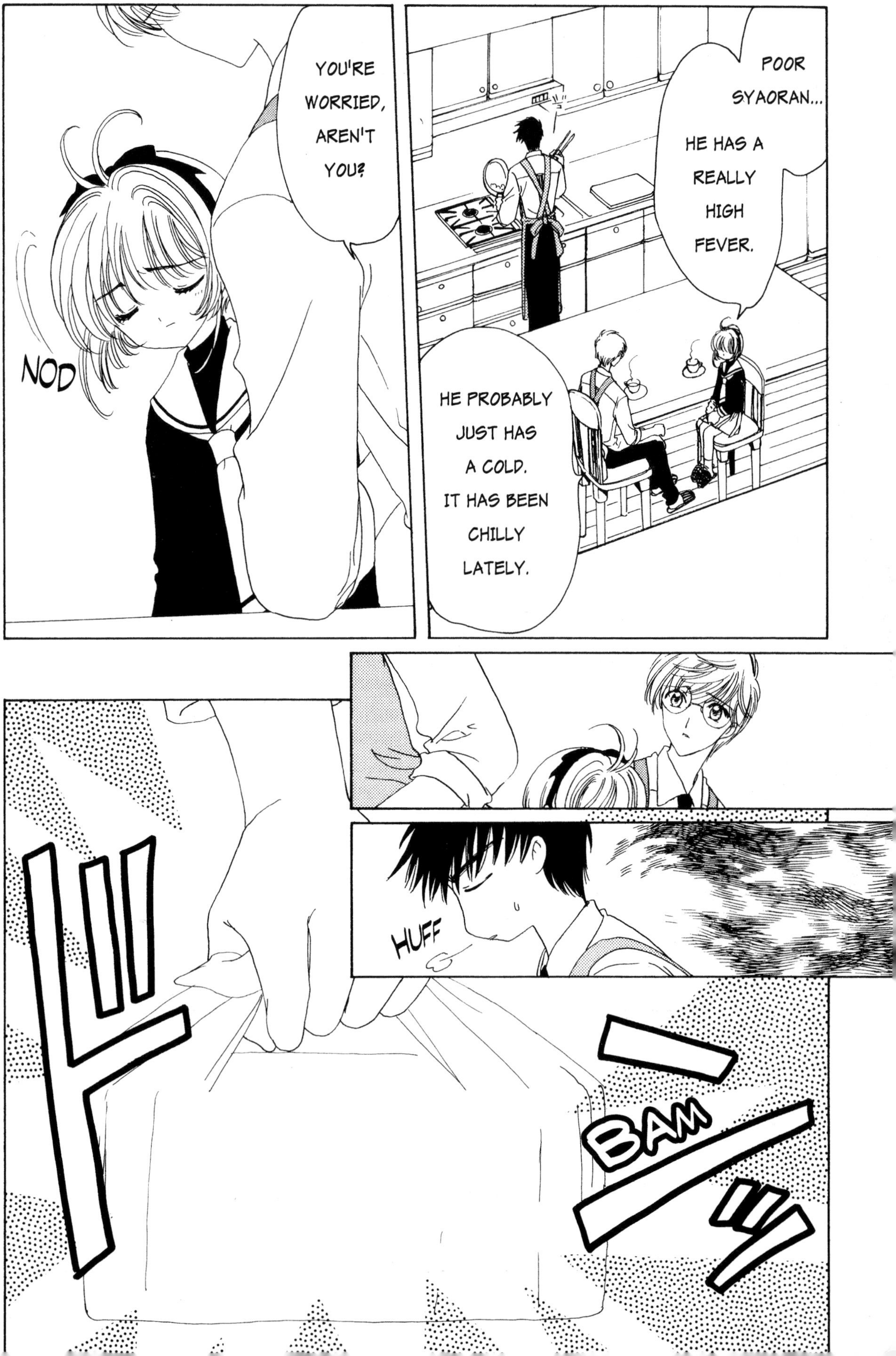
POOR SYAORAN...
HE HAS A REALLY HIGH FEVER.
HE PROBABLY JUST HAS A COLD. IT HAS BEEN CHILLY LATELY.
YOU'RE WORRIED, AREN'T YOU?
NOD
HUFF
BAM

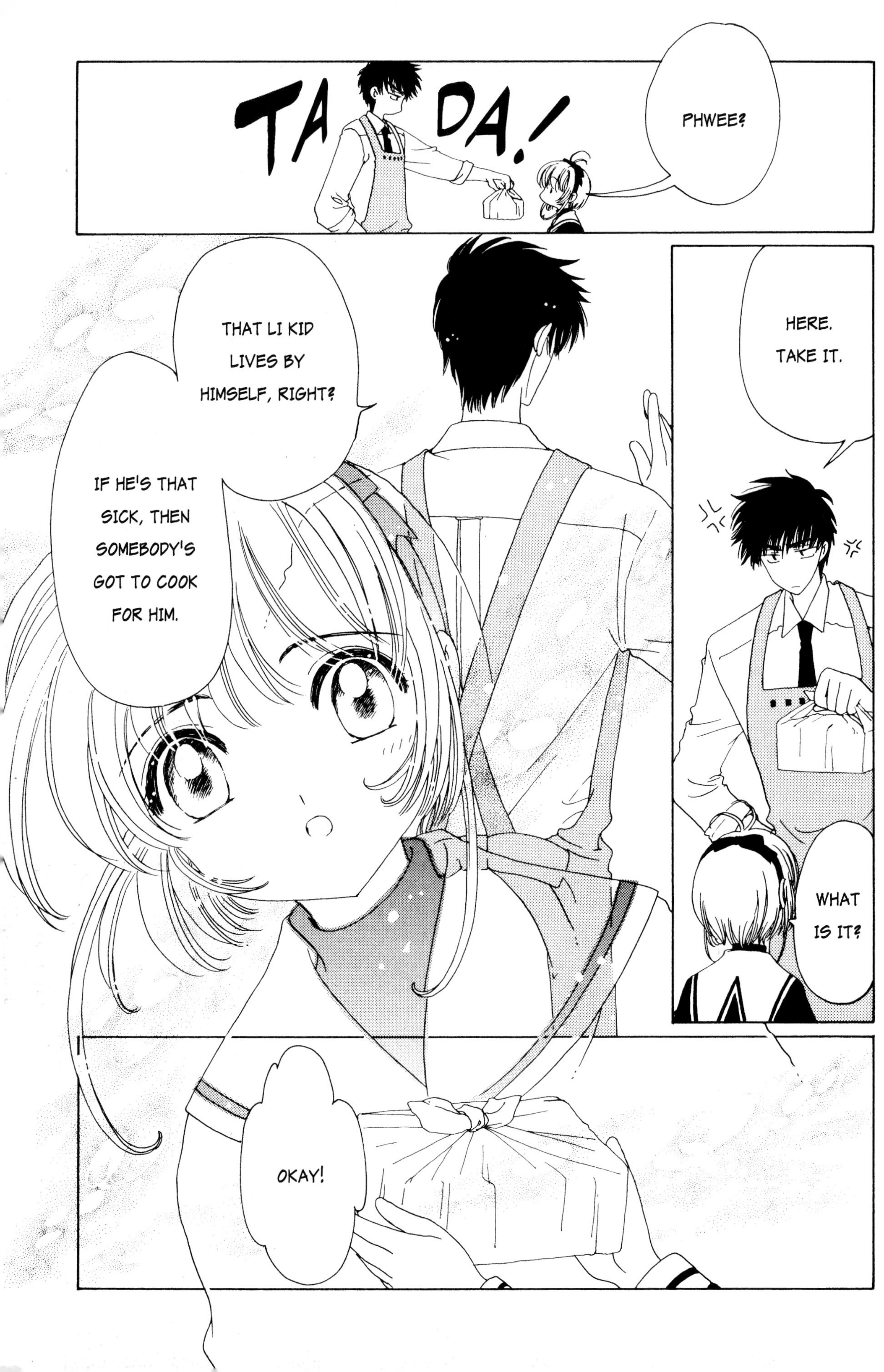
TA DA!
PHWEE?
HERE. TAKE IT.
WHAT IS IT?
THAT LI KID LIVES BY HIMSELF, RIGHT?
IF HE'S THAT SICK, THEN SOMEBODY'S GOT TO COOK FOR HIM.
OKAY!

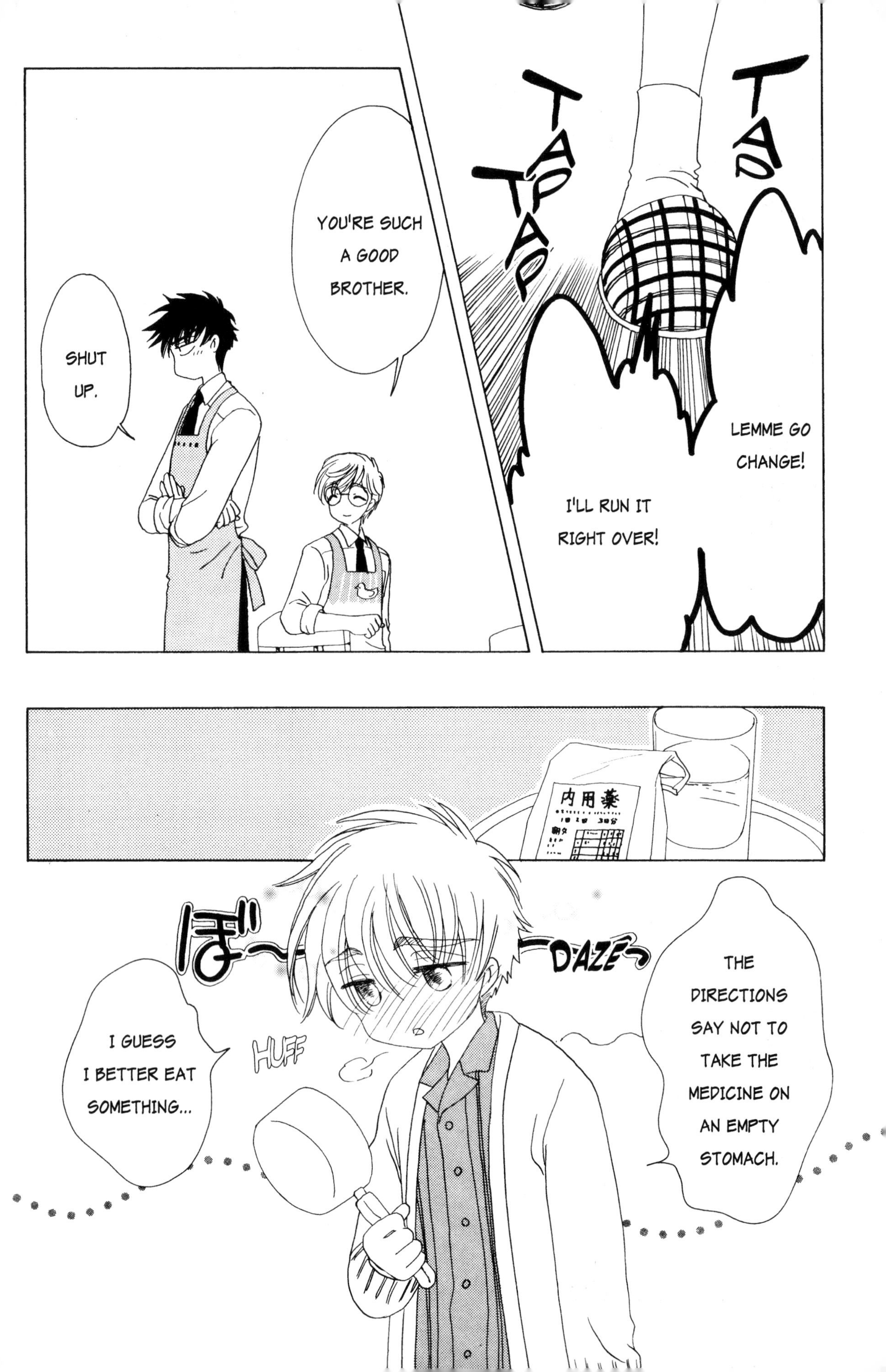
TAP TAP TAP
LEMME GO CHANGE!
I'LL RUN IT RIGHT OVER!
YOU'RE SUCH A GOOD BROTHER.
SHUT UP.
内用薬
ぼ~
DAZE
THE DIRECTIONS SAY NOT TO TAKE THE MEDICINE ON AN EMPTY STOMACH.
HUFF
I GUESS I BETTER EAT SOMETHING...

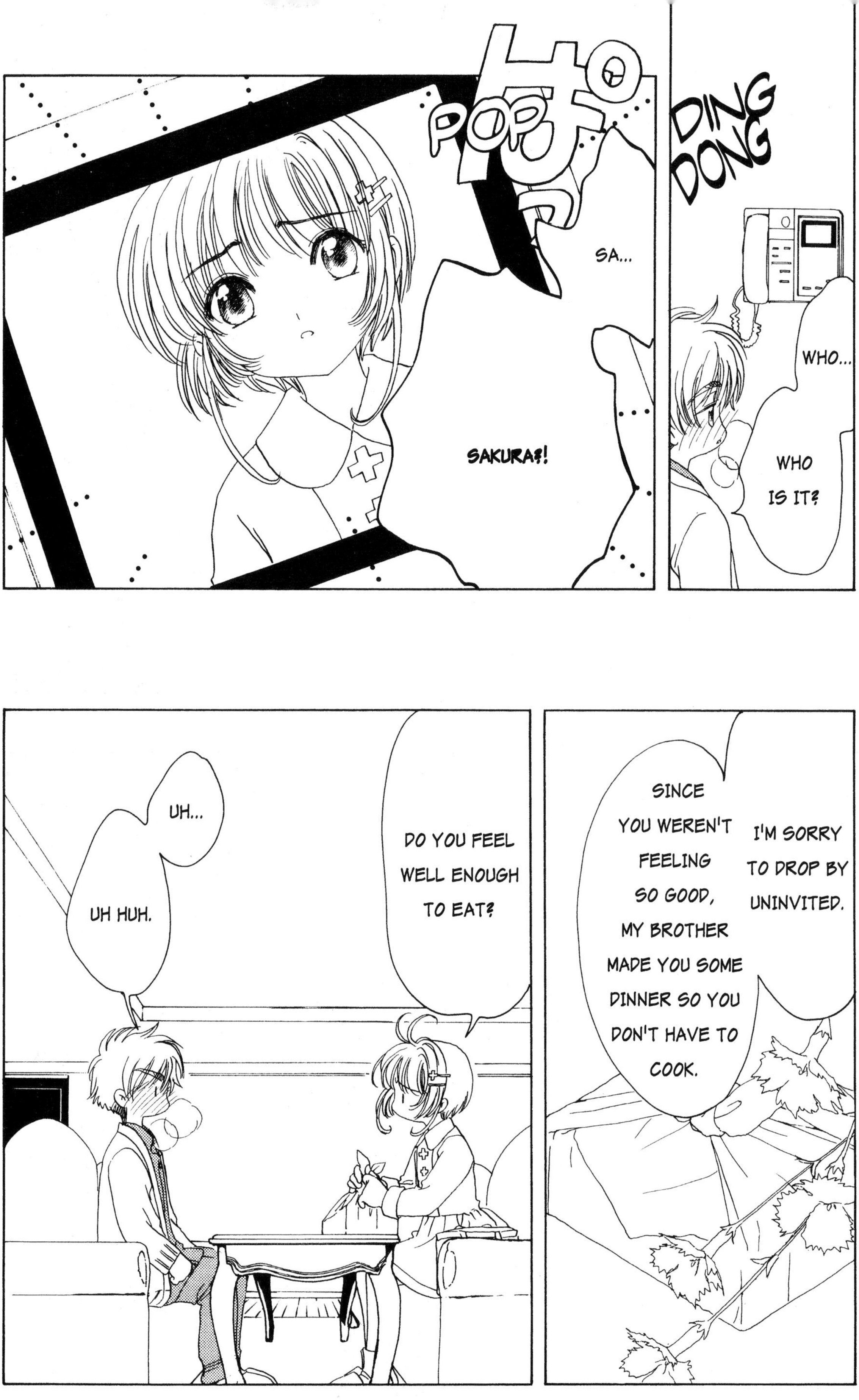
DING DONG
WHO...
WHO IS IT?
POP
SA...
SAKURA?!
I'M SORRY TO DROP BY UNINVITED.
SINCE YOU WEREN'T FEELING SO GOOD, MY BROTHER MADE YOU SOME DINNER SO YOU DON'T HAVE TO COOK.
DO YOU FEEL WELL ENOUGH TO EAT?
UH...
UH HUH.

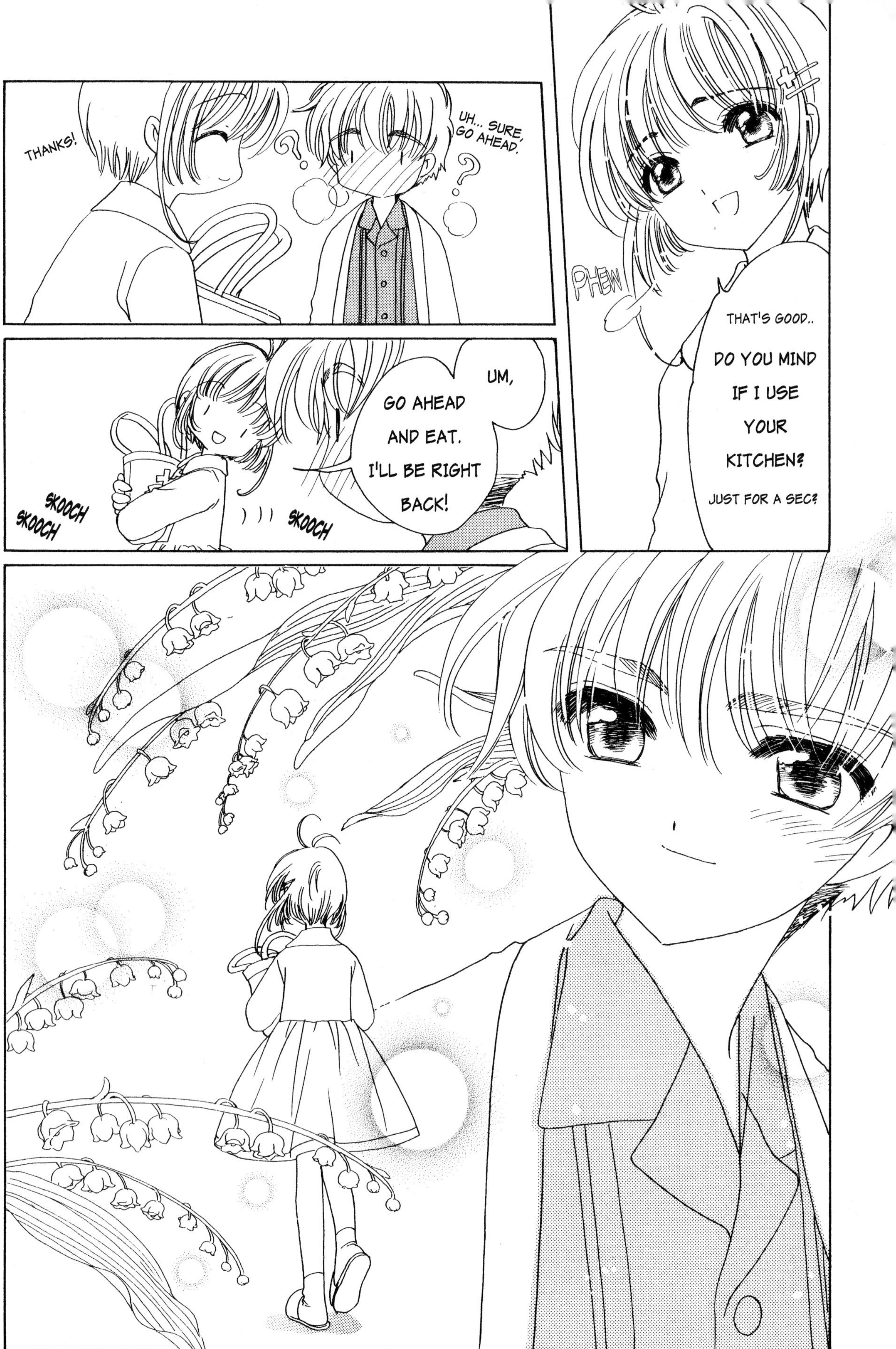
PHEW
THAT'S GOOD..
DO YOU MIND IF I USE YOUR KITCHEN?
JUST FOR A SEC?
UH... SURE, GO AHEAD.
THANKS!
UM,
GO AHEAD AND EAT. I'LL BE RIGHT BACK!
SKOOCH
SKOOCH SKOOCH

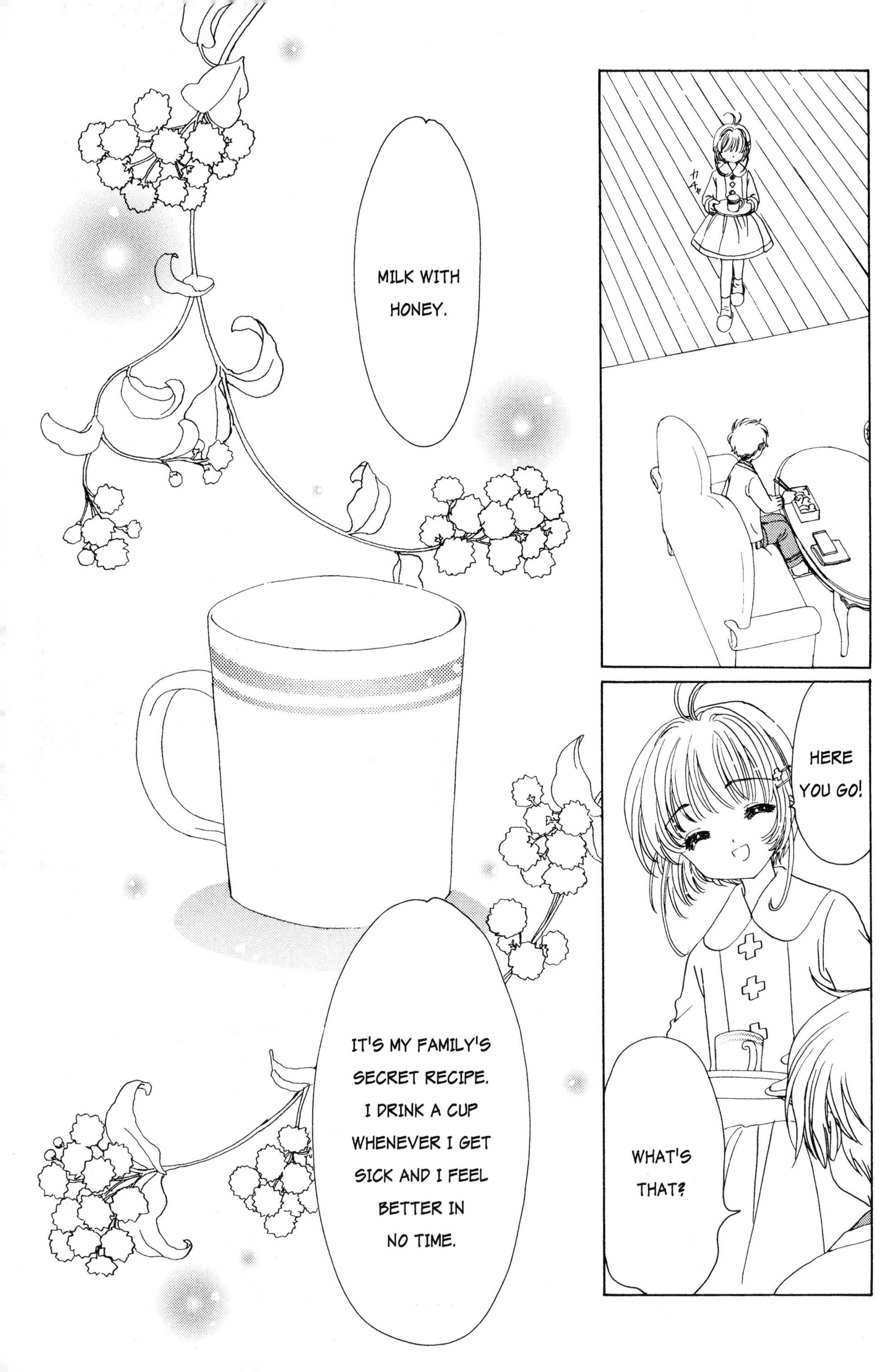
HERE YOU GO!
WHAT'S THAT?
MILK WITH HONEY.
IT'S MY FAMILY'S SECRET RECIPE. I DRINK A CUP WHENEVER I GET SICK AND I FEEL BETTER IN NO TIME.

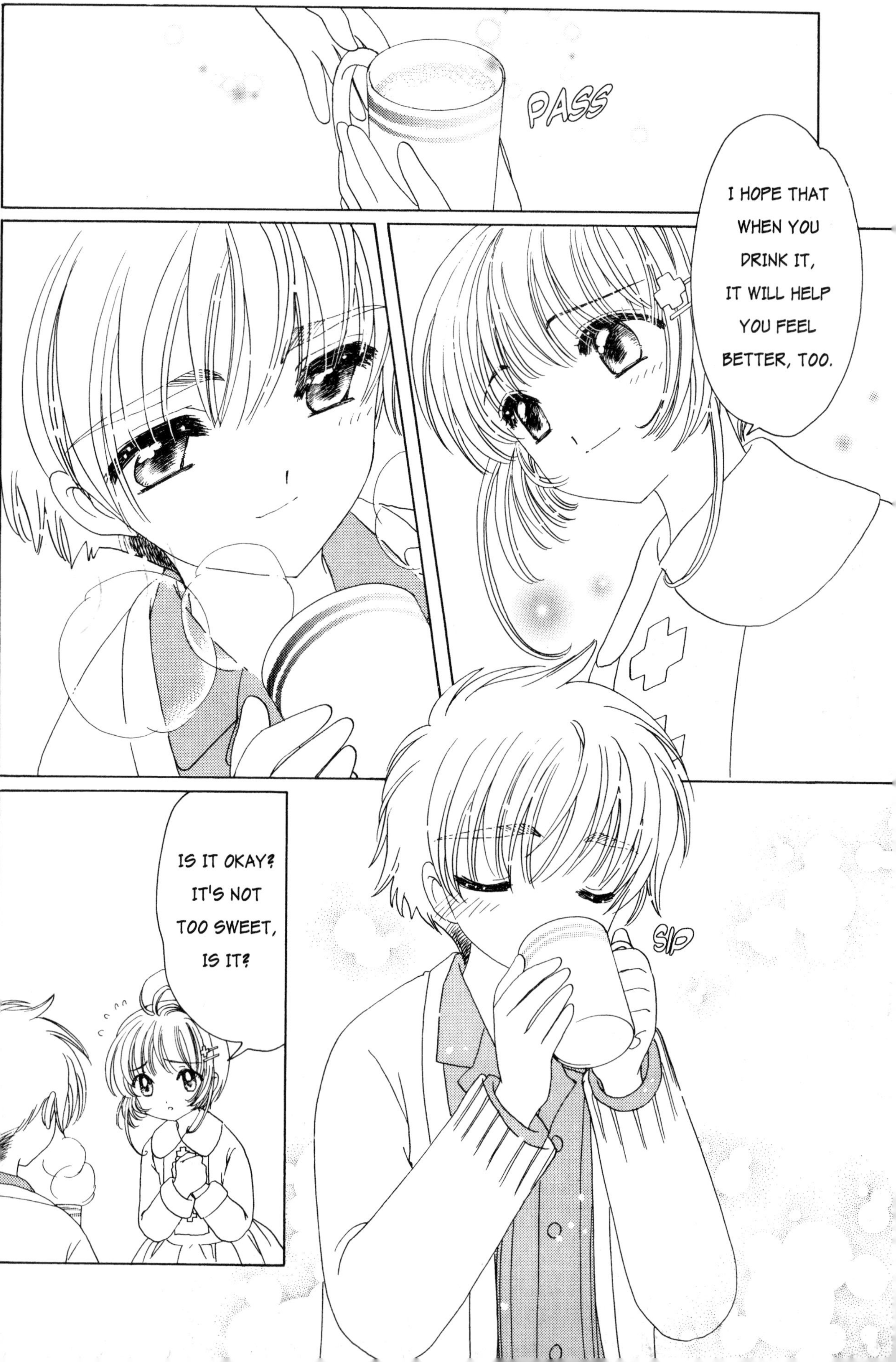
PASS
I HOPE THAT WHEN YOU DRINK IT, IT WILL HELP YOU FEEL BETTER, TOO.
SIP
IS IT OKAY? IT'S NOT TOO SWEET, IS IT?

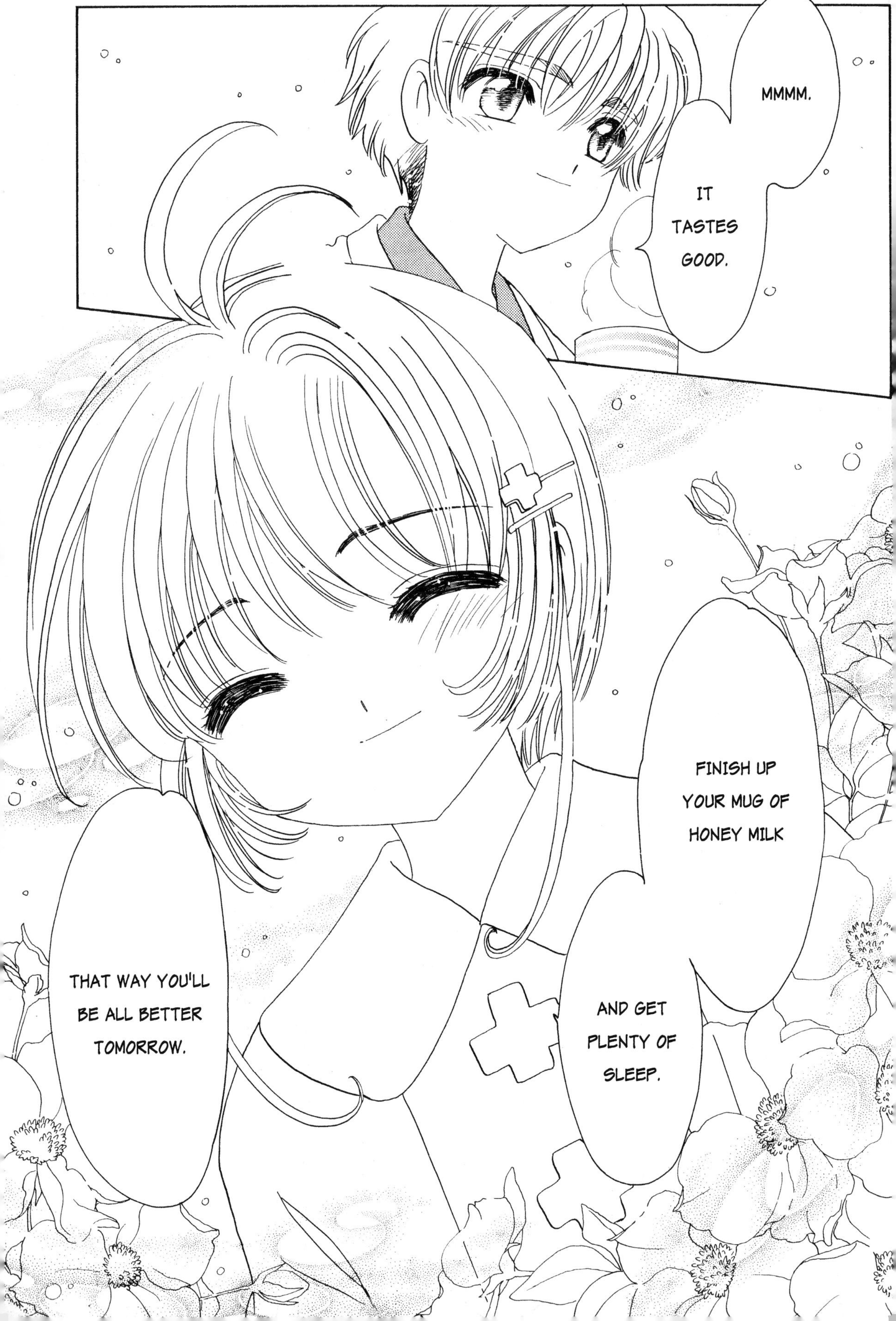
MMMM.
IT TASTES GOOD.
FINISH UP YOUR MUG OF HONEY MILK
AND GET PLENTY OF SLEEP.
THAT WAY YOU'LL BE ALL BETTER TOMORROW.

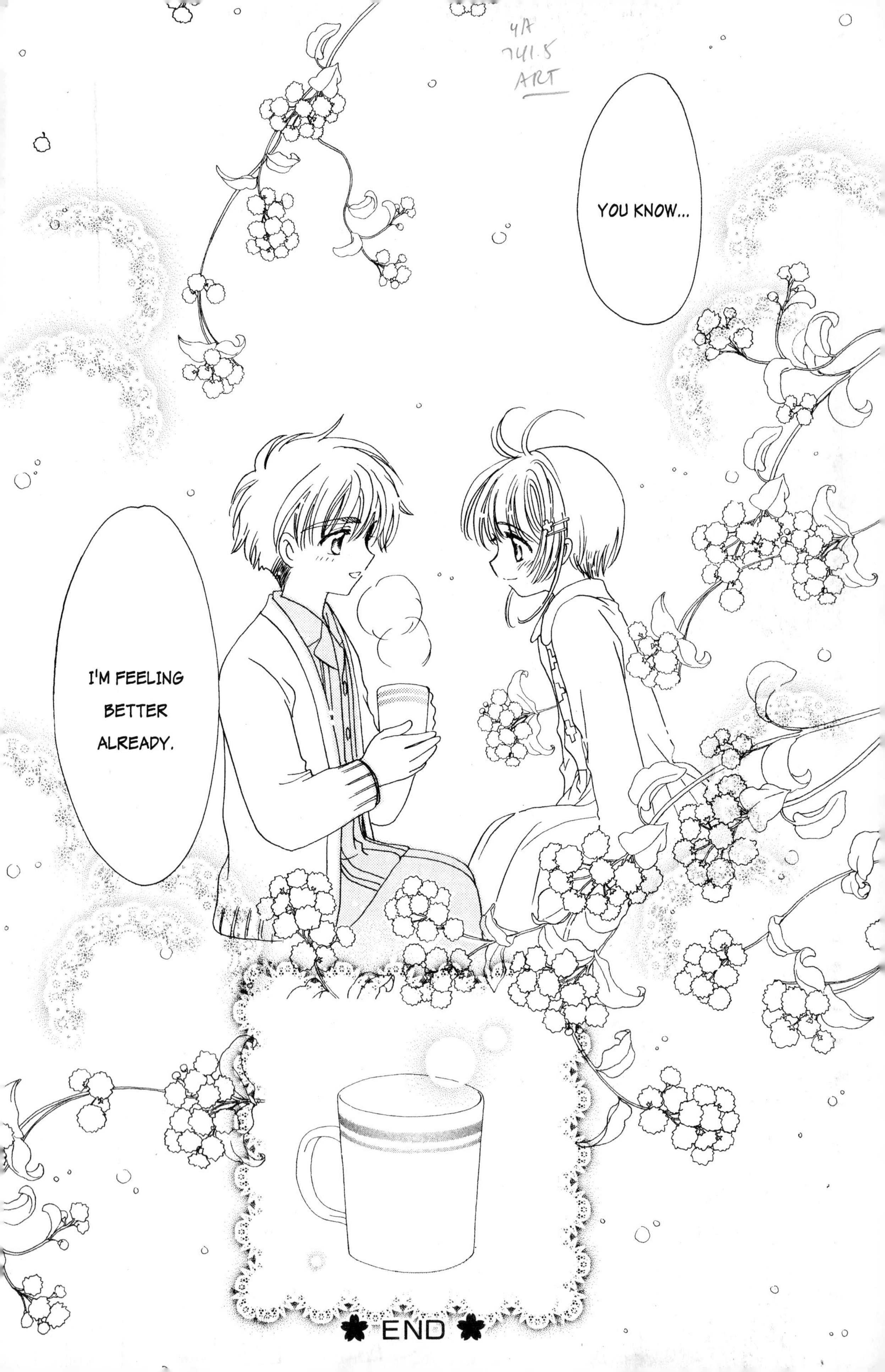
YOU KNOW...
I'M FEELING BETTER ALREADY.
END

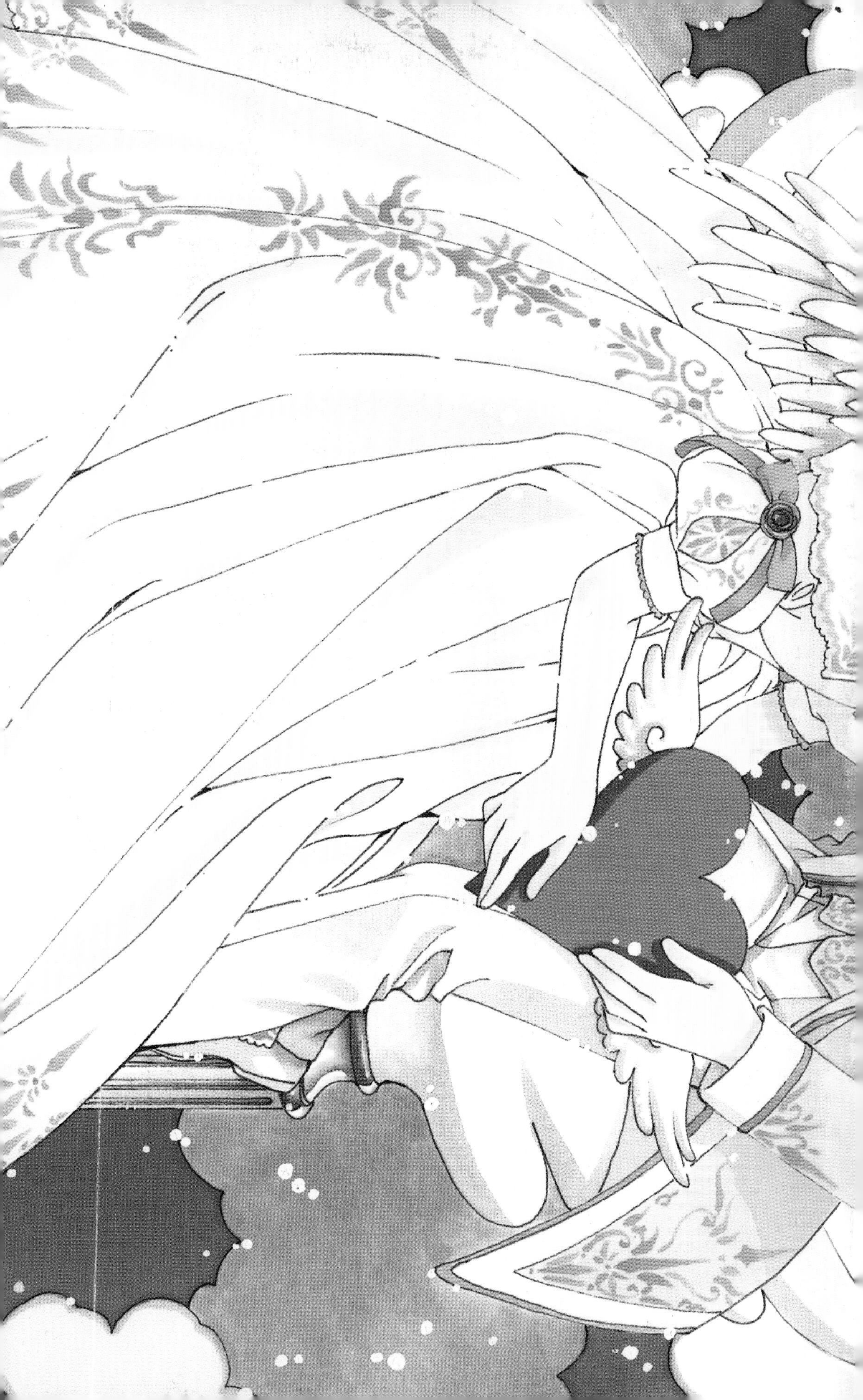

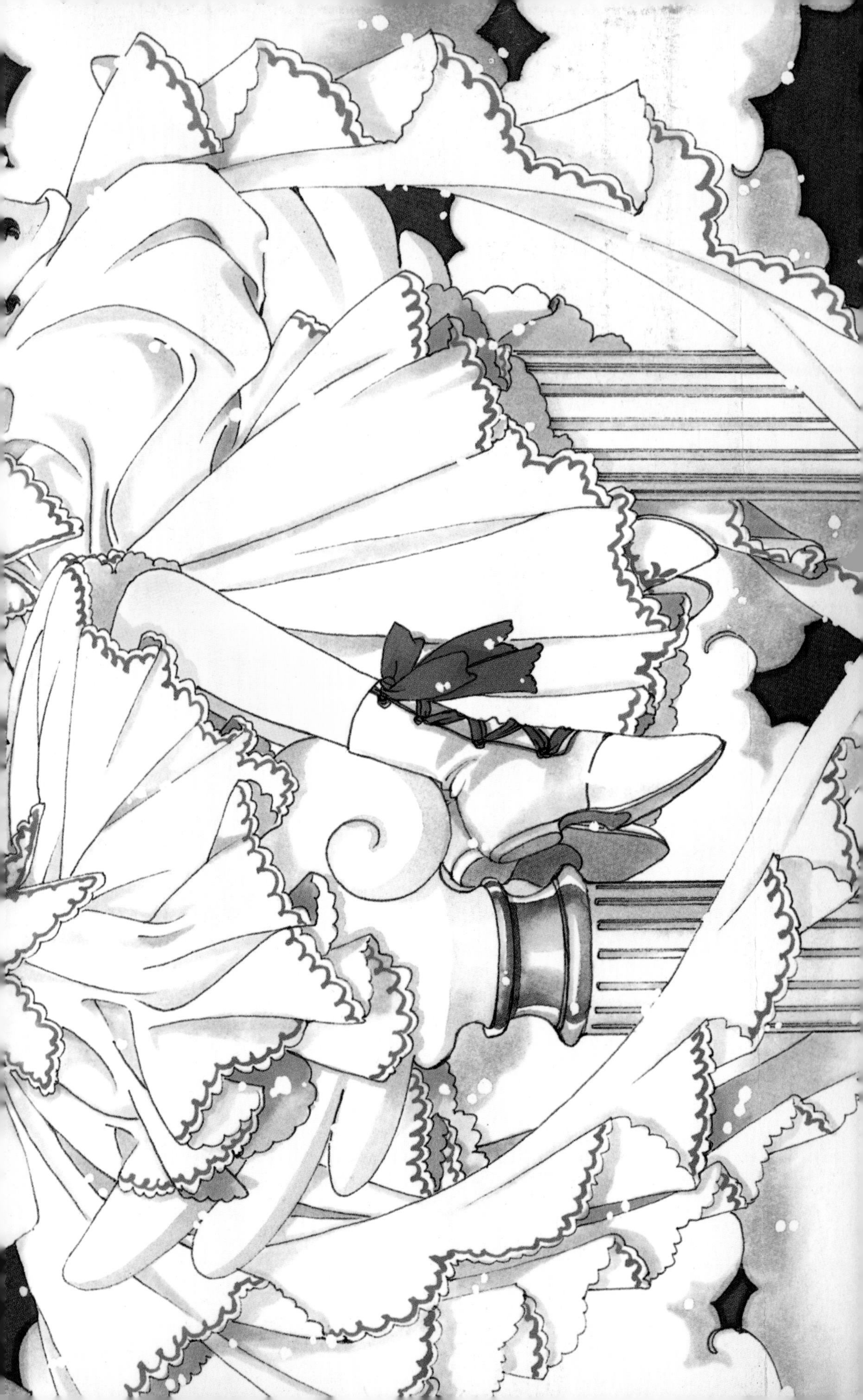

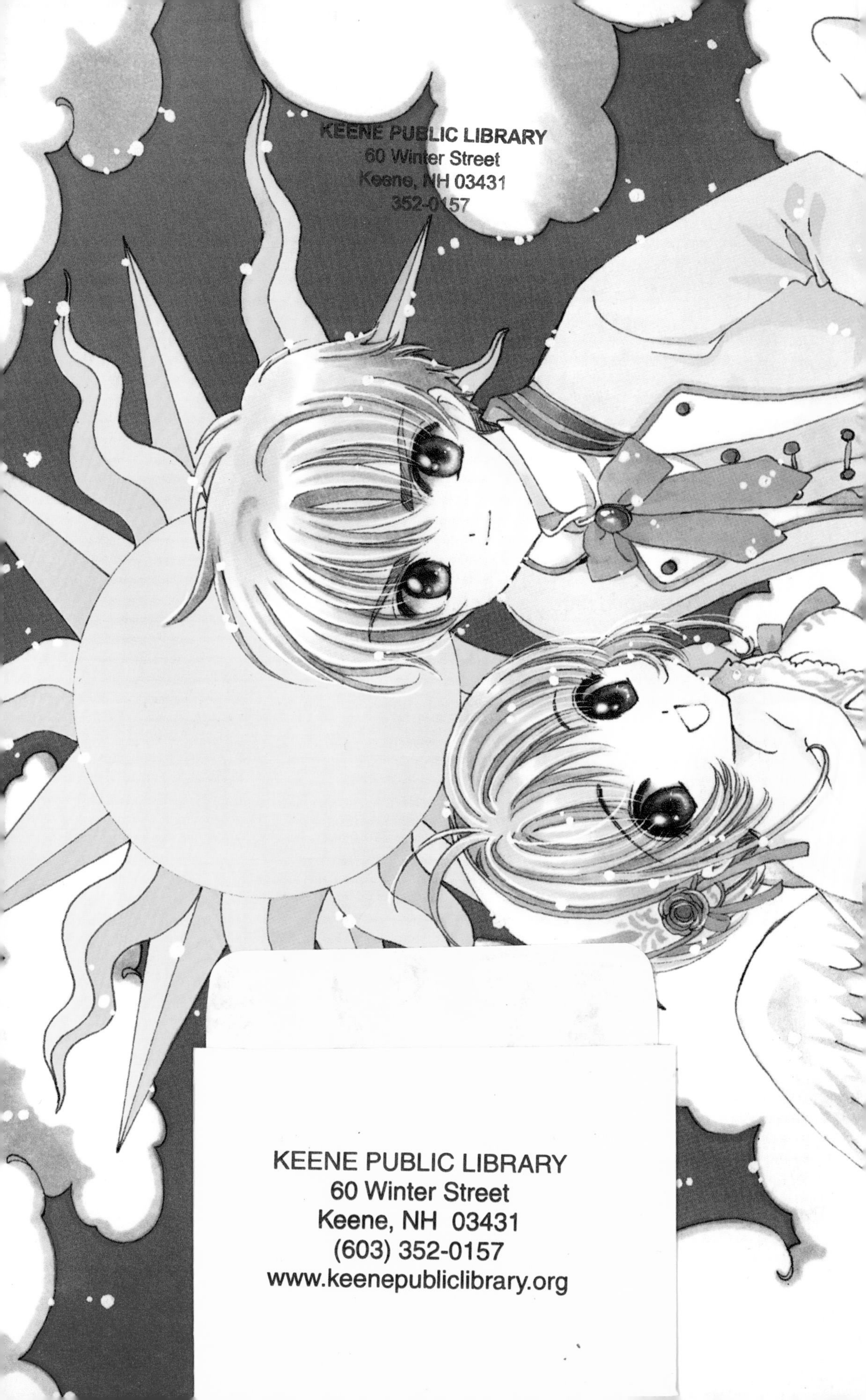

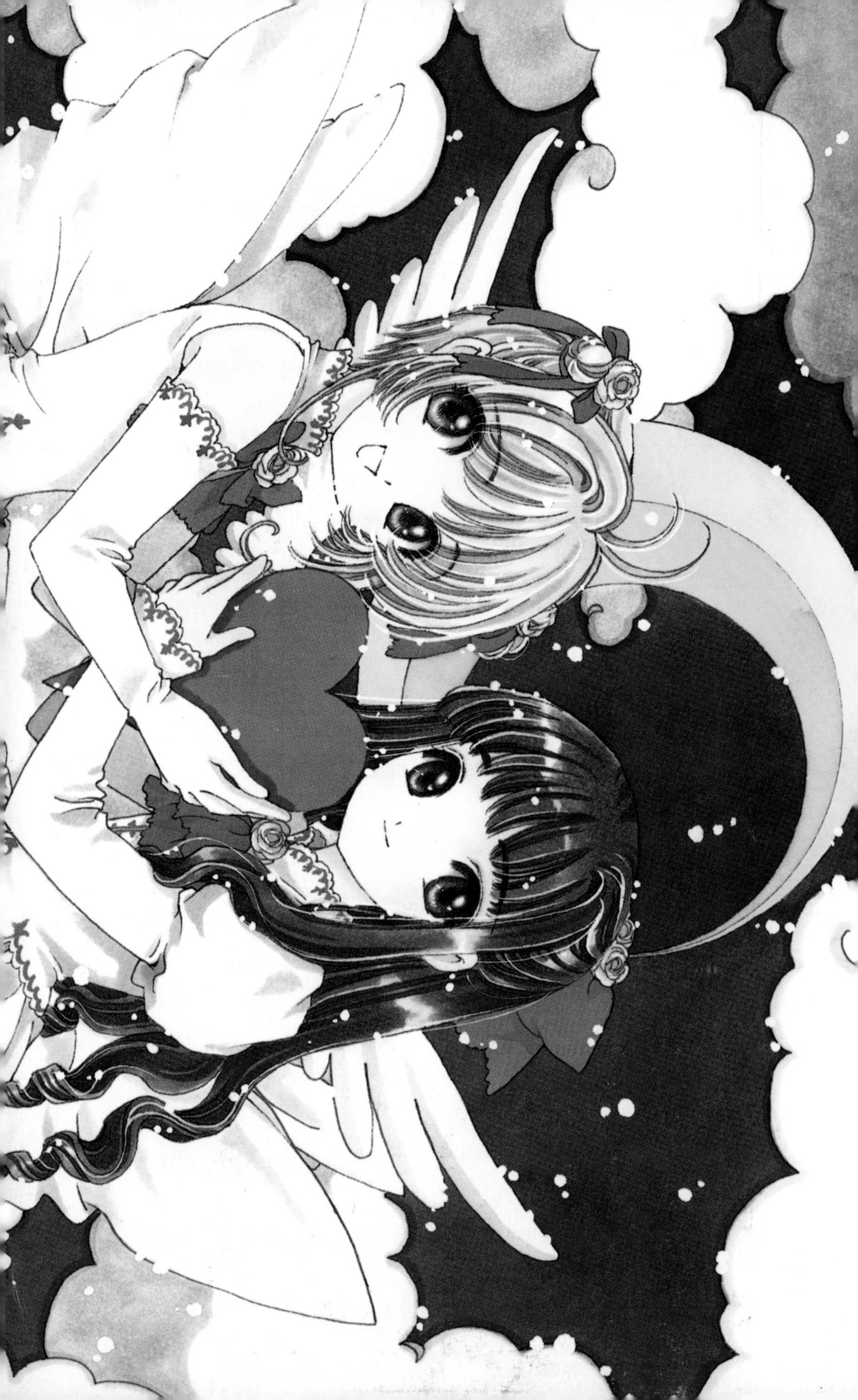